Praise for DEREK RYDALL *and*

THE
ABUNDANCE
PROJECT

"Creating a life of real abundance isn't accidental or only available to the lucky few. As Derek Rydall shows in this book, you can create a life where you have more than enough of everything you need when you understand and apply certain principles and practices. In *The Abundance Project*, you will find a simple and fun step-by-step way to release your fear and baggage around abundance and begin living the life you were born for!"

—**Marci Shimoff**, *New York Times* bestselling
author of *Happy for No Reason*, *Love for No Reason*,
and *Chicken Soup for the Woman's Soul*

"The moment I first interviewed Derek, I knew I had met a teacher who truly lived his teaching. He stood out amongst the hundreds of speakers, authors, and transformational icons I hosted on my show as not only brilliant, but also honest and authentic. In *The Abundance Project* he shows us how we too can live a congruent life. He doesn't promise it will be easy but that's part of why you want to listen to what he has to say. There's no hype here—only Truth. And it's shared in a way that you don't have to wait to get results. Read Derek's book and you can start living the Abundance Principle in all areas of your life—not someday, but now."

—**Debra Poneman**, bestselling author, founder of Yes to Success, Inc.
and cofounder of Your Year of Miracles, LLC

"Derek Rydall lays out spiritual truths that will help you transcend your limited beliefs, tap into your true power, and fulfill your higher purpose!"

—**Mark Harris**, producer of *Crash* (Academy Award for Best Picture)

"We've been conducting business and creating under false assumptions. Derek challenges us to open up to a fresh world view where we can work from our true nature: whole, abundant."

—**Lindsay Crouse**, Oscar-nominated actress, *The Insider*, *The Verdict*, *Places in the Heart*

"Derek Rydall's work is invaluable for any creative soul who wants to channel material the world is waiting for!"

—**Dee Wallace**, healer, author, teacher, and actress, *E. T. The Extra Terrestrial*, *Cujo*

"As a professional writer, I consider Derek's work one of the most valuable resources I have. It has been invaluable in helping me grow personally and believe in the possibility of what I create truly having a higher purpose."

—**Erik Bork**, two-time Emmy Award-winning writer–producer of *Band of Brothers* and *From Here to the Moon*

"My income went from barely making it to earning $8,500 in one month! That's more than I have ever experienced in my life! Thank you, Derek, for being my teacher, guide, and coach! I can hardly wait for my next breakthrough!"

—**Terrie Marie**, the Angel Lady

"When I found Derek's work, I was on the verge of losing my house. Last month, I made more money in one week than I make in a month. Derek is a true Master. He has the ability to get to the heart of any issue in a short time, then give us exactly what we need to continue the momentum of the breakthrough."

—Kim Marino

"One of my goals when I started Derek's work was to sell some property. Hadn't managed to do so thus far, but today *we just closed a deal for three parcels*. The intent is to be completely out of debt by the end of the year, and we're nearly there. So jazzed! Thank you!"

—Susan Barrow

"I am on my third money wealth module. Derek, please hear this, I have been a counselor for twenty years. I have worked with many people. Your work is the first I can say is truly coming from greatness, wealth, abundance, and love. I feel it every time I do another piece of this. Thank you, thank you!"

—Judi Larson

"Derek, thank you so much! I am now experiencing a life of happiness and joy from within. My health has transformed from problems in my kidney to great function, I have a great career, and my bosses love me! From being a person who felt like nothing, I now love my life and have deep gratitude and appreciation!"

—Efrat, Israel

THE
ABUNDANCE
PROJECT

THE
ABUNDANCE
PROJECT

40 DAYS TO MORE WEALTH, HEALTH, LOVE, AND HAPPINESS

DEREK RYDALL

x

ATRIA PAPERBACK
New York London Toronto Sydney New Delhi

BEYOND WORDS
Portland, Oregon

ATRIA PAPERBACK
An Imprint of Simon & Schuster, Inc.
1230 Avenue of the Americas
New York, NY 10020

BEYOND WORDS
1750 S.W. Skyline Blvd., Suite 20
Portland, Oregon 97221-2543
503-531-8700 / 503-531-8773 fax
www.beyondword.com

Managing editor: Lindsay S. Easterbrooks-Brown
Editor: Emily Han
Copyeditor: Jen Weaver-Neist
Proofreader: Michelle Blair
Design: Devon Smith
Composition: William H. Brunson Typography Services

First Beyond Words/Atria Paperback edition February 2022

ATRIA PAPERBACK and colophon are trademarks of Simon & Schuster, Inc.
BEYOND WORDS PUBLISHING and colophon are registered trademarks of Beyond Words Publishing. Beyond Words is an imprint of Simon & Schuster, Inc.

For more information about special discounts for bulk purchases, please contact Simon & Schuster Special Sales at 1-866-506-1949 or business@simonandschuster.com.

The Simon & Schuster Speakers Bureau can bring authors to your live event. For more information or to book an event, contact the Simon & Schuster Speakers Bureau at 1-866-248-3049 or visit our website at www.simonspeakers.com.

Manufactured in the United States of America

10 9 8 7 6 5 4 3 2 1

Library of Congress Cataloging-in-Progress Data

Names: Rydall, Derek
Title: The abundance project : 40 days to more wealth, health, love, and happiness / Derek Rydall.
Description: Hillsboro, Oregon : Atria Books/Beyond Words, 2018.
Identifiers: LCCN 2017033108| ISBN 9781582706528 (hardback) | ISBN 9781582706535 (paperback) | ISBN 9781501167690 (ebook)
Subjects: LCSH: Self-actualization (Psychology) | Motivation (Psychology) | Inspiration. | BISAC: SELF-HELP / Motivational & Inspirational. | BODY, MIND & SPIRIT / Inspiration & Personal Growth. | SELF-HELP / Personal Growth / General.
Classification: LCC BF637.S4 R937 2018 | DDC 158.1—dc23
LC record available at https://lccn.loc.gov/2017033108

The corporate mission of Beyond Words Publishing, Inc.: *Inspire to Integrity*

To Nirvana Reginald Gayle, my spiritual father.
You found me when I was just an ignorant boy and helped
me grow into a (hopefully) wiser man. I don't know what I
would have become without your unconditional love
and support (and style). I know you're guiding me from the
other side now, but I would gladly have one less angel on
my shoulder if I could have one more session with you.
(And maybe a pair of your best shoes.)
I love you, Nirv. Mad love.

CONTENTS

INTRODUCTION

MORE THAN ENOUGH

The key to abundance is meeting limited circumstances with
unlimited thoughts.
—MARIANNE WILLIAMSON

This book is about having enough. More than enough. In every area
of your life. More than enough money, time, love, connection, and
creativity—regardless of the circumstances you've been through or
are currently facing. It's about having the ability to generate an abundance of everything you need no matter what's going on in the world,
because the world is no longer your Source.

That may sound like a big promise, but when you understand what
you're really made of, and what the real nature, source, and substance
of abundance is, you'll no longer question whether this is possible,
because you'll be too busy living it!

Even so, this is not a get-rich-quick program—it's not a get-
anything program; you can't get what you already have. (That may not
make sense now, but it will by the time you're done with this book.)
This is a time-tested, proven system to unlock your natural abundance-
creating capacity and unleash your divine inheritance, no matter what.
That's one of the principles you'll discover in these pages: your circumstances have no ultimate power to determine your life.

I imagine you're reading this now because there's some area in your life that appears to be lacking. Maybe it's a cash-flow problem—you're living paycheck to paycheck, with no clear path to get out of that cycle. Perhaps it's a lack of love or connection to others—you feel lonely, even in a crowded room, or feel unappreciated and invisible, yearning for a rich life of relationships. If you're a creative type, maybe you find yourself at a loss for fresh ideas and inspiration. Or if you're a busy parent, student, executive, or entrepreneur, you may feel like you don't have an abundance of time. The bottom line is that there's some level of lack in your life that seems to be holding you back from living and fulfilling your greatest potential.

But it doesn't have to be that way. You were designed for so much more.

Look around you. Everywhere you look is abundance. The trees don't have just enough leaves to get by; they have more than enough. The night sky doesn't have just enough stars to illuminate our path; it has more than we can count. The universe didn't churn out the bare minimum of planets to create life; there are billions of heavenly bodies, and it expands every second.

Abundance is the nature of life—in fact, it's a synonym for it. And you, being a unique expression of life, are meant to reflect that abundance. Not just enough to get by—*more than enough*. It's not personal, it's principle. It's not luck, it's law. And when you understand the principles and laws of abundance, and design a life of integrity with it, you'll experience this prosperity, affluence (which means "flow"), and more than enough.

This isn't just about having more fame, fortune, or greater possessions in the world; it's about having a greater possession of yourself—it's about freedom. Freedom to be who you really are. Freedom to do what you're here to do. And freedom to take care of your loved ones in the deepest way possible.

● ● ● ● ● ● ●

I've always felt that developing this consciousness of abundance was important, but a few years ago, I had an experience that made me realize that, for many, it's a matter of life and death . . .

It was a Friday afternoon when I got the news. I was sitting in the sun outside Starbucks. It came by text: "It's cancer."

It was from my wife. It was in both breasts.

The message was meant for a friend—she planned on telling me in person—but a slip of the finger sent it to me instead. I sat, staring at the text, stunned. Then I called her. It was a serious case, she said, and we needed to act fast.

At the same time, our son was about to go off to college. My little boy was leaving home. When I say "at the same time," I mean literally: he had to be driven to college, in another state, the following weekend. It was supposed to be a family thing—all of us sending him off together; a week of fun and games, laughter, and bittersweet tears. Instead, I had to drive him to college on Sunday, turn around, and drive back the same day (over fourteen hours of driving) so I could be with my wife in the hospital on Monday.

I remember hugging him good-bye on the steps of his dorm, not knowing what to say; not knowing if he'd have a mother to come home to; not knowing anything except how much I loved him, how much I was going to miss him, how quickly life can change, and how insanely fast it all goes by.

"I guess . . . I'll see you later, buddy," was all I could get out. Then I turned away quickly and headed to the car, so he wouldn't see his dad fall apart. That's the last thing the kid needed to deal with.

I got the tears all right, but not so much of the fun and games. As I drove off, it began to rain, and I began to cry. It was pouring so hard outside and inside that I could barely see the road for hours.

The following weeks were some of the hardest of my life. Walking by my son's empty room. Wheeling my wife into surgery. At the same time, my first big book was due to my publisher, and my business was putting a lot of demands on me. To say I was tapped out was an understatement.

So what does this have to do with the topic of this book?

Well, the one thing I *did not* have to worry about through this and the months that followed, when my wife had to stop working and I had to get more help, was having enough of whatever we needed. When it was time to send my son off to college, I wasn't worried about cost. And when my wife's pay stopped coming but the bills didn't, I wasn't worried if we would have enough; I just wrote the checks.

In the midst of one of the worst economies in the United States since the Great Depression, while friends were losing their jobs and homes, I knew we were safe and secure. In fact, those financial issues existed in a world I rarely lived in anymore. Not because of some pile of cash in my bedroom closet but because of a knowing in my "inner closet"—*a conscious connection with the real source of supply, built on an understanding of the principles of abundance contained in these pages.*

But it wasn't just a wealth of money—there was a wealth of everything. When my family needed more of my time, I could give it to them. When my business required me to deliver on a creative project, my muse was waiting. When the days were so filled that we couldn't cook or shop, friends appeared to take care of us (often with more food than we could eat!). I could be with my wife and with my daughter, and do whatever they needed—and still take care of myself. I'm not saying it wasn't challenging, but because there was such abundance—of money, time, love, inspiration, and support—there was the inner and outer spaciousness to see what was needed and to meet that need with a level of ease and grace I had never experienced before.

All I kept thinking was, *Thank God I learned to create a conscious-ness of abundance that gives my loved ones and me the peace to know our needs are met.* So many were suffering through challenging life experiences like this or worse, which were made all the more diffi-cult by the fact that they had to worry about having enough—enough time, enough money, enough opportunity, enough of everything. At a time when they needed to be supported the most, many were strug-gling just to support themselves.

I was struck with an awareness of how much pain others were experiencing. They didn't know how to make ends meet, or even which end was up when it came to creating real abundance. I'm not just talking about money—that's only one symbol of abundance. Even if you have a lot of money, if you're not connected to the source of it all, you'll never be free. How many people get bigger paychecks yet only end up being "broke" at a higher income bracket? I've known people with a lot of money who were really living in poverty—a poverty of rich relationships, creative fulfillment, life purpose and meaning, and time to do the things that matter most.

Even if you have all the money in the world, if you don't have the time to live a life that deeply fulfills you, you're broke. Even if you have a big balance in your bank account, if you're not doing work that deeply fulfills you, you're bankrupt. Even if you have a magnifi-cent mansion on a hill, if your house isn't filled with an abundance of love, laughter, and the things that make life worth living, you're really homeless.

The truth is that our relationship to abundance—to having all of our needs met on every level—is less about the objects we have and more about issues of worth, survival, security, and power. Few topics are as charged as the subject of wealth or abundance, simultaneously stirring one's mind to visions of power while making another feel impotent; unleashing a sense of possibility that lifts one to new heights of potential while sending another plummeting into a pit of despair; driving some to do anything while repelling others with equal force.

Since the beginning of recorded history, people have begged, betrayed, lied, cheated, attacked, killed—even their own loved ones— and sent whole countries to war to get more: more money, more land, more power, more people, more reach, more resources. All of it is largely propelled by a primal belief that the more we have, the more powerful, worthy, and secure we'll be; but the result is often the exact opposite. In the western world, we are more materially wealthy than ever before—even the poor have more stuff than some royalty of past centuries—yet on the whole, we feel less secure and more depressed. In the extreme, those who are willing to do anything in their pursuit of more often destroy themselves in the process.

Our social and economic systems are largely based on an outside-in paradigm of scarcity that says, "We're separate from what we need; our good is 'out there,' belonging to someone else; and there's not enough to go around." When it comes to money, we look at our economy, job, or bank balance to determine how well we're doing and what's possible, then expand or contract our behaviors accordingly. This often leads to a never-ending yo-yo cycle of feeling victimized or rewarded based on arbitrary events seemingly outside of our control, increasing our sense of powerlessness and our ability to take authentic action in the direction of our highest vision.

In relationships, it causes us to look to other people—family, friends, and intimate partners—as our source of love, support, or validation, keeping us in a power struggle where we'll never have enough. This zero-sum model of life that has put most of our needs outside of us in scarce amounts creates the experience of lack, or not enough, in virtually every area of our life. It also creates an unhealthy mentality that translates into *I'd better get what I can when I can.*

The problem with this paradigm is that it's all a lie.

The model of what abundance is—where it comes from and how to generate it—is backward, which is why people are rarely satisfied, even when they attain it through traditional routes. They eventually find themselves asking, "Is this all there is?" Yet this never-ending quest for more usually continues all the same. And there will never be an end to the struggle and suffering caused by this experience of lack until a new paradigm of real abundance—and abundance creation—is understood and applied.

The Abundance Project is that system.

This book is built on universal principles, tested and refined over two decades, that have helped thousands of people around the world transform their experience of abundance. These people are living their *ideal* life, creating more time for themselves and with their loved ones, launching their own businesses, pursuing their deepest creative desires, finding the home of their dreams, healing their relationships, gaining the courage to ask for anything they want (and often getting it), charging what they're really worth, erasing tons of debt, and even adding millions of dollars to their income.

With my book *Emergence*, I revealed the missing link in personal development, offering a revolutionary principle that frees people from the struggle of self-improvement and sets them on the path of effortless achievement. In this book, I reveal how this same principle applies to the sustainable creation of abundance—an infinite-sum paradigm that turns transactional relationships into transformational ones, allowing every exchange to increase *the good for everyone involved*—whether you're trying to get more time, more love, more opportunity, more money, or more of anything.

Imagine a world in which you're not dependent on anyone or anything outside of you, but instead, you are a source of unlimited support, supply, and security—more than enough to meet your own needs, and the needs of your family and community. Now imagine people all over the world with this new awareness. There go most acts of violence. There go most wars. Here comes a golden age of abundance for all!

The Awakened Abundance Principle

I wasn't always this optimistic about abundance. I wasn't raised in a home with an abundance mind-set. Even when my family seemed to have a modest amount of one thing, it would cause a shortage of something else. When we finally started having enough money, there wasn't enough time to enjoy it as a family. When we had the time to be together, there wasn't an abundance of love and connection, which often led to conflict. It always seemed like a zero-sum game—two steps forward, three steps back. And it only got worse with time.

Eventually, my parents divorced and I ended up living in a house with no electricity or water, taking sponge baths, ashamed to have friends over. Then we lost everything and ended up staying in a friend's garage—my mom, sister, and I all living in a ten-by-ten space, sleeping on the same mattress. Everything was in short supply: time, space, money, patience, and the bathroom. It got so bad sometimes that I would sleep in our friend's boat in the driveway, under a tarp, breathing in the stale, putrid odor of dead fish. And things didn't get much better from there. At the age of sixteen, I ran away from home and lived under a friend's staircase, my whole life's belongings in a pineapple box beside me. Then in my early twenties, I survived off of nineteen-cent boxes of Kraft mac 'n' cheese in a one-room apartment.

The worst part about all of this wasn't only the lack of abundance; it was the fear, powerlessness, shame, and confusion. I didn't know how to make enough or keep enough of what I made; and even when I did make it, I often felt guilty for having it. Feeling like I had a lack of freedom and space led to a sense of isolation. My childhood experience of being controlled by my parents and their constant conflicts had me believing that I never had enough time to do what mattered to me, creating a hypervigilance to make the most of every minute I had. Because there never seemed to be enough of anything I could count on at home, I developed the perception that I constantly needed to protect what little I had.

This was my reality for several decades. I scrimped, scratched, and clawed my way through each day, trying to stay afloat and just survive. Then a near-death experience in my twenties cracked me open, shattering that old reality, leading me to explore and discover a radically different view on life that revealed the true substance and source of abundance and how it's generated, without limits. I call it the Awakened Abundance Principle, because it's not so much that you achieve, attract, or even create abundance; rather, it's like opening your eyes and realizing you're already surrounded by it.

Imagine thinking you're running late, then discovering you have all the time in the world; or feeling like you're all alone, then waking up to find the love of your life sleeping next to you; or believing you're broke, then getting a call that there's a trust account in your name that's always been there, with more than enough to meet all your needs for the rest of your life. Imagine all of this abundance being available no matter where you've come from, what you've been through, or what circumstance you find yourself in. What would you do differently? Who would you become? What would you create or contribute?

The Awakened Abundance Principle can make it possible to:

- Earn what you deserve
- Launch that dream business or project
- Invest in your future
- Become more creative and productive

- Have the time and energy to give your gifts to the world
- Be surrounded by people who love and support you
- Live a fulfilling and meaningful life

Imagine having no more fear, judgment, or resistance around having all the abundance you want, and not just making a living doing what you love but living a life that reflects your deepest values and highest aspirations. This is not only possible, *it's already been given to you*. And this book shows you how to finally experience it. There are no tricks here, only principles and practices that form the path of true abundance in this world.

Like electricity, the substance of real abundance is everywhere. But merely knowing that intellectually won't turn your lights on; you must build the infrastructure (in this case, internally) and plug in. The ability to create computers, fly planes, and send a rocket into space existed when humans dwelled in caves; but without the right understanding of the principles and practices to channel these hidden forces, they were stuck with sticks and stones. This is the same with your abundance: *it's already right where you are*. And when you understand and apply the Awakened Abundance Principle, you can access, activate, and express a virtually unlimited amount of it.

This doesn't necessarily mean having as much money or material things as the super rich—most people don't actually want that. It means that you have the same inner source and capacity to generate this infinite supply, in whatever form that abundance needs to take. How it manifests will depend on your soul's unique pattern and purpose. But one thing is for sure: *it will manifest as fulfillment*.

Ultimately, the Awakened Abundance Principle is about becoming free. Free to be who you really are, to do your deepest work, to take care of your loved ones, and to have the lifestyle that supports it all. It's about becoming so connected to the source of real substance and supply that you never have to worry about having enough. You become free from the fear and guilt that has held you back, and all the energy that used to be sapped by the need to survive becomes available to thrive.

● ● ● ● ● ● ●

By the way, my wife is healthy again, and has one heck of a tennis serve. My son is thriving in his creative endeavors, my daughter has begun her college journey, and we're richer in many ways as a result of all we've been through. And me, well, my work has grown every year, my faith has deepened, and I get to be here, serving you. How does it get any better than that?

If you're ready to get free of all the fear, shame, and pain around abundance and the core issues related to it, and ready to begin to manifest abundance the world can never take away, then it's time to start on this new path. I look forward to walking it with you.

HOW TO USE THIS BOOK

Abundance is not something we acquire.
It is something we tune in to.

—WAYNE DYER

This book will help you create a life of more than enough without the toxic byproducts. But it will do more than that—having a great outer life is only the beginning. As I practiced these principles, especially during the difficult times, it wasn't just more abundance that emerged; more of *me* emerged. In a situation where it would have been so easy to fall apart, give up, and stop growing, these abundance tools helped me turn the problems into greater possibilities.

I want this for you.

I want you to have the freedom, passion, resources, and resourcefulness to take your life to the next level and live your full potential. Maybe it means paying off money you owe, like Sarah did when she went through this program, proclaiming, "After years of struggling with finances, my husband and I are finally on track to being debt free this year!"

Perhaps it's about having a financial cushion or getting more clients, as it was with Christy, who started doing this work and earned more in a month than she had the year before. Abundance for you might look like getting a better job, launching a dream business, or starting a creative endeavor, like Lars, who went from being on the verge of bankruptcy to having more business than he could handle, later using that momentum to open his own healing center. Or maybe it's about cultivating relationships or creating an abundance of time and energy to do the things that matter most the way Judi did—who went from living out of her car to getting engaged and moving in with the man of her dreams. Or Tom, who finally found the space to create more time, take better care of himself, and live a life of adventure!

All of this and more have happened for thousands of people as they've worked—and played—through this system. And it can happen for you; because this isn't personal, it's principle. And when you understand and apply a principle correctly, it works.

●●●●●●●

The Abundance Project is structured to be your personal path; and like any journey of transformation, it takes a certain amount of curiosity, commitment, determination, and time. Results come when you take your desire for change and harness that intention into real action. I suggest taking your time as you read through the book for the first time, from beginning to end. Let yourself become familiar with these new concepts, exercises, and tools, some of which may be contrary to long-held beliefs.

When you have a clearer sense of the breadth and depth of what this book has to offer you, feel free to go back to specific chapters you want to focus on. I recommend creating an abundance journal or diary to track your ideas, questions, experiences, and feelings as you travel this new path. Writing is a powerful tool for gaining clarity, accessing guidance, and activating your power to manifest the life you dream of.

You can also invite a partner to play along. (When two or more come together in agreement on what's possible, you create a new contract with life that can override limited beliefs.) Maybe you and your spouse want to manifest a dream home or start a family, or you and a colleague want to launch a new company or expand your current projects. If the result you want is more abundance in any area, this book can be a great tool to achieve that.

What to Expect

The Abundance Project is not designed to just give you new theories and concepts, or even to merely inspire you about what's possible; it's designed to provide the specific practices that will allow you to access, activate, and embody this potential in a real-world way. As stated above, you can read this more casually at first, then go back and do the exercises. You don't have to do them all to get results, but the more you engage in this process, the more you'll get out of it. There's also a convenient index at the back of the book that lists the practices by chapter for quick reference.

In chapter 1, you'll learn about the "Real Source and Substance of Abundance," and about the "Great Reversal," which will take you out of the old mind-set of trying to get something from the outside and show you how to let out what's already inside. You'll also discover a unique principle called the "Big Betrayal," which explains why anytime you make something or someone outside of you a source of your security, support, or supply, it will ultimately fail you.

From there, chapter 2 will help you see through the "Five Abundance Blind Spots"—the unconscious trances that keep most people stuck in patterns of lack and limitation. You can't wake up if you don't realize you're dreaming. You don't have free will or true choice until you have an expanded awareness of what's really running you.

By the time you're finished with this section, you'll be living with eyes wide open.

In chapter 3, we'll dive into one of the most important frameworks you must master for generating abundance: "The Seven Gifts that Give You Everything" (also known as the "Wealth Activators"). This will show you how to turn on that inner abundance machine and start generating this substance in every area of your life.

In chapter 4, you'll learn one of the most fundamental but often overlooked principles: the "Law of Circulation." This will clarify why things stop flowing in your life, why you get stuck and feel stagnant, and how to create a flow of life-sustaining, abundance-creating energy that never runs out.

Chapter 5 will teach you one of the most critical truths to abundance freedom: "Everyone is Your Channel; Nobody is Your Source." This is a master teaching that will show you how to ask for what you want, earn what you're worth, share more of what you have, and turn every transactional relationship into a transformational one that magnifies abundance for all.

We'll move into a powerful healing and transformational stage in chapter 6 by uncovering the "Healing Abundance Shadows and Values Conflicts"—the unconscious patterns that have been driving many of your compulsive, self-sabotaging actions. Understanding how to spot and heal these limited beliefs and coping mechanisms is one of the most revolutionary and liberating experiences someone can have on the path of personal growth.

Finally, in chapter 7, we put it all together in a program for creating real, lasting results—the "Abundance Boot Camp"—which takes your "Abundance Mastery Goal" and turns it into a 40-day actionable plan, switching on your inner-wealth-creating capacity so that you can start generating everything that appears to be missing in your life. And we'll close with "Unconditional Living," where you will learn how to live in the world without seeking to get anything, magnifying the good for everyone by being what ancient Sanskrit defines for *man*: "the dispenser of Divine gifts."

The Abundance Project is not just a system for getting more material things in the world; it's a way of life. When you plant a seed and cultivate the right conditions, the laws of nature will grow that seed. If you design a plane and fly it in accordance with the laws of aerodynamics, it will take flight. If you understand the principle and align with it, it must produce results. Period. The same is true with the Awakened Abundance Principle: if you commit to aligning your life with this principle, you will experience the true meaning of having more than enough.

THE
ABUNDANCE
PROJECT

1

THE REAL SOURCE AND SUBSTANCE OF ABUNDANCE

Wealth is the ability to fully experience life.
—HENRY DAVID THOREAU

Picture a flourishing apple tree burgeoning with ripe, golden, delicious fruit. There's something almost magical—even mystical—about it. Maybe that's why the apple has been such a prominent symbol throughout the ages. But in all the stories where apples play a part, the tree only gets a little mention, if at all. It's the fruit, forbidden or otherwise, that we're most focused on. It's like telling the story of eggs without giving much consideration to the chickens they came from. However, like the old question of which came first, the chicken or the egg, we must ask the same query of the fruit: which came first, the tree or the fruit . . . or the seed?

(The answer might surprise you.)

None of them.

Sure, there couldn't be fruit without the tree. And there couldn't be a tree without a seed. But there couldn't be any of it without an intelligent life that created the seed and placed the pattern of the tree inside it. That intelligent, invisible life is the real Source—the source of the fruit and the egg, the tree and the chicken. Without Source, this same nothingness out of which the Big Bang created the universe, there would be no creation.

You might argue that evolution is the process by which the seed was created—that it was all a random act of mutation and adaptation. And I would suggest that the likelihood of a universe filled with such complexity and diversity emerging out of random chaos is about as possible as an explosion in a junkyard eventually creating a Boeing 747; or an explosion in a printing press evolving into the collective works of Shakespeare. Some would argue that it's irrational to believe in an invisible, conscious force behind creation; however, I would suggest that to believe all of the beauty, complexity, and order in the universe is the result of *unintelligent* particles slamming into each other is much more illogical. Nevertheless, this book isn't about creationism versus evolution; and you don't have to take a position on either to put this principle into practice.

The point is that the fruit isn't the source of itself; therefore, it's not the real wealth of the tree. *The real wealth is the inherent, transformational* process that turns the seed into a sapling, then a tree that blossoms, and finally, a tree that bears fruit. That's why, after the fruit has been harvested, the farmer doesn't look out at a field of barren trees and think, *Well, those trees are all broken. Better cut them down and plant new ones.* No, the farmer sees just as much abundance as before, and knows that if he keeps watering, weeding, and feeding them, in due season, they'll produce another bountiful crop. The same goes for the egg. The farmer doesn't gather up a basket of eggs then throw away the chicken; he knows that if he takes good care of the chicken, more eggs will be produced over and over again.

The classic fable of "The Goose and the Golden Egg" illustrates the folly of giving value in the wrong place. As long as the goose was taken care of, it produced golden eggs—a state of abundance consciousness. But when the goose (the Awakened Abundance Principle) was taken for granted and, through fear or greed, violated, the wealth-creation process stopped. Similarly, the farmer understands that you can't just focus on the fruit but must tend to the root, or you'll eventually destroy the very source of the fruit.

The fruit, the eggs, and all forms of abundance are the effects, or byproducts, of this intelligent principle of creation. They're the outer symbols and results of abundance. But we've been conditioned to believe the opposite—that outside, material things are the source of other material things, that *things* are what have real value. This is why, at least in the western world, we put more stock in a "quantity life" rather than a quality one, and have bottom lines that are largely about profits instead of the deeper values that impact people and the planet.

This is the real meaning of the age-old saying, "The love of money is the root of all evil" (1 Timothy 6:10). First of all, that saying is often misquoted as "Money is the root of all evil," which completely misses the point. This misunderstanding has contributed to many people's fear, guilt, and shame around money or wealth. But even when you understand the full saying, it's still easy to misinterpret if you don't know what money is.

Money is just a medium of exchange. In certain cultures, instead of dollars, they trade chickens, cows, or furs. In fact, the word *salary* comes from the Latin word for salt, the currency Roman soldiers were paid in. So would you say, "The love of chickens, cows, furs, and salt is the root of all evil"? It doesn't make sense until you see that, because money is just one outer symbol of abundance. What this is really saying: "The love of the *symbols of abundance* is the root of all evil."

If you believe some outer symbol is the source of your abundance, you'll believe the abundance is finite; and you'll struggle, strive, fight, kill, and even die to get it—since it appears to be the very substance of survival. Again, the exact *opposite* of where abundance really comes from. So when you're identifying, attaching, and grasping at the

3

symbols, you're living in opposition to the real principles of abundance. And when you live in opposition to the principles of life, problems ensue (interestingly, *evil* is *live* spelled backward). If you were to wire your electrical circuits backward, in opposition to the laws of electrical conductivity, they would not only fail to work properly, they could start a fire and burn your house down!

When you realize, however, that the source of abundance is spiritual or energetic—the substance of consciousness or spirit—and become unattached to any of its outward symbols, then you begin to generate prosperity that takes nothing from anyone and benefits everyone. *You live in harmony and alignment while ending the war for wealth, once and for all.*

This is not magical thinking; it's scientific. We already know that energy is never created or destroyed. And new discoveries are proving we live in a field of infinite energy out of which we can draw without limits, putting us on the verge of a revolution where energy could become free. I've heard of studies where researchers placed a tree in a tub, measured the volume of the soil, and then grew the tree to the point where it produced fruit. At the end of the study, researchers measured the soil again, *and it had the same volume as it did before it fruited.* The tree didn't deplete the soil; it used the conditions of the soil—and the natural byproducts of its growth and environment—to make its invisible potential tangible. If every tree that grew used up the soil, the Earth would have run out of dirt a long time ago! The only reason we erode our soil or run out of resources is because we're not in harmony with the natural rhythms of renewal. The entire visible universe came out of the invisible, out of nothing. This is a clue about how creation is meant to occur. As we align with this principle and learn to lean more on the invisible Source versus visible resources, we will develop a capacity to create without limits and without taking anything from anyone—instead, we will continuously add to the abundance of the world.

When you understand that wealth is not dollars, apples, eggs, cabbages, or property but the intelligent process that turns the raw material of life itself into the forms of abundance that surround you—and when you design a life around that—you'll activate the same potential to produce a bountiful harvest season after season. You'll begin to realize you can create everything in your life out of seemingly nothing and have the confidence to know you can draw out of this infinite Source everything you'll ever need.

The Great Reversal

As we begin to understand the real nature of wealth and abundance, this is the next core principle we must organize our life around: "Everything is within us; therefore, life flows from us, not to us." This is a foundational truth from my book *Emergence*. It turns inside out the whole model of how we've been conditioned to believe life works. And that's exactly what it should do, because it really is an inside-out world. The world has nothing to give us except feedback and an opportunity to express. Just as a mirror can't reflect back to you any more or less than what you're doing in front of it, this world can only reflect back to you what you express into it.

The Great Reversal is the realization that all the issues of life emanate from our mind: *we aren't in the world; the world is in us*, in our consciousness. We are completely self-contained, self-maintained universes, experiencing whatever is active in our consciousness. There's no "blame the victim" here. Even so, if you're experiencing what the world calls "terrible things," there's no value in blaming yourself for it; that's just a trick of the ego to keep you stuck. Instead, the value is in using our experience to show us what we really believe, so we can grow. Plus, most of what we have in our consciousness is the result of many years of experience (even lifetimes, if you believe in that) in

5

which we were operating from very limited awareness. We've always been doing our best, based on our narrow perception of reality.

If we knew better, we would do better.

All great masters have taught that the source of all creation is within us—whether they called it the kingdom of Heaven, nirvana, the Tao, or paradise. If we had only gotten that part right, we would be having quite a different experience. The implications of this one principle alone are a total game changer. If you want more to come into your life, you must let more life come out of you. If you want more inspiration to show up, you have to act like an inspired person to activate more of this energy of inspiration. If you want more love to show up, you have to act more loving to generate a greater abundance of love.

It all starts with you.

I had a client, Mona, who was a shut-in for most of her adult life because of a childhood illness that made her feel terribly isolated. As she began the Awakened Abundance process, she stopped waiting for opportunities for greater connection and started generating them. She began to extend herself to whatever was available—befriending the plants, communing with the stars, being a good companion to whoever showed up in her space. As her feeling of connection and confidence grew, she stretched her capacity further, forgiving the people in her past (another form of love) and expressing more love to herself and to those around her. Within several months, she met someone and fell completely in love for the first time in her life.

Remember, the word for *man* in Sanskrit means "the dispenser of divine gifts," and that's what you are—a dispenser of the gifts of life, an opening through which all of eternity can pour into expression. Think about how this would radically change your relationship to everyone and everything out there if you actually understood, believed, and acted from this truth.

Everything out there is an effect of an internal cause. There are no other mitigating factors; no other powers, substances, or laws operating upon us. *Nothing* has the power to increase or diminish your capacity for abundance—not your parents, your social status, the economy, the government, your employer, your partner, or anything else. We are reaping what we sow, harvesting what we've planted. Whatever we're experiencing now is the fruit of some previous planting, and whatever we're planting now is the seed of our future crop.

Nobody else can plant for us, and nobody else can dig up what we've planted; nobody can determine whether we have sweet fruit, bitter fruit, abundant fruit, or no fruit. It's an inside job. But there's no judgment here, just a spiritual principle—the most empowering of all principles if we embrace it.

Think of all the examples of people who have come from seemingly insurmountable challenges and risen above these challenges, because they refused to let anyone or anything else determine their destiny. The stories are too numerous to recount. But in all of them, a principle is being revealed—that the locus of power, the main determining factor of our destiny, is *within* you; and it is based on whether you see yourself as a victim of circumstances or the author of them. When you finally accept this, taking 100 percent responsibility for your thoughts, words, and actions, then directing those energies toward your highest vision, things can truly change for the better.

I've worked with many people who have turned their lives around when they started to see how the seeds of their thinking, feeling, and doing were directly creating the fruits of their experience. Another of my clients, Claire, came to me at her wit's end after experiencing a string of setbacks: a painful relationship breakup, a business deal that had gone awry, and the possibility of losing her house. She felt betrayed, abandoned by God, and angry at how everything she had worked so hard for was failing her.

From her initial story, I could already see a core pattern: in every one of these instances, she had betrayed or abandoned *herself* at some point by not trusting her intuition or listening to her guidance for fear of making the wrong choice or losing out. As we dug deeper, we found the seeds of this behavior early in her life, when she had accepted the belief that her judgment wasn't good; that she wasn't as smart as others; and that deep down, she didn't deserve better. The result was that she struggled to overcome this belief, creating coping mechanisms to repress her real feelings about herself.

She became a hard worker and developed a lot of great skills that took her pretty far. But eventually, those seeds of self-judgment bore fruit. They showed up first by her not acknowledging the red flags she saw in her relationship until they blossomed into a full-blown act of betrayal by the man she was with. Then, in a business deal, because she didn't listen to her inner guidance to protect her intellectual property, her partner was able to do things that ultimately destroyed their project. All of this led to a breakdown in her overall confidence, and a lack of momentum and follow-through that put her in the place she was now, on the verge of losing her home.

When she was able to see all of these stories together, she could see that it was *she* who had betrayed her trust long before her boyfriend had, and *she* who had abandoned her needs for healthy boundaries in her business dealings long before her partner had. This new awareness led her to commit to expressing herself in very different ways moving forward. Instead of looking to others and waiting for validation, giving away her power, she began giving herself more love, trust, and respect. She began treating her ideas, her intuition, and her needs the way she wanted others to treat her; and within less than a year, she turned all of her prospects around. But she didn't just have more possessions at the end of that year; she had a greater possession of herself, of her power.

That's Awakened Abundance!

So if everything is within us, the key to creating a life of never-ending growth and expansion is summed up in one word: *giving*. Or in any of its synonyms: sharing, serving, circulating, radiating, blessing, expressing—anything that activates more of the abundance that's in us and allows us to pour it into our experience. This is what Claire discovered in the story above. When she could finally see the areas where she had cut herself off from her Source by trying to "get" something (including love, approval, and validation) by waiting for that something to come *to* her, she could reconnect to her inner source and start generating what she needed. She could see how her actions were separating her from the life, love, and potential already within her. (We'll dive more deeply into this with the Seven Gifts and the Law of Circulation discussed in chapters 3 and 4.) Suffice it to say, understanding this core concept is the beginning of true freedom and a life of limitless abundance.

Now I understand this might still sound esoteric and intangible, like a bunch of theoretical or conceptual ideas that you aren't quite sure how to apply. You might be thinking, *I need to pay my rent . . . I'm in a loveless marriage . . . I'm stuck on an important project and could lose my job . . . I need* real *help, not just abstract concepts*. And I get it. That's how our ego responds to things we can't immediately touch, taste, or measure. The human mind is always seeking something concrete to rely on, because it only believes in that which we can experience with the senses. Ironically, it's the opposite: if you can measure it, it's *not* real. As stated before, the real source and substance of life is invisible and intangible, manifested only through our conscious contact with it. This is why the Tao says, "The Tao that can be expressed is not the eternal Tao; the name that can be defined is not the unchanging name."

This wisdom has been expressed throughout most of the great teachings of the world as mystics pierced the veil of materiality and discovered what's really running things behind "the seen." Bottom line: anything we can perceive with the senses is a concept, belief, or symbol of the "real thing"—what Plato called a shadow of the realm of perfect forms, or what I call "a relative expression of the Infinite Perfection." The more we become interested in, identified with, and anchored to the real Source—the invisible qualities and principles behind the appearances—the more our life will manifest an unlimited good. The more we are attached to the outer symbols, the more we will block our greatest good, limit our abundance, and ultimately, stagnate. This is one meaning behind the biblical statement from Galatians 6:8: "Whoever sows to please their flesh, from the flesh will reap destruction; whoever sows to please the Spirit, from the Spirit will reap eternal life."

Let's make this more tangible with the following practice, so that we can have a direct experience of the truth that everything is within you, just waiting for you to activate it, rather than keeping it in the realm of the conceptual.

Manifest Abundance Now!

Turning On Your Divine Power Plant

- Get comfortable and close your eyes. Recall a time when you felt loving or loved. See the object of affection, feel the love you feel.
- Take a breath and, as you exhale, let that feeling of love expand to fill your chest, then your whole body. *Really* feel it. Give it a color, then take another breath; and as you exhale, see and feel this color expanding to fill your whole body.
- Now radiate that love into your life, and see it saturating everyone and everything. See people's reaction as they feel your love enveloping them. See how it blesses, heals, and inspires them. *Feel how*

good that feels. Experience its expansion as you radiate it, seeking nothing but to give and generate that love.

- Rest in that for a moment. When you're ready, write down your experience in your journal. Describe what you experienced—the sensations in your body; the emotions; the color, images, or people you saw.

Now what just happened? A moment ago, you probably weren't feeling love or joy, at least not like you just experienced. And nothing physically changed in your world. Nobody gave you a gift, you didn't win the lottery, and you didn't meet your soul mate. There was no external object that gave you that love. So where did it come from? And where does it go when you're not feeling it? The same place it's always been and will always be: within you—within your consciousness.

It's always there, always playing on your own personal radio station ("KLUV"), but you have to tune in to that broadcast to experience it. Then you can crank up the volume, expand it into your life, and with regular practice, create a preset on the dial so the frequency of love becomes a permanent part of your bandwidth. You can also do this for any other positive quality you want more of in your life. Once you understand the vibration or feeling behind any object or appearance, you can radiate it into your experience. I recommend doing this daily—ideally in the morning, to set a powerful tone for the rest of your day. The more you generate and circulate these qualities, the more of them you'll have.

And here's where the magic happens: as you activate more love, it will eventually manifest as more loving experiences. That could be a new pet, a new partner, a new friend, a new child, or some other new expression of love in your life. Likewise, if you embody more gratitude, the universe will give you more experiences to feel grateful about, and on and on. *It's all within you.* That's why one of my principles of Emergence is that whatever's missing in your life is whatever you're not giving—whatever you're not activating or generating.

You Can't Get What You Don't Have

Besides understanding the truth that you already have everything within you, the cornerstone of the Awakened Abundance Principle is also about developing and expanding your "have consciousness"—that inner feeling that you already have whatever you want or need. It's not enough to just know about this truth; you need to embody it and live from it. Like electricity, the fact that it's everywhere does you no good unless you're plugged into it. If you're in a state of having, the law of mind operates on that consciousness and manifests more having. Whereas, if you're in a state of not having, even if you currently have a lot or do a lot to have more, the law operates on your consciousness and manifests more not having, which appears as loss and lack.

This is why a person who suddenly gets a new job, a new opportunity, a new relationship, or an unexpected windfall of money (externally) is still filled with the fear of losing, failing, or being rejected (internally), which then leads to self-sabotage and a self-fulfilling prophecy of lack. The person had a state of not-having consciousness. Conversely, a person who has very little outwardly but begins to build a state-of-having consciousness will start to experience an increase in their outer abundance—and sometimes in dramatic, seemingly miraculous ways. This is one meaning of the metaphysical axiom, "To he who is right in mind, he can do all the wrong things, and it will still turn out right. But to he who is wrong in mind, he can do all the right things, and it will still turn out wrong."

When I wanted to be more philanthropic in my life but didn't feel like I had any extra money, I began to take what little money I could spare and go through a process that put me into a state of *feeling* like I had an abundance to give. I would bless the money, activating a feeling of gratitude for what I had, where it came from, and all the good it was already doing. Then I began to imagine all the good it could do as it was circulated, and this filled me with an expanded feeling. I would dedicate my offering to creating more abundance for everyone it touched, then give it away. As I practiced this, I found myself having spontaneous moments of feeling so rich and so inspired—like something magical was happening. I noticed more abundance starting to flow into my life, along with more opportunities to give. Eventually, this became a habit; and within about a year, I was giving thousands of dollars to charity.

I used this same practice to expand my creative and writing capacity. Instead of waiting for the right or perfect idea to come before I would engage in the creative process, I took whatever idea I had, however seemingly small, and put it to work, giving it a chance to flourish into something more. When I wanted to write books, I just started writing *as if* I was already a prolific author. It wasn't easy. My mind put up a lot of resistance, telling me I wasn't good enough, my writing wasn't strong enough, the process was too hard, it would take too long, and besides, who did I think I was to presume I had anything worth saying? I thanked my mind for sharing and wrote anyway.

I wrote slowly. I wrote quickly. I wrote badly. But I just kept writing. I took everything I had—all my knowledge, experience, and passion—and poured it onto the page, day after day. Pretty soon, moments of inspiration broke through, and I found myself in the flow. And it just kept coming. Where there had been a barren desert, there was now a forest of ideas. This led to my first book proposal and my first book. From believing I had nothing to write about and could never write a whole book to four books later—this is the power of coming from a state of have consciousness.

●●●●●●●

I've used the Awakened Abundance practice for myself and with clients to generate more money, better opportunities, relationships, dream homes, vacations, and even a family. The key is that if we take what we have, what we've been given, whatever's showing up and use it, invest it, circulate it—because we have a mind-set of trusting life and believing we're supported—life will reward us by giving us even more to use.

Why does this work?

Because life wants to express more of itself.

In fact, that's the only impulse of life—to manifest more life. So, in its perfect system of efficiency, life diverts energy from those places not willing to invest and express it and sends it to those willing to use it fully, as bigger channels of it. Put another way: "Use it or lose it." But the overriding idea is about the importance of being in a state of having versus a state of not having, or being in a state of having enough versus a state of not having enough.

To begin building this state-of-having consciousness, don't allow yourself to entertain loss or lack. The reason is that, in reality, there is no such thing; there is only infinite abundance, wholeness, and perfection, forever unfolding as our moment-to-moment experience. Our limited perceptions are what tell us otherwise. Though we can definitely *experience* lack and loss, we're not experiencing reality; it's just our relative perception of it. And if we react to that appearance, we develop a mind-set of lack. Then the law of mind in action must operate on that, giving us more lack in return.

That doesn't mean we deny the facts. Facts are facts, but they're not truth. If you break your leg, you don't limp around affirming, "My leg is fine, my leg is fine." Doing nothing about it will likely make it worse. Likewise, if your bank account is empty and you have bills due, you don't skip around singing, "I'm rich! I'm rich!" and hope the bill fairy will leave a mortgage payment under your pillow!

Nevertheless, even as you continue to be a good steward to whatever obligations face you, the moment an appearance of lack tries to tempt you into believing you're actually lacking something or have lost something of true value, you must work at realizing the truth that you have infinite abundance—even if, right now, you can't see it. By whatever means you have, you must claim it and work with this principle until you feel it and shift to an upward spiral of having.

Even while you knock on doors, cold call, pound the pavement, go on blind dates, or stare at a blank screen trying to write the next great novel—whatever you do to be resourceful and create momentum—don't let your energy or feeling around the condition continue on a downward, have-not spiral, because soon, you'll manifest even more not having.

Again, this is not about denying the "facts," and it's certainly not about resisting or wrestling with the appearances. If you're fighting or resisting things—even trying to pray or affirm them away—it's because you've already been caught in the belief of lack. And what you resist, persists; what you fight, you fuel. So it will likely get worse.

But if, instead of reacting, you stop, become still, breathe, and reconnect to the true Awakened Abundance Principle—to the Source of Life within you—you come home to the realization of your wholeness, your "have-ness." Now you're back in alignment, and your actions from that place are right actions.

The Big Betrayal

For years, I had been a struggling actor, chasing fame and fortune but really chasing self-acceptance. I almost killed myself with an alcohol overdose that landed me in the ER, and then I nearly drowned during a film shoot when I recklessly went diving alone after the movie fell apart. That near-death experience was so traumatic that it ripped my ego from its moorings, and in a blinding aha moment, revealed that everything I believed about how to make life work was backward.

I decided to pull out of society to become a monk; but when a silent, fasting retreat in a traditional monastery caused me to break into the monk's kitchen and steal food in the middle of the night, I decided that maybe the monk life wasn't for me. So I cloistered myself in my apartment and began a two-year spiritual journey to understand the miraculous glimpse I had been shown.

During those years, I was happier than ever. I had a contentment I didn't know was possible; I thought I had "arrived." Then my savings account began to dwindle...and dwindle. I burned through everything, exhausted all external means of support, and had no prospects in sight. My "trust account" went to zero and my peace went to pieces—I was literally living on a prayer. I was also, to be honest, pretty pissed off at God. I mean, here I was dedicating my life to being of service and all my services were being canceled!

So one day, after groveling for another rent extension from my landlord, I sat in my worn faux-leather meditation chair and laid down the gauntlet: "God, either you really exist and I can rely on you, or this is all a bunch of bull. Either way, I'm gonna find out today, because I'm not getting up until I have my answer—even if they have to pry my cold, penniless hands from this chair!"

As I describe in my previous book, *Emergence*, that moment of intention when I took a stand (or rather, a sit) for knowing the truth, led to a powerful revelation—the most important insight after my near-death experience. After sitting and struggling for hours with waves of emotional turmoil, somewhere in the middle of the night, something cracked open inside of me and a divine guidance came through, showing me why I was going broke and why nothing was working anymore: I had made my bank account my Source, my God, and "You shall have no other gods before me" (Exodus 20:3).

As this awareness came through, a peace washed over me, and all the fear and stress was released. I didn't know what had happened, but I knew I was free—I knew I was taken care of. A few days later, I got a call from a former acting agent that led to an audition for a commercial, which I booked. The resulting few days of work ultimately paid me more than enough to live off of for the next year.

The money was great, but the awareness that there really was something within me that could meet my needs—beyond what I could imagine, regardless of conditions—was a life changer. It began my journey of learning to lean less on resources and more on the true Source of Life. I now knew, viscerally, that everything was inside, and that the only way more could come into my life was by letting more come *out* of me. This idea became a process for consciously activating my inner abundance-creating power without having to hit a wall or have my back against one. It also revealed one of the key reasons people suffer and feel powerless when it comes to creating a life of real abundance and freedom—what I came to call the Big Betrayal. The basic principle states that:

Anytime we make someone or something outside of us
our source of supply (or anything else), the universe
is set up to fail us in that area.

The reason is both simple and profound: if we believe that someone or something outside of us is our Source, we must give it our power, contorting ourselves into whatever shape we think is necessary to get what we don't have or to keep what we fear losing. This leads to control and manipulation, including various forms of violence toward ourselves or toward another. But more importantly, it makes it nearly impossible for us to show up authentically—to be the person we were created to be, giving the gifts we came here to give and fulfilling the greater purpose life has for us.

Left unchecked, this would eventually lead to a breakdown of the major systems of life, *but life will not be denied.* The divine or evolutionary plan will win the day—either by bringing us to our knees and taking away all means of outer support, forcing us to turn within and find our connection to Source again; or by removing us from the picture and replacing us with someone willing to act from his or her power.

Life is designed for living in an ever-increasing, ever-expanded way. Anything that limits, denies, or blocks this will ultimately be removed. Just as a branch on a tree gets pruned when it isn't producing flowers or fruit, life prunes away those parts that aren't revealing and reflecting its true nature and purpose. This is a natural process in nature, but we often forget that we are part of that same natural process. The result is that we misdiagnose the problems in our life as being random, accidental, karmic, or someone else's fault instead of seeing that our chronic problems are an indication that we're trying to survive in a paradigm that is too small for what's trying to emerge from us. We've created coping mechanisms out of fear and a sense of separation from our true Source and are now putting all our energy into staying safe, not losing or failing, and creating mere comfort or convenience.

This disconnection from Source prevents our life force from flowing until, like a tree whose roots have begun to rot, the many branches of our life stagnate: health, wealth, work, relationships, personal growth, spirituality. We're filled with fear, guilt, shame, or resentment because we've given away our power in exchange for some outer form of safety or security—mere symbols of Source—then we try to fix those branches by exerting more control and manipulation, or just withdrawing. The result is that our branches wither, and our life stops flowering and bearing fruit. We lose our job and increase our debt; our relationships suffer or completely fall apart; and our sense of purpose, passion, and inspiration dry up.

We may rail against things, blaming God, life, the universe, or whoever is within earshot—like I did that fateful night. We may dig in our heels and stubbornly try to make our small life better by working harder, smarter, faster; or by straining to attract or achieve more. But because we've become cut off from our true Source, we run out of energy; become overwhelmed, burned out; and eventually break down. It seems like life is against us. But actually, life is completely *for* us, trying to bring us back home again, to the real source of our power and prosperity, which is and has always been within.

Interestingly, the more personal growth or spiritual work we've done, the more intense and accelerated this process often is—because you've activated a bigger life, and it's determined to break through the hard shell of your myopic perceptions. You're trying to stay an acorn and just be the best nut in the forest; but a mighty oak is emerging, and it will win the day!

Perhaps it hasn't become quite as desperate as this yet. But if there are any areas of your life where you're making someone or something your Source, you're setting yourself up for pain and suffering, sooner or later.

We've been conditioned since birth that someone outside of us is our Source. First it was Mommy and Daddy, who really did appear to be our source of survival—not just in terms of putting a roof over our head and food in our stomach, but giving us the love and attention fundamental to our well-being. When we receive this love and attention, we feel seen, valued, and supported for who we really are; we don't become more dependent *but* less. However, to the extent that we don't feel fully nurtured in our family, we begin to look to others—friends, romantic partners, or other authority figures—for validation and a sense of belonging, making their opinions our source of well-being.

If we lacked specific recognition or support from a parent, we might look to our teachers or coaches or mentors for approval and self-worth, making them or our performance the source of our self-esteem. If we haven't been anchored in a deep sense of safety and self-confidence, we will likely look to a job, a boss, a spouse, the economy, the government, or some other outside entity as our source of supply and security. And as we grow older, we're trained to believe doctors are the source of our health—the true authority over our body—making the "MD" stand for "minor deity"!

On and on, we're made to believe we need someone or something outside to complete us. But the truth is *nobody completes you.* In any real partnership, as Michael Beckwith said in an Agape Church service, "Two 'halves' don't make a whole; two 'haves' do." If you don't bring wholeness with you, you'll never experience wholeness from something or someone. If you feel cut off and alone, other people won't cure your loneliness. If you feel unworthy, no level of outside validations will make you feel good enough. If you feel lacking, no amount of wealth or opportunity will make you feel abundant, safe, or secure.

When you connect with what you need within, however, and build that inner trust account and greater resourcefulness (which I call being "full of Source"), then no matter what appears to be lacking, no matter what anyone does or doesn't do, says or doesn't say, you'll always have enough, be enough, and experience fulfillment. The world can never add anything to you because you already have it all. The even better news is that, because the world didn't give it to you, the world can never take it away. It's spiritual, infinite, and can be infinitely and eternally activated within you.

Manifest Abundance Now!

Resourcing: Part I

- Look at an area where you've made someone or something your outside Source. Maybe it's your job, your bank account, your spouse, some other family member, or a friend. It can be about money, but because we're dealing with abundance in a broader sense, you can focus on any area where there appears to be a lack of something (for example, you don't feel validated by your boss or appreciated by your spouse).

- Close your eyes and visualize your relationship to that outside Source. How does that relationship make you feel—empowered or disempowered? Peaceful or stressed? Safe or insecure? Are you able to gracefully be yourself, or do you feel compelled to do certain things that are inauthentic in order to get what you believe you need or to keep what you already have? Notice any feelings of resentment, guilt, shame, or blame—no judgment, just awareness. Let yourself feel the pain and suffering this relationship is causing you, and the impact it's having on your wealth, security, and power. Reflect and write down your feelings.

- Now ask yourself: *What is this relationship costing me?* In terms of self-worth and self-esteem, when you say yes and you really mean no, or when you say no to yourself and you really want to say yes, are you paying a high price for this? Write down your thoughts.

From this practice, you may notice that, despite all the effort you're expending to maintain your relationship with that outside Source, you still don't feel safe, secure, or worthy, let alone have enough of whatever you've been struggling for to meet your needs or to live the life of your dreams. Maybe the relationship has even backfired and things have become worse. Maybe after all your attempts to get what you believed was missing, you lost your job or your mate, or you become estranged from your family or friends.

Recognize where life seems to be failing you in this area, and remember the principle that the universe is set up to betray you when you make anything outside of yourself the Source. You might even discover that the more you've prayed, affirmed, or done spiritual work around having more abundance in this area, the *worse* this area has become, because you're still seeing these people or places as your Source.

Let's start healing this Big Betrayal with the following practice.

Manifest Abundance Now!

Resourcing: Part II

- You begin healing the Big Betrayal by first understanding what's really true: that outside person, place, or thing you've been focused on was never your Source. At best, they were a potential channel for your good; but to whatever extent that good came through them, it originally had to come *from* your consciousness. *Nothing* can come into your life except as an activity of your consciousness.

- Next, work your way back to the truth that everything you could ever need is already within you—actually generate the *feeling* of this. Then make a sacred commitment to embody this truth and live from it fully. To help you with this, recall a time when you felt like you *had* whatever you currently feel is missing. For example, if you've been trying to get validation from someone, remember a moment when you felt this quality. If you can't find a moment in your life when you felt this, imagine a scenario where you receive whatever appears missing and feel what that feels like. Breathe and let that feeling expand to fill your body.

- Focusing on the current area of lack, imagine you got whatever money, opportunity, or emotional response you wanted/needed. See yourself getting that call, that check, or that experience— whatever represents fulfillment in this area. Visualize your reaction. See how you would live differently as a result.
- *Now multiply that experience times ten.* See yourself completing that dream project; having a huge growth spurt in your business; becoming a superstar in your area of work; being deeply seen, valued, loved—whatever would represent a massive breakthrough and success. *Feel what it feels like.* Breathe and let those feelings expand to fill your whole body.
- Now radiate this energy to everyone in your current life, including the people or places you've believed were your Source. Feel how good it feels to be a giver in your life, the source of all good, and how it feels to have more than you need—so much that you can share and circulate it.
- From this place, look at the relationship or situation you believed was your Source and ask the following questions:

  - *If I really knew and believed the Source of Life was within me, always available, how would I be different in this relationship or situation?*
  - *How would I hold myself, treat myself, or express myself?*
  - *What would I start doing, stop doing, do more or less of, or do differently?*

- Listen for the guidance in the answers to these questions. Then ask, *How can I start living into this truth of my abundant being and be the Source of my life today, this week?* Take a breath and receive your inner wisdom.

- When you're ready, write what came through. Then pick something you can do today, (or at the latest, tomorrow) to begin acting from this truth. Commit to activating the feelings associated with this truth and go back to them every time you're tempted to believe this person or place is your source of anything. Give thanks for the capacity to activate these feelings regardless of conditions, knowing that these feelings are the very substance of the next stage of your abundance.

- To further embody the energy of this potential, visualize already having whatever it is you're waiting for, trying to get, or believe is lacking, really *feeling* what it feels like. Then notice who you are *being* in this vision. What are the qualities of being/embodying this desire? (Some examples could be spontaneous, generous, playful, bold, or outgoing.) Write down whatever comes to mind.

- Either in meditation or with your journal, ask, *What would it look like to step into being this person in my life now? Where am I called to be more of this?* Listen for specific guidance and actions you can take or stop taking, then commit to taking that action.

- As you visualize your ideal outcome, activate and radiate the qualities that appear missing, and begin to "act as if" you already are the person experiencing these qualities. In doing so, you *activate* this latent energy of abundance within you and begin to circulate it into your life. And because whatever's missing is what you're not giving, as you start to give what appeared missing, you start experiencing the truth that you already have it.

Becoming the Source of your life is a process. Developing the capacity to trust in this part of yourself enough to lean on it and live from it, regardless of conditions, is a muscle you have to build by working it out. And like working out your body, you don't always want to exercise, you don't always enjoy the exercise, and you sometimes feel sore after. What's more, you usually don't see the results for some time, and it's very tempting to give up too soon.

But if you'll stay committed to the goal, be kind and patient with yourself along the way, get whatever help you need to stay accountable, and simply refuse to give up until you get results, you can turn your life around no matter what. And once Source starts flowing from the inside out, you'll be in a success pattern that will start gaining its own momentum—until you're living by grace, not personal power. When that happens, life is no longer a problem to be solved but an adventure to be lived!

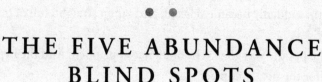

THE FIVE ABUNDANCE
BLIND SPOTS

Wealth is the product of man's capacity to think.

—AYN RAND

The man tried desperately to chase the white poodle off the stage as the person conducting the exercise had directed him to do. But no matter how much he dodged and darted, trying to cut the poodle off, scare the poodle, or grab the poodle, his attempts failed. Exhausted, the man collapsed in his onstage chair, frustrated, staring out of the corner of his eye at that godforsaken white poodle standing just a few feet out of his reach.

The audience watched in awe, some covering their mouths in shock at the antics of this person; because from their perspective, all they saw was a wild man chasing *nothing* around the stage, driving himself crazy until he collapsed in a pool of anger and perspiration. You see, the man had been hypnotized to believe there was a white poodle, and to his awareness, the poodle was as real as anyone else in the room.

"I'm going to count backwards from five to one now," the hypnotist said in a calm, steady voice. "And when I reach one, you'll wake up, feeling refreshed and rejuvenated. Five, four, three, two, one . . ."

He snapped his fingers.

Like a curtain pulling back, the man's face grew brighter. He took a breath, suddenly became relaxed, and sat up straight, full of renewed energy.

The poodle was gone. The audience applauded. And the hypnotist asked for the next volunteer...

So where was that poodle? Where did it come from and where did it go? To the hypnotized man, it appeared to be there. But in truth, it was all a projection of his mind, which had been implanted with a hypnotic suggestion, creating a cognitive blind spot. He wasn't seeing what was *really* there; he was seeing his own *belief* of a white poodle and reacting to that. This same trick has caused many people to do strange things and to have a wide variety of experiences that defy logic. They've been hypnotized to believe they can't move and, try as they might, they're stuck, as if in concrete. They've been hypnotized to believe they're surrounded by snakes and are cowering in fear, completely paralyzed.

There are various studies in which people were "primed" with ideas and then observed as they acted out these hypnotic suggestions: from forming heat blisters when they were touched with a cold match they believed was hot, to displaying symptoms of youth or age in their body posture or the speed and gait of their walk based on auto-suggestions that had been planted in the text they read or the words they heard.

There is an experiment with a group of elderly men who were put in a house that had been converted to reflect the environment of their youth through music, television shows, books, furniture, and so on. The result? After a week of being in this environment, they showed significant signs of age reversal. Some who arrived in wheelchairs came out with only a cane. Some who couldn't even pull up their own socks ended the week playing touch football. But as they returned to the world full of suggestions that they were old, they soon reverted back.[1]

So where were the qualities of youthfulness and old age, the heat of the match, and the white poodle? *They were all in the mind of the subject.* Please don't brush over that sentence, because if you can truly understand that, your life will never be the same. All of these examples and numerous more have proven over and over that we don't experience life as it is; we experience life through the filters of our conditioned beliefs, our expectations, and our stories. We are so susceptible to such suggestions that we can be primed in a matter of minutes and, without even knowing, experience a reality that isn't really there.

Subliminal advertising, which is supposedly illegal and not used anymore, showed just how easy it was to cause people to take action without knowing they were being manipulated. The first major study of this was with ads for snacks during a movie. They would flash an image of popcorn, candy, or soda fast enough so that the conscious mind didn't see it but long enough to enter the unconscious mind. Result: there was a significant increase in concession sales. If we can be made to buy popcorn when we don't really want it, without even knowing we're being influenced, how much more might we be influenced by the subtle and not-so-subtle suggestions from our environment, family, friends, schooling, media, and society?

This book is not a thesis on the power of persuasion or the broad impact of mass propaganda; the key takeaway is that each of us has been influenced by these suggestions. And beyond our own personal lives, we've been soaking in a sea of universal beliefs—beliefs about life that are specific to whatever culture we're a part of—that act as a larger agreement shaping our reality. These create a paradigm of what's possible, what's not, what works, and what doesn't. Over time, they turn into our own unique story of lack and limitation, putting us asleep and playing a part that we didn't even know we were cast in. We think we're walking around with free will, making conscious choices, but often, we're responding to a script we didn't write, blind to all the abundance that's really here. Even as we work on our personal issues, these larger universal beliefs usually remain intact, obscuring our vision of what's true because they're tribal, and to break them would be to come out from the pack and risk rejection.

These universal, limited beliefs act as filters to our perception, narrowing our capacity to see what's possible and putting us into a trance, or hypnotic state, that causes us to keep reacting to these unconscious patterns until we can snap out of them. As I've worked in the area of wealth and abundance, coaching tens of thousands of people around the world, I've identified five of these false, universal beliefs—what I call the Five Abundance Blind Spots—and their corresponding Awakened Abundance Truths. Learning how to identify the signs that you've got one of these blind spots and then how to remove it is the key to creating sustainable abundance in every area.

Now, there are probably more than five, and many distinctions and permutations of each of these. However, in coaching hard-working, conscientious people who sincerely want to have more abundance but are struggling to make it happen, these are the core patterns I've uncovered. Let's dive into them.

ABUNDANCE BLIND SPOT #1
We are separate from our good and must get it, achieve it, or attract it.

AWAKENED ABUNDANCE TRUTH #1
We are one with all good—we can't add or lose anything.

The idea that goodness is outside of us is the number-one lie that hobbles many people in their ability to achieve abundance in any sustainable way. We touched upon it in chapter 1, when I discussed how the substance of all creation is within us and we can never be separate from it. Here, I want to expand on the characteristics of someone blinded by this belief and someone free from it, so you can identify when you've fallen under its spell and have practices for snapping out of it.

We've been conditioned from birth to believe that we're separate—separate from each other, separate from our environment, and separate from the things we want and need. In fact, the ego is basically a separation-creating program. That's actually its job—to create programs that ensure the survival of the separate self and its body. It allows us to experience ourselves as distinct from the environment so we don't walk into a tree or off a cliff; it causes us to feel separate from other animals so we don't hug a lion; and it makes us feel separate from other humans so we don't blindly trust everyone and walk into a dangerous situation unprotected. This separation-creating program extends to our family, friends, ethnicity, tribe, village, nation, and planet.

Clearly, this separation had its benefits at some point in our history. As we were evolving and didn't have the brain capacity to question our perceptions and beliefs (metacognition), it created in us an instinctive mechanism that increased our chances of survival. By seeing ourselves as separate, we protected our body. By seeing our family as separate, we could more easily protect that unit within the tribe. By seeing our ethnicity as separate, we could honor its unique heritage and bring forth its specific gifts. By seeing our tribe, village, and nation as separate, we could develop the diverse qualities, capacities, and ultimate purpose of this larger unit of life. It makes sense in the same way that our behavior makes sense when we really want to master a thing: we isolate this thing and dive deeply into it until we discover, extract, and integrate its potential.

The problem, however, is that a paradigm of separation can only take us so far. It can help us understand or preserve an isolated, distinct part, but it can never bring us to an awareness of the whole and how it all operates together. This is also the problem with much of modern medicine. It has been built on dissecting the parts of the body, often after death, versus understanding how all the parts fit together as a greater whole—not to mention the rest of the being's mental, emotional, energetic, and spiritual influences. The same problem shows up in politics, race relations, and basic human relations.

Nationalism, which has at its divine roots an impulse to distinguish the benefits, values, and purpose of a country or culture, becomes a disease when it judges others as less than and cuts itself off from the whole world. Racial pride, while striving to bring forth the unique gifts of a race, becomes racism or worse when it's rooted in fear and divisiveness. Ultimately, our sense of separation from each other is the cause of all our human conflicts. Over and over, we see the negative consequences of separation playing out in every area of life: how we treat animals like fodder for factory farming, with little awareness of the impact on every area of life; how we treat the environment as if it's just a bunch of separate resources to be plundered and turned into mountains of waste, with little concern of the garbage dump we're creating in our own backyard and the complex ecosystem we're destroying.

But the greatest sense of separation—the one that actually leads to all the rest—is our fundamental sense of separation from Source itself, or what some would call God. In fact, this is *the only real problem we have—our sense of separation from God.* Our belief that we are separate from our Source of Life is the primary cause behind *all* acts of violence and cruelty against ourselves and against others—all wars, all destruction of our precious planet, all suffering. And the only solution to our personal and global problems is to come back into a realization of our oneness with Source and all that it entails. When we know—*truly know*—that we are one with our Source of Life and with everything else that comes from Source, what could we possibly want for? Why would we ever lie, cheat, steal, harm, or kill anyone or anything when we know we *all* are connected to the source of all creation, including its capacity to create whatever we truly need? The answer is *we wouldn't.*

When the Bible refers to being one with the Father and everything that the Father has made, it's speaking of this realization of oneness with the Fountain of All Creation. The Bible talks about the "prodigal son" who leaves his father's house, takes his inheritance, and tries to make it on his own only to become broke and broken, and finally return home again. This story describes the human journey of separation and reconnection—of leaving our sense of oneness with Source to create a separate sense of existence only to experience all the pain and suffering of the human drama; until one day, we wake up in a hovel and realize, *I am alone and lost—what the heck was I thinking?* This is also the meaning behind the Biblical metaphor of the vine and its branches, and how a human is like a branch that withers and dies when cut off from the vine.

Once you understand this principle, if you go back and read the great scriptures of the world (from all religions), you'll start to see what they're really teaching. And it boils down to this:

We are dreaming we're separate from God/Source, which creates all our suffering. We must remove this blind spot to realize our oneness again.

Another important implication: as long as we have this abundance blind spot putting us in a trance of limitation, no amount of good deeds or right actions will solve our problems—as it was with the man wildly trying to catch the white poodle without success. Whatever the strategy or technique used, even the popular law of attraction, if it comes from *within* this blind spot, or hypnotic spell of separation, it will not work.

The law of attraction, while an important metaphysical step, is just training wheels for those who feel that life is happening *to* them; it helps them to begin to move into the second stage of manifestation in which *they* are happening to life. This law is useful because it moves us from being a victim to being a creator, but it's still a form of manipulation that can produce many negative byproducts (as many have attested to and my personal struggle with self-improvement has shown).

I'm not saying that this and other modalities are wrong—many things within this blind spot serve to free us from it eventually. I am saying, however, that some of the ways we've attempted to improve our lives and create more abundance fail or fall short because they exist within this matrix of separation. They're a product of this trance, and like the white poodle, they'll keep us chasing after—or running away from—things that aren't really there until we eventually collapse in exhaustion.

So how do you remove this abundance blind spot and snap out of this spell? Well, first, you have to recognize you're in it. The following are some of the signs that you have been blinded by a sense of separation:

- Feeling that you're incomplete without something, someone, or some condition and that you will only be complete once you have it.
- Feeling unsafe, unsupported, insecure, unworthy (or the many subqualities of this category) because you don't have something or someone, and believing that you'll only be "enough" or feel safe and secure once you have it—similar to the first bullet point but more specific. (These underlying beliefs and their accompanying

emotional patterns are what most advertising is built on. They create an emotional experience of someone feeling happy, safe, secure, and so on, associating that feeling with the product they're selling. If you're buying into ads like this—and buying things based on them—you might have this blind spot!)

- Finding yourself fantasizing about some future goal and telling yourself, *Someday, when I [fill in the blank], I'll be happy, I'll be enough, and all will be well.* (In fact, anytime you put your sense of freedom, fulfillment, or well-being in the future, you've been caught in this blind spot.)

- Feeling a compulsive need to use various "success" strategies to attract or achieve something. (This doesn't mean you can't use these tools; but if you feel you must use them or you'll lose out, or if you feel a sense of fear, excitement, or pushiness when it comes to your goals, you might be chasing a white poodle.)

- Comparing yourself to others in order to feel superior *or* inferior to them, thereby giving away your power to name, fame, fortune, and material things.

- Overworking to achieve or attain anything to the detriment of other important areas—in a way that damages your health, your relationships, or your creative contributions.

- Judging others as "less than" who aren't working hard enough or achieving what you consider success. (This indicates both a shadow [such as "lazy" or "failure"] as well as a sense of separation. [We'll dive into more about shadows in chapter 6.])

- Believing nothing will happen if you don't work consistently, struggle, strive, or push. (This doesn't mean you shouldn't dig in, dig deeper, and work hard sometimes. But if it becomes a compulsive habit accompanied by the fear that if you stop or slow down everything will fall apart, you are caught in the separation blind spot.)

This list isn't meant to be exhaustive; there are many other possible clues that you have fallen under the spell of an abundance blind spot. However, it's enough to alert you when you've taken the bait and are walking asleep, *dreaming you're awake*.

Once you become aware that you've got this blind spot, you can begin the process of removing it. In fact, the moment you realize you're not seeing things as they really are, you've already begun to awaken. In general, if you have a daily meditation practice such as mindfulness and journaling, you'll create a more expansive awareness and greater dominion over your attention; you'll become less likely to be hypnotized. It won't completely inoculate you, but it will definitely build up your immunity.

In addition to—or sometimes in place of—long meditation sittings, you can also do the following "One-Minute Mystic" practice (which I first talked about in my previous book, *Emergence*). This is about stopping throughout the day to practice mystical moments of remembering what's true (about you and life in general), remembering what's important, and feeling grateful for it all. As this becomes a habit, you create a new subjective tendency that operates in the background of your awareness, keeping you open to guidance and inspiration all day.

Manifest Abundance Now!

The One-Minute Mystic Practice

Here's a simple exercise you can do in a minute that will help you embody a greater *feeling* of your oneness with the source of all creation:

- When you find yourself in a fearful, limited, or reactive state of mind (based on any of the clues listed on pages 34 and 35), take a breath and remind yourself that you're not experiencing reality; you're in a blind spot.

- Whatever condition is confronting you, imagine getting what you need, experiencing the outcome you want and really *feeling* the energy of that reality—the "feeling tone" of it. This is the very substance of your abundance.

- Breathe and let that "feeling tone" expand to fill your chest, then your whole body. See it radiating beyond you, filling every area of your life, and saturating everyone and everything.

- From this vibration of abundance, speak some affirmation to yourself about the situation. For example, if you're experiencing some kind of financial lack, tell yourself that all of your needs are abundantly met and that everything is working together for the highest good. By *feeling* this energy and then *affirming* it, you create the condition for integration.

Whenever you can get multiple aspects of your being to "agree" with the truth you want to experience, you accelerate the process of embodiment and awakening.

ABUNDANCE BLIND SPOT #2
Money and material things are wealth.

AWAKENED ABUNDANCE TRUTH #2
Real wealth is invisible, infinite, and within you.

We touched upon this in chapter 1 and will expand upon it here, anchoring the spiritual truth that what most people strive after isn't really what they want; rather, it's the inner quality, the inner connection they desire. What everyone is actually going for, even when they think otherwise, is a *state of being*, whether that's peace, love, joy, freedom, or fulfillment. The belief is that we must purchase this state of being by attaining a certain level of external wealth or things. The irony is that, for many people, the struggle to get the outer things they believe will finally give them this inner experience often robs them of the very state of being they were striving for in the first place.

As we already discussed, the outer expressions of abundance are mere symbols of the real substance, just as the fruit on a tree is not the wealth of the tree but an effect of the invisible process within the tree—the real source of its wealth. As we come to truly understand this, we no longer strive and struggle after the outer things—the effects—but become more interested and invested in the Source, the real cause. Our value system begins to change; we don't value material things as much as we used to. We value people more than profits, quality over quantity, connection over commerce, transformation over transaction. When we really know that the source of all creation is our consciousness, we start to live in consciousness more than appearances. And there, we begin to find the substance of real fulfillment, because that's the only place it can be found. This world is just a canvas upon which we are painting with the colors of our soul, a screen upon which we are projecting the story in our heart. The world can't give us anything except feedback—a reflection of where we are in consciousness and an opportunity to express ourselves. Likewise, it can't take anything away.

Remember, *it's all within us.*

All of the issues of life emerge from mind or consciousness. If we want more of anything, we must touch more of it first within ourselves, then begin to generate or radiate it from our own being. This is why all the great masters have taught us to make that inner connection, whether they called it the kingdom of Heaven, nirvana, the

Tao, or any of the various names this inner dimension has been given. Jesus told us "do not worry about your life" (Matthew 6:25) or any of the things of life, but instead, "seek first his kingdom and his righteousness," which he said was *within* us, and "all these things will be given to you as well" (Matthew 6:33). Buddha taught the same thing, in his own way.

This isn't a religious teaching; it's a perennial truth, a universal principle. In other words, when we make that inner connection with the real substance of life, it always takes form in our experience. But the form is the "added thing," not the thing itself. And when we're anchored to the real thing, or Source, within us, no matter what seemingly threatens, diminishes, or even destroys the outer form, we can always re-create it out of the indestructible, incorruptible reality of our being, from which it came.

This is the real power of removing the abundance blind spot and snapping out of the hypnotic spell it puts us in. When you believe that money and things are wealth, you must give your power away to them. You become attached to them, and you fear all the many ways the world can take them away. This leads to all manner of conflict and control until we're twisted into such a pretzel that we can barely function as the authentic, brilliant beings we truly are. When you understand that all those outer things are just the fruit of an invisible principle, however, you know that no matter how much you have hanging on your branches—no matter how much has been eaten by the birds, blown away by the winds, or dried out from temporary droughts—you can always generate a whole new harvest.

Now, the fact that everything out there is nothing more than a symbol of something real within you doesn't make the symbols bad or unimportant; it just puts them in their proper perspective. And this is not an absolutist teaching that says this world doesn't matter, that it's nothing but an illusion, that we should only care about waking up and getting out of here! There have been many teachings that have made this world bad, unimportant, or just illusion, separating it from God or Source (which has led, in part, to our willingness to allow Earth and its creatures to be destroyed)—an incomplete understanding of reality.

It's true that the world you see, taste, touch, and sense is not real in the absolute sense because it's temporary, always changing; and everything that appears eventually disappears. But that doesn't mean the physical/external world has no value. A painting or photograph of a person or landscape isn't the real person or territory, but it can still be a valuable memento or work of art. We can gain many insights and other benefits from the capacity art gives us to slow things down, focus on the details, discover the distinctions, unpack different interpretations, and activate our feelings.

We can experience great joy, love, laughter, inspiration, and enlightenment from our interaction with the world of appearances, like we can with great works of art. But while we may enjoy and learn from a beautiful painting or a powerful story, we don't want to lose ourselves in it or become so identified with it that we forget who we are separate from it. You can paint a beautiful picture of a road, but it won't take you anywhere; you can snap amazing photographs of food, but none of them will feed you; and you can admire masterpieces of human portraiture, but you'll never know true love and connection by staring at a picture of someone. As with much of this work, it's about being in the world but not *of* it; it's about enjoying all the fruits, all the outer symbols without becoming attached to them or believing they're your Source.

Imagine the power you could possess if you no longer believed the outer world was your Source and no longer worried that it could take anything away? Imagine what you would be capable of if you no longer wasted time and energy struggling for the outer symbols, defending what you have, fearing its loss, or fighting to get it back? Imagine who you could become if you knew all wealth and abundance was within you—infinite, inexhaustible, and unconditional—merely awaiting your activation and expression. This is not only possible, it's how you were designed to live!

So what are some signs that you have an abundance blind spot?

- You judge how much you have or what you're capable of doing based on your bank balance, material possessions, or worldly opportunities.
- You're willing to sacrifice your authentic values or the things and people that truly matter to you for some level of name, fame, or fortune.
- You're willing to sacrifice your true calling, your deeper purpose, the work you most want to do for a job or opportunity that only brings you money. (This doesn't mean you don't sometimes have to work a regular job or work part of the time to pay the bills so you can use the rest of your time to pursue your passion; that's a perfectly legitimate path. The key is that you don't let your pursuit of money or security replace the pursuit of your deeper purpose.)
- You're willing to lie, cheat, steal, or harm someone or something in order to get some level of name, fame, or fortune. (This can be as simple as cheating on your taxes, lying on your resumé, or emotionally betraying someone—including yourself—to get what you want.)
- You're willing to be disrespected or mistreated on some level in order to maintain your outer source of safety, security, support, or supply. (This includes staying in a job that treats you badly, not speaking up to change it, or putting up with unloving or unkind behavior from a spouse, parent, or partner to avoid losing them as your source of something.)
- You find your sense of safety or security in the material things of the world. For instance, you have a job or savings account and,

therefore, feel financially secure. Or you have a home and spouse and feel safe and supported. (This doesn't mean it's wrong to have these things, but you must check yourself on a regular basis to see if you've begun to lean on the outer world and become complacent with the inner work to anchor yourself in Source. You don't want to lean on a resource; you want to lean on *the* Source. If you're finding safety, security, and most of your satisfaction externally, you've made the material world your god. And when you make your Source anything outside of you, the universe is set up to fail you—to force you to return to the true Source within and live an empowered life.)

- You're putting your real life on the layaway plan, waiting for some future condition when you'll have enough of whatever you think you need (time, money, ability, relationships) to go for what you really want, be who you really are, and fulfill the deeper reason you're here. The only reason you would do this is because you believe some outer symbol is the Source. When you know that the source of all abundance—an abundance of time, money, ability, love, and so on—is within you, then there's nothing to wait for.
- You admire or value people with a lot of outer symbols of wealth— name, fame, or fortune—more than you admire or value people who have an abundance of inner resources. When your criteria for the most "successful" people on the planet or throughout history tends to be more material and external rather than spiritual and internal, you have an abundance blind spot.

It's not wrong to have an outer goal of name, fame, or fortune. The problem comes when you believe that the outer goal is the source of your inner well-being and fulfillment, or when you pursue it to the detriment of your inner connection to the real source of creation. As long as your primary goal is to have an ever-deeper connection to the real source of abundance and power within you—to live in peace, love, joy, and gratitude regardless of conditions—then there's no problem having a big outer goal too.

If you want to live a truly abundant, happy, fulfilled life, your deepest devotion, investment, priority, and attachment must remain on the inner goal, the inner connection. If you have that, you have the real riches of life, and they will appear outside as the "added things." But if you pursue the outer things and lose that inner connection, no matter how much you get out there, you'll be in poverty. This is one way to understand the ancient text, "What good will it be for someone to gain the whole world, yet forfeit their soul?" (Matthew 16:26). All you end up with is a gallery full of pictures that can't feed you, comfort you, hold your hand, or love you. You'll wander the gallery of your mind, staring at one-dimensional images of reality—lost, alone, and asleep—until they eventually fade and turn to dust in your hands.

So what can you do to remove this blind spot and snap out of this hypnotic spell? As with all of these, there are the staples of waking up: a daily practice of meditation, prayer, affirmation, journaling, inspirational reading, and moment-to-moment mindfulness (remember the "One-Minute Mystic" practice on page 36). As these things become a way of life, you become a candidate for real revelation, gaining real insight into the ultimate nature of life. Beyond that, this next exercise is a fun and powerful practice for building your awareness of the real wealth behind the symbols of wealth.

Manifest Abundance Now!

Mastering the Energy of Money

- Every time you participate in a transaction, instead of focusing on the money being exchanged, whether you're giving or receiving it, bring your attention to the energy behind the exchange. For example, if you're filling your car with gas (or whatever fuel you prefer, including electricity), contemplate all the many people and aspects of creation that went into bringing that fuel to you: the attendees running the filling station; the people who built that station; the truck drivers who deliver the fuel; the business people who manage all the administrative details; the executives who run the companies involved; and all the many industries, resources, and people required to find and extract the oil, build and run the refineries or power stations, mine the raw materials that are turned into all the equipment, and even all the farmers and grocers who harvest and sell the food that feeds all these people. Expanding even further, you begin to realize that all of nature—indeed the whole universe—has conspired in a grand circle of life to bring this fuel to you.

- As you bring all of this into your awareness, consciously give thanks to everyone and everything that is part of this circle of life, love, support, and supply. Bless it all. Feel the perfection of it all. Feel and sense how there really is only One Life and one omni-activity appearing as the many expressions of diversity. Allow yourself to expand into a sense of awe and wonder at how perfectly it orchestrates this symphony of life.

- Breathe and let that feeling expand to fill your being. Let it loosen any places where you're holding on tightly, believing you're in control. Breathe and receive *this enormous gift of grace that we call life*, recognizing that you didn't do anything to earn it and that there's no way you ever could. You didn't set up all the systems that allow this fuel to get to you; you didn't create those farms, raise those farmers, teach those truck drivers, drill for oil or mine the raw materials, build the electric power stations, create those solar panels, wind turbines, or put the sun in the sky—it wasn't your time, energy, or education that made all of that happen. No single person, no matter how brilliant they are, could ever begin to create, master, or manage such a diverse, complex system—all of which is required to deliver that fuel to you. Only grace and an inherent pattern of emerging wholeness has made it so.

• As you rest in this grace, turn your attention to all the ways this fuel serves you, your family, your friends, and your loved ones. See all the possibilities it gives you. You can drive to a job that employs you, pick up your children from school, take your family on a fun vacation, explore and experience the world, deliver your gifts, and so much more. Expand your vision to imagine all the ripple effects of your activities.

For example, because you can bring your child to school, they can become an educated citizen who then goes out into the world and adds their contribution. Because you can go to work, you can give gifts that help all the people your business serves and you can earn money to support your family in their endeavors. If you run out of ways this fuel blesses you, imagine all the ways it blesses others, allowing firefighters, police officers, paramedics, and many more people to help those in need, saving lives and keeping the peace. Truly, the blessings of this one thing are far and wide.

• As you imagine all these different benefits, allow yourself to feel the qualities of it—the love, peace, joy, inspiration, and gratitude. *Really feel it all.* Feel how abundant you are. Breathe and let that energy expand to fill your entire body; then breathe and radiate it out to the world, blessing everyone and everything. Feel how the more you pay attention to it and share it, the more of this feeling and energy you have. That feeling tone of abundance, gratitude, and joy is the real activity of wealth within you.

• As you practice this process, you'll start to fall more in love with the energy and qualities behind the outer symbols, until that's where you're predominantly living. When you live more in the invisible energy of life, you have more and more access to the real substance of all creation, and your outer world expands to express this unlimited abundance.

Now, this was just one small area of your life—the fuel you put in your car. You could do it around the food that fuels your body; the books, programs, and other mental practices that feed your mind; and anything else that nourishes your heart and soul or those you love. There's virtually no end to how many ways you can practice tapping into the energy of abundance behind every form and experience. But as you do, you change the nature of your interaction with everyone and everything. It becomes more about an exchange of energy that expands the good for all involved, ultimately turning every transactional relationship into a transformational one.

ABUNDANCE BLIND SPOT #3
You have to believe to receive.

AWAKENED ABUNDANCE TRUTH #3
You have to ask to receive.

This limited perception has caused so much pain and frustration, as countless sincere seekers have put their life on a layaway plan, thinking they couldn't go for what they wanted until they believed in themselves or the goal enough—until they felt good about it, worthy of it, confident they could do it, or at least unafraid. While our feelings can exert a powerful force in our life, they don't *actually* have the power to determine what we go for, ask for, or in many cases, what we get. Often, just acting or asking opens the channels for receiving, or activates an inner feeling that starts generating the necessary energy to bring it to fruition. Removing this abundance blind spot will free you from the waiting game and move you to take the bold action necessary to achieve your vision of Awakened Abundance.

The first layer of conditioning that has bred this limited perception is the idea that our feelings or emotions control us—an easy assumption to make. At first glance, it does appear to be the case. If we don't feel motivated to do something, we usually don't do it; and if we do feel motivated, we're more likely to take action. If we feel confident about some activity, we're more likely to engage in it and take more risks than if we lack confidence in that task. This is what leads to the confidence–competence loop: we experience positive feedback from doing something and getting better at it, increasing our level of confidence, and motivating us to take more action and develop more competence—all in an upward spiral. Conversely, if we don't feel confident in something, we stop taking progressive action, get worse at it, or never develop the necessary skills, leading to less competence, less confidence, and less action—a downward spiral that perpetuates the belief that we lack any capacity in that area.

Even so, while the confidence–competence loop is useful in creating this upward momentum, it's not necessary to feel confident to get started. In fact, the tendency to let our feelings determine what we do or don't do is categorized as a cognitive disorder called "emotional reasoning." Unfortunately, a vast majority of people suffer from it. The truth, however, is that our feelings don't determine our action. They have no power beyond the power we've been giving them. They also don't tell us the truth; they tell us what we *believe* is true. They're a reaction to our thoughts—a useful guidance system to uncover what we believe, especially if the belief is creating emotional pain. Our feelings also offer a powerful way to know when we're in or out of alignment with our deepest truth: when you're *in* alignment, you feel good; when you're *out* of alignment, you feel bad.

So how can we prove to ourselves that our emotions or feelings don't determine what we can or can't do? Simply by doing the thing we're committed to do or want to do *regardless of how we feel*, and by seeing that, in fact, we can do it. I've demonstrated this many times with clients. In a session, they'd tell me they couldn't do something they committed to because they weren't inspired—or worse, because they were paralyzed with fear. First, I would playfully tease them with something like, "Oh my god, how did you get out of paralysis? Did you have to call the paramedics and get a shot or something?" They would usually get the joke or respond that they weren't literally para-lyzed. I would remind them that the words they tell themselves are a form of autosuggestion that can hypnotize them—like the hypnotist telling the volunteer that their arm is so heavy they can't lift it.

I would then show them how they could snap out of this form of self-hypnosis by simply doing the thing they don't feel capable of. For instance, if they're trying to write something, I would invite them to open up their computer and start writing for a few minutes. Sure enough, once they began to type, they often got quite involved in it. I would then stop them and proclaim that a miracle had occurred! They would, again, usually get the joke. And they would also start to understand that it was never their emotions that stopped them; it was that they didn't *do* the thing. *That's it.* This has been demonstrated with everything from household chores to creative projects, exercise and spiritual practice to difficult relationship conversations. Regard-less of whether they "felt like it," they were able to do the task before them. Even more encouraging, once they did the action, they usually *activated* the feeling—revealing the key principle of Emergence: *whatever's missing is what we're not giving.* We are divine power plants, and a power plant doesn't *receive* energy or even *have* energy; *it generates it.*

Perhaps this all seems obvious; but the implications of being able to do what you want, regardless of how you feel, can be one of the most liberating realizations when it comes to developing a whole new level of productivity and empowerment. And this is just the beginning of this insight. Often, even when we understand that our emotions don't determine our actions, we still think our beliefs determine our experience.

Now, to be clear, our beliefs *do* have a tremendous impact on our experience. A belief is a composite of thoughts that form a specific paradigm, like one of those filters on the end of a pasta maker that determines the shape of the pasta that comes out. Our beliefs filter Ultimate Reality in all its infinite potential, determining how much or how little of life we allow in or out. But we are not our beliefs and are not at the mercy of them. This means that even when we have limited beliefs that are hard to overcome, we can begin to override them by *acting according to our vision regardless of our belief*. Our actions then become like affirmations in work clothes—what I call "active believing." This is akin to active imagination, generating new energy that accelerates our more empowered belief or completely shatters the old one.

When the Bible says, "Ask, and it will be given to you" (Matthew 7:7), it's pointing us to this powerful principle. The reason this works is because everything is already here—already happening—in the quantum field, or spiritual reality. Even more, it's actively seeking to find outlets for its expression. So the act of asking opens the channel to receive what is always being given. The verse continues with, "seek and you will find; knock and the door will be opened to you." All of these instructions illustrate a practice for making ourselves available to the good that's always trying to flow to and through us, but we have to open the channel by asking, seeking, and knocking—not by waiting to believe it's possible.

The second layer of conditioning we have to release is the teaching of many spiritual, self-help, and new-thought practices, which puts a great emphasis on the idea that our thoughts and beliefs create our experience. While this is true, it's also misleading. First, it's not just our thoughts and beliefs that create our reality; it's the activity of our consciousness, to be more specific. And our consciousness includes thoughts, beliefs, feelings, *and* actions—*all* are an extension of it. When we use our actions as moving affirmations, or active believing, we stimulate consciousness and accelerate our expanded beliefs.

The more important distinction: Our thoughts and beliefs create our experience; they don't prevent us from thinking and, ultimately, acting *independently of our thoughts and beliefs*—because we are not our thoughts and beliefs. We have the capacity of metacognition, which means our ability to think about what we're thinking about. So regardless of what we think or believe, or even what appears possible, with expanded awareness, we can choose to act in alignment with our higher vision, activating higher vibrational feelings and moving out of those limited perceptions.

The biggest side effect of all the teachings about how our beliefs create our reality is the inadvertent *belief* that we are victims of our current mind-set, causing us to think we can't create a new reality until we *believe* and *feel* it. Like the emotional reasoning disorder, we fall prey to an equivalent mental disorder—a "belief reasoning," if you will. We look within ourselves and see that we don't believe we're worthy or capable enough yet, which generates fear, sadness, confusion, or overwhelm, among other feelings. This leads us to tell ourselves, *Well, I guess I'm not ready to ask for the promotion, raise my prices, start this project, ask this person out . . . I'll have to do more work on my thoughts, beliefs, and feelings until I feel and believe I'm worthy and capable*; then *I'll take that action*. Hence, the legions of navel-gazing aspirants who embark on the path—or I should say, sit on the *side* of the path—praying, affirming, and waiting for their beliefs and feelings to be at a certain level before they can start moving toward what they really want.

Maybe that's you. Maybe you've been doing all this inner work—going to classes, reading books, trying to build a sense of confidence and a belief in yourself or your dream in order to finally take bold action toward it. If so, I have some good news: you can stop waiting! The truth is that whatever you're waiting for, you're waiting *with*, often weighing it down. Source / God / the universe is not saying, "I would really love to give you everything, but you just need to believe more." Yes, as we've already discussed, belief and feeling are important elements for permanently establishing yourself at a new level; but *in the absence of them*, your *action* can begin the cycle of activation that opens you to higher energies, ideas, insights, and ultimately, expanded beliefs and feelings.

That's why I say that this work is the ultimate "wait-loss program." Life isn't holding anything back from us; we are holding ourselves back from life, because we've been hypnotized into believing we have to be more, feel more, and believe more before we can ask, seek, knock, and act from our highest vision. But not anymore! You are removing this abundance blind spot, snapping out of this hypnotic spell, and stepping onto the path of real progress.

One personal story brought this truth home for me. I had taken a consulting job that involved evaluating an outline for a film project; and at the end of the work, the client wanted to hire me to write the film. Up to that point, I had charged a certain amount based on what I felt I could realistically get, but I aspired to raise my rates to the market value for a professional of a higher caliber. I didn't think I could raise my prices, though, because inside, I didn't *believe* I could get it or that I was truly worth it. I was also afraid I would lose business if I charged too much. At the same time, I felt this deep desire to increase my rates and take a stand for who I wanted to be in the world. So I worked on my belief: praying, affirming, meditating, visualizing, doing all manner of things to think and feel like a person who charged that higher rate. Despite all these efforts, however, I was still too scared to charge it. I just didn't *feel* confident.

Then an opportunity came. There I was, standing with this client, who had just offered me the job to rewrite his project, and the big question came: "How much will it cost?"

I paused a beat, feeling my desire to charge more being choked by my fear of blowing this opportunity. But something in me—maybe inspiration or just a moment of boldness—caused me to blurt out the number I really wanted. Instantly, I regretted it. I was freaking out inside: *How could you do that? That was so stupid. He's never going to give you that! You just blew this job . . .*

Surprisingly, I remained calm on the outside, watching as he stared back at me, then down at his papers for what seemed like an eternity.

Oh man, I am so greedy, my self-talk continued. *I can't believe I did that! Why didn't I just quote my normal price? But it's too late to take it back now. I'll just look desperate.*

I was a mess! Inside, I was wilting.

Then he looked back up at me, extended his hand, and said, "Okay, I'll have my office cut you a check at the end of the week."

I shook his hand, somewhat in shock, and that was that. I had the job at the price I wanted, without *believing* I could. I nodded calmly—as if this was something I did every day—then showed myself out, got in my car, drove about a block, and proceeded to scream like a teenage girl at a rock concert!

I couldn't believe what had just happened—it didn't make sense. How could I receive so much when I didn't believe or feel worthy of it? *When, in fact, I felt and believed the opposite?* I contemplated it all the way home (as I also fantasized about how I would spend my new-found fortune).

What I realized was that the inner work I had done had not been for nothing. It had built up an inner pressure; it was valuable. But the inner work alone wasn't enough. If I merely stayed in the realm of the theoretical—in the praying, the affirming, and the "waiting for magic to happen" mind-set—I was stagnating, becoming spiritually and energetically constipated. I realized that the real breakthrough I was seeking couldn't happen until I *acted* upon the vision *as if it were already true*—that was the missing piece. After that, I practiced this "as if" action more and more, and began to experience the fruition of many of the things I had been praying about, affirming, and hoping for. I had finally replaced my wishbone with a backbone. I had lost all the waiting and had real momentum at last.

Here's another little-known secret: if you're waiting to have all the details, to know all the directions, or to be sure that where you're heading is the right path before you act, *you'll be waiting forever*. Most of those answers will not come until after you've acted. It's like an explorer waiting to know all the terrain ahead before she climbs that first mountain, but she can't know it *until* she climbs to the top and sees what's on the other side. It's like sitting in your driveway, staring at the GPS and waiting for it to give you all the directions before you start driving, but it won't start guiding you until you start moving. Even then, how do you know it is guiding you correctly? You won't until you reach the destination!

Life comes on a need-to-know basis: it doesn't give you much more information than what you need to take the next couple steps—especially if it's a journey of transformation. The reason? It's the journey itself that makes you increasingly able to receive the next piece of the puzzle. If you got all the information immediately, it would either confuse or scare you, and you wouldn't keep moving.

But the good news is that, just as you can drive across the country in the dark of night with only a small space illuminated in front of you by your headlights, you can still get anywhere you need to go with the limited awareness you presently have. You're only required to take the next step.

So what are some signs that you've got this abundance blind spot?

- You have a deep desire to do something, say something, create or contribute something (have important conversations, start a project or business, ask for a raise, move to the next level professionally, ask your spouse for something), but you're *waiting* to feel good enough, strong enough, talented enough—or at least to *not* feel so scared, intimidated, or unworthy.
- You deflect positive feedback or compliments from others, deny gifts, and even find yourself trying to talk others out of their positive perspective of you.
- You hear yourself saying, internally or out loud, that you need to do more research, study more, or make more improvements before you're ready to pursue the thing you truly want. This doesn't mean you don't need to study, improve, or get support, but if this has been a chronic story keeping you from stepping out, you're caught in this blind spot!
- You're a perpetual student, always taking classes and "preparing" to someday be enough, know enough, or have enough to be worthy, credible, and ready for the thing you want (more money, a better job, a new business, more clients, and so on). Again, this doesn't mean you shouldn't keep learning, growing, studying—I'm a perpetual student myself, always reading new books and taking new programs—but if you're not also taking progressive actions toward achieving your vision, you might have the reception blind spot.

- You hear yourself saying or thinking, "Someday, when I [insert what you're waiting for here], I will [insert your aspiration/goal/dream] . . ."
- You judge others who seem to be average or who lack confidence but still get the great job, the great date, and all the great breaks. This is your "light shadow," your disowned power or potential that you project out to others.
- You feel jealous or envious of others who are confidently pursuing their dreams and just seem to "have it all together." (This is another example of the light shadow projection.)
- You're doing the inner work—praying, affirming, meditating, visualizing—and waiting for something magical to happen instead of taking continuous action in the direction of your vision.
- You're doing your best at the outer work—preparing; studying; developing yourself; doing your research, your due diligence; getting support, striving for excellence—but are still waiting to feel a certain way before you really go for it in a newer, bigger way. (Remember, you can plan every detail of a journey, but it doesn't truly start until you embark on it—and even then, you can't account for everything that may happen along the way. That's what makes it a memorable adventure!)

The process for removing the reception blind spot includes all the foundational practices already mentioned before. Cultivating these practices as a way of life will build up greater resistance to forming these blind spots in the future. Just the expanded awareness this new knowledge is creating in you is already progressively setting you free, but there's more you can and must do to wake up from this permanently. And it's summed up in the iconic advertising slogan of Nike . . .

Manifest Abundance Now!

Just Do It

To begin breaking through this abundance blind spot, try this practice:

- Make a list of the things you are waiting to feel a certain way about before taking action—things you are scared to do or don't feel confident enough to ask for. These can be big or small actions, from asking your partner to put the toilet seat down to asking your boss for a raise.
- Pick the easiest one on the list and do it today or tomorrow. (I know, I know. Even asking your husband to stop drying his hands on the dish towels feels like a dangerous request! Try it anyway—I promise you'll live.) And when you do, you'll begin the process of discovering that you don't have to wait until you feel a certain way or you ask or act in a certain way in order to get the results you want.
- If you want to accelerate this process, pick something to ask for or act on every day for the next fourteen days. Journal about the experience—the good, the bad, and the ugly. It's all part of the growth process.
- If you're really courageous, pick one of the hardest or scariest asks or actions on your list and commit to doing it in the next forty-eight hours.

As it becomes a regular practice to go for what you really want—regardless of whether you believe you can—and you start seeing the positive results, you develop a mental and emotional habit. You may still feel the fear or lack of confidence, but you start to know it doesn't matter. Your experience of *feeling the fear and doing it anyway* builds a real wisdom that overrides the cognitive disorder of emotional reasoning. You also start to understand that fear, doubt, and a lack of confidence are not necessarily signs of neurosis or proof that you're not ready; they're simply the energetic signals that arise when you're at the threshold of new growth. The mind has just been conditioned to label anything outside of your comfort zone or current self-concept as bad or dangerous.

I know that the guidance to "Just Do It" sounds simplistic, but one of the things you're hopefully realizing as we go through these abundance blind spots is that our thoughts, beliefs, and feelings don't have any real power over us; our capacity to move and change the energy in our lives is much greater than we know. Regardless of what's churning inside emotionally, if we just take positive, productive action in the direction of our dreams, we can begin to activate the energy, inspiration, and transformation we've been waiting for.

Make no mistake: we *do* need to work on the inner world—that's critical—but because of our ability to think and act independently of our thoughts and feelings, we don't have to put our life on the layaway plan, waiting for some big inner change. We can step into the life we deeply desire today—*right now*. All you have to do is shift into an abundance mind-set and act as if you're truly supported. This will activate the latent potential within you and begin to circulate this energy into your life. As you begin to stretch and see new results, you'll turn on the confidence–competence loop, create new success patterns, and create real momentum in the direction of your dreams.

ABUNDANCE BLIND SPOT #4
You have to adapt to circumstances.

AWAKENED ABUNDANCE TRUTH #4
You must expand in the face of contraction/limitation.

To "adapt" to something, from its definition, is to "adjust or fit into" some new condition. In its most basic sense, it's a capacity we have to cope and survive against all odds. In our evolutionary history, when the weather turned harsh, our ability to find shelter, create clothing, and store food were adaptive abilities that allowed our species to stay alive. Evolution is the story of how things learned to adapt in order to survive, and how that drove change and growth in certain areas. And it's a good thing we had this capacity. It was a necessary mechanism to increase the chances that this human experiment would work out.

But natural evolution can only take us so far. Its purpose was not necessarily progress but protection. It was more about surviving than thriving and revealing our full potential. This is especially important for species without the capacity to think independent of circumstances—something only humans seem to have. But for humans, the natural flow of evolution and adaptation is not enough. Worse, the very thing that previously helped us survive now puts us on the brink of extinction—if not a literal death, then at least a stagnation of our full capacity.

The process of adapting is about surviving and mitigating loss; it's not about progress and innovation—something we must embrace consciously. We must cocreate with life to bring forth our true potential; it won't just happen. The problem is that we've been so conditioned to adapt that it's hard to override this impulse. When conditions contract, our tendency is to merely problem solve or shrink to fit the problem so that it doesn't hurt so much. If we lose our job, we view it as a bad thing, fall into survival mode, cut back, become less creative, and simply try to find a new job. It seems perfectly logical—and it *is* logical (of the left, instinctual brain)—but it's not progressive; and it won't lead to a greater, more abundant expression of life. From a spiritual evolutionary perspective, adapting is the worst thing we can do. When we adapt in the face of limited conditions, we shrink the channels of our capacity and end up smaller on the other side.

This doesn't mean we shouldn't adjust, be flexible, and do what we need to in a survival situation; but it does mean we shouldn't limit ourselves to fit the limited conditions that face us, which is often what "adapt to circumstances" looks like for people. A recession hits and we cut back, not only in our circulation of supply but in our vision of possibility. The result: on the other side of the limited condition, we're smaller mentally, emotionally, energetically, and often financially. The Awakened Abundance Principle, however, is quite different. It states that we must "expand in the face of contraction," which activates a powerful progressive force within us that uses the limited experience to make us bigger and stronger—better able to carry more energy and bring forth new and improved ways of living. On the other side of that, our ability to generate and circulate more of this vital energy of abundance also increases.

The challenge, of course, is that this goes against most of our instincts, which have been geared toward preventing more loss and staying alive. It makes perfect sense that if there's a sudden shortage of food or water, we should cut back on our consumption and ration our supply. I'm not saying there's never an appropriate time to manage our resources according to conditions; but if that's all we do, we're never going to get stronger or more resourceful (like working to build a better system for sustainable water and food supply, for example). The Awakened Abundance approach—coming from the premise that life happens *through* us and *for* us, not *to* us—looks at the limited condition and asks, *How do I need to grow to become an even bigger channel in this situation? What's the opportunity for growth, expansion, and new possibilities in this situation?*

Remember, there is infinite potential locked up within you. So if you want more to come into your life, you must find a way to let more life come out of you. It doesn't matter what the outer circumstances are—they have no power to determine what you can create and contribute. *Your potential is always greater than the problem.* All power, all supply, truly everything that you could ever need is within you. If you shrink to fit a condition, you constrict the channel through which the solution and evolution can flow. If you expand in the face of contraction, becoming a *big enough, strong enough channel,* you embody the answer you're looking for—and probably the answer many people are looking for—regardless of outer limitations. This excerpt from Robert Browning's powerful poem "Paracelsus" speaks to this "imprisoned splendor":

> Truth is within ourselves; it takes no rise
> From outward things, whatever you may believe.
> There is an inmost center in us all,
> Where truth abides in fullness; and around,
> Wall upon wall, the gross flesh hems it in,
> This perfect, clear perception—which is truth.
> A baffling and perverting carnal mesh
> Binds it, and makes all error: and, to know,
> Rather consists in opening out a way
> Whence the imprisoned splendor may escape,
> Than in effecting an entry for a light
> Supposed to be without.

As this poem expresses, life doesn't come to you; it comes *from* you. And the whole universe is set up to support you in uncovering and expressing more of this imprisoned splendor. So the limited situations are not appearing to make you smaller or weaker; they're happening to make you bigger and stronger.

There are many examples in life and nature that reveal this principle. When you begin exercising to become more fit, you don't lower the weight to what you can easily adapt to and handle; you raise the weight beyond your capacity to tear your muscles and make you stronger. And if you can lift a certain weight—let's say, for ten reps—where does all the growth happen? *On the eleventh rep.* As you stretch beyond your known ability, it activates the growth process, creating new tissues and new potential. The same is true in every area of your life, including your capacity for creating more abundance.

People who are successful in the stock market understand this principle, if only instinctually. When the market is going down, and everyone else is selling stocks and running away, the savvy investor doesn't shrink to fit that situation; they start bargain shopping. When housing prices go down, the unknowledgeable sell while the wise investors buy. The average person buys high (when prices are going up) and sells low (when prices decline), while the smart moneymakers buy low (when everyone else is selling) and sell high (when everyone else is buying). That's why during the down markets, the rich get richer and the poor get poorer. The wise investor doesn't merely adapt; they expand to embrace the larger possibilities.

You can take this same principle of "buy low, sell high" and apply it to any area of life where you want more abundance. When a relationship is struggling—perhaps because one partner is angry or unhappy with the other—the natural human response is to react by defending, attacking, withdrawing, or even leaving. This is shrinking to fit: lowering the emotional, mental, spiritual, and energetic set point to the level of the unhappy partner (selling when things go down). But the savvy partner does the opposite: when there's a low point in the relationship or in their partner, they expand in the face of it and bring an increase of love, wisdom, service, energy, and so on—they buy or invest *more.*

This isn't always easy. You might have to dig deeper in yourself, release resistance and fear, and heal old wounds. The key is that during the low or contracted points, you bring *more of yourself, not less*. And when the high point comes again (if not before), you reap the rewards. This is one of the deeper interpretations of Jesus's statement, "If anyone slaps you on the right cheek, turn to them the other cheek also" (Matthew 5:39). It doesn't mean to let someone hit you on the other side of the face! It means to return a *different, higher energy* than the one you received—to return love for hate, peace for chaos, or generosity for limitation.

We can see this same principle play out in business. When everyone else is watching the clock, trying to make sure they don't give more time than they're being paid for, it's the one who shows up early and leaves late that ultimately gets promoted. When the boss is not appreciating the employees or is more of a dominating, controlling type, it's the employee that focuses on how they can serve and add value to the boss or company who gets noticed and ultimately treated better.

Stephen Covey, author of the classic *The 7 Habits of Highly Effective People*, called this being a "trim tab." A trim tab is the small rudder that moves the big rudder on a ship. It appears to be very tiny compared to the large rudder—and to the size of the ship—but it's what moves the whole thing. He gives an example of a person in a company who could have easily felt like they had little power in the face of the hierarchical structure but, nonetheless, decided to give their all, give their best, and continuously add value. The result was that they eventually rose to the top, while the others who were just "giving as good as they got" or were adapting to the circumstances remained stuck at their level or worse.

There are examples of this in nature as well. Certain plants require rough soil to activate their potential. When the ground gets hard and rocky, they don't give up, give in, or lower their ability to grow based on the harsh conditions; they activate certain enzymes to develop thicker bark and a heartier system that allows them to thrive in those conditions. They dig deep and grow to be *more* than they were before the challenge.

This is what all great individuals have done, whether they're athletes, politicians, entrepreneurs, or spiritual leaders. The ones that rise to the top don't adapt—they *expand*. They go to the deeper well within them; they call forth more of themselves; they look for the blessing, the lesson, the opportunity to become more than they ever thought possible. This isn't to say that there's never a time to "sell on the downswing" or adapt temporarily, until you have the strength or resources to expand, but it should be the exception to the rule, not the predominant strategy that governs your life.

You can see this principle play out for many of the great leaders throughout history, such as Nelson Mandela, Mother Teresa, Gandhi, Queen Victoria, Martin Luther King Jr., or Joan of Arc, as well as many great artists, scientists, and innovators who weren't appreciated initially—or were even attacked and vilified. Through their continued growth, expansion, and dedication to the bigger vision, they prevailed, brought forth their gifts, and changed the world. I've practiced this principle in numerous arenas, using it to rise to higher positions of authority. But there was one simple moment when this principle came home to me in an area that had often made me shrink.

The economy was in a recession, and it had hit people pretty hard, including some of my clients. Business had gone down, and there was a general sense of fear and lack in the air. Friends were losing their jobs and homes; and much of the conversation was around how we needed to cut back, lower our expectations, buckle down, and ride out the storm. For a while, I unconsciously got swept up in this trend of thought. Then one day, while sitting out in the sun, contemplating the possibility of cutting back our budget (including reducing our charitable giving), I felt that something wasn't sitting right with me. I went into meditation and a thought suddenly struck me:

If I am a unique expression of infinite potential, why would I ever adapt to a limited situation? The truth is that conditions have no power—all power and substance are within me. So rather than adapting to this situation, I need to expand and prove the principle of infinite abundance.

This insight was powerful, and I could feel a shift inside me. A new energy emerged, and with it the decision that, not only would I not reduce my charitable contributions—I would *increase* them. I would expand in the face of this contraction; stretch my channel; and grow my capacity for giving, being of service, and generating abundance. It was scary, but the call was clear. So I doubled my contributions; expanded my vision; and dug in to be, do, and create even more. As a result, on the other side of the recession, though friends and colleagues had significantly downsized their businesses or lost their jobs and homes, I had nearly *doubled* my income; had many new opportunities; and felt more empowered, inspired, and abundant than ever before.

So what are some signs you've become caught in the limitation blind spot and have adapted to circumstances instead of expanding in the face of them?

- Your normal reaction to people mistreating you is to defend, attack, or shrink—to "give as good as you get."
- You let your bank account, income, family budget, or economy determine what you're willing to do, be, and pursue. (If your reaction to this is something like, "Well, yeah, that's just being smart. That's just common sense!" then you're definitely in this blind spot!)
- You let external conditions determine what you will or won't do. For example, you have plans to do some outdoor activity and the

weather changes (becomes too hot or too cold), so you cancel the plans. Sometimes, it's impossible to do the activity, but how do you react? Do you give up, or do you ask questions to find the next best—or even better—possibility? It's often more about the *energy you give* as a response than the action, because your energy, or consciousness, is the first step in expanding.

- When times get tough financially, your first response is always to cut back and "budget" rather than expanding and finding ways to earn (and even give) more.
- When you hit a wall with a creative project, you want to give up, withdraw, or just try to get past it rather than looking for new, more innovative ideas. Some of the greatest breakthroughs have come from someone hitting a major setback and using it to dig deeper, stretch further, and ask bigger questions.
- When talking with others about problems with yourself, them, or the world, you tend to commiserate around how bad things are instead of offering up ideas for how to make things better. You might even feel embarrassed by the idea of being positive or expansive in the face of these challenges—as if people will judge or attack you for being unrealistic, insensitive, naive, Pollyanna-ish, or just ignorant of the realities of the situation.
- You view challenges, setbacks, and unexpected change as a bad thing; and your emotional default when situations don't work out is to either blame someone or something outside of you or to feel sorry for yourself, feel like a failure or a victim, or feel powerless or helpless. Then you contract, withdraw, or shrink.

So how do you remove this limitation blind spot? Besides the foundational suggestions I've given for the other blind spots, this one is about the practice of stretching yourself beyond your comfort zone, giving more than you're getting, and continuing to go for your big vision regardless of conditions. As you do this, you'll invariably come up against all the reasons why you can't do it, don't want to do it, or feel it's not fair that you have to! The mental patterns of lack, limitation, and feeling like a victim will most assuredly be stirred to the surface, as will the undigested emotions from past wounds. Then your work will be to address those and to reaffirm the truth of your inherent power and abundance until it's more real to you than the experience. You'll need to feel your feelings fully, until they've run their course.

This means you can't wait for it to feel safe, secure, comfortable, or convenient. You must be brave and become a hero to yourself. It didn't feel safe or secure for me to double my charitable contributions when the economy turned. It didn't feel comfortable for me to give my best at a job where I was routinely being unappreciated. And I'm sure it isn't fun or convenient for anyone striving to grow or make a difference to keep getting up after being attacked, blamed, rejected, betrayed, or let down, over and over. Adapting to our conditions is the path of least resistance, although not always pleasant. But to expand in the face of limitation, giving more than we appear to have, without any guarantee of a return—this is real labor of the heart and soul. It tears the muscles of our character but also makes us stronger, more resilient, and a bigger channel to increased abundance in every area we're willing to expand.

Manifest Abundance Now!

The Expansion Practice

- Pick an area that feels limiting or constricting—an area you wish was different or better, like your job, your relationship, or your home environment. If you have several areas that fit these criteria, make a list and choose one that feels like a stretch—but not so much that you might pull a muscle!

- Imagine your ideal version of this situation. If you aren't happy at your job, visualize your ideal work. If you're in a relationship that's not fulfilling, imagine the relationship of your dreams. As you visualize this ideal scenario, notice how you *feel*, who you're *being*, and what you're *doing* on a regular basis. Write these under three categories: feeling, being, and doing.

- Pick one thing from each category to begin bringing to the current situation. For example, if you are more joyful in your ideal job, your practice will be to bring more joy to your current job, regardless of conditions. If you are *being* more creative, spontaneous, or playful in your ideal job, your work is to *be* more of that in your current job. And if you would give a certain level of excellence or a higher work ethic to your ideal job, the challenge now will be to bring that same level to your current job.

    You're no longer going to wait for things to change, and you're no longer going to shrink to fit the limited situation you're facing. You're going to consciously and proactively *expand* yourself and your capacity in the face of this contracted condition. As you act from this higher place, you'll *activate* latent gifts, talents, abilities, and energies. And as these become embodied, your condition will either change or you'll move into an environment that can match you.

- As you're doing this practice, you will sometimes be met with resistance and challenges, and be tempted to shrink again. When this happens, your work is to dig deeper and stay the course. If you can get some support from a like-minded friend, coach, or accountability partner, that will go a long way in helping you stay committed.

A final note on this process: if you know in your heart that your current job, home, relationship isn't your ideal, it's perfectly okay to pursue your dream at the same time as you are bringing more of yourself to the current condition. The key is that wherever you are in the present moment, you are engaging it fully—as if it's your ideal—rather than waiting for things to change before you show up completely. This is what activates and unlocks your greater potential. If you're waiting, hoping, wishing but not expanding in whatever condition you find yourself in, you're blocking your potential from emerging.

ABUNDANCE BLIND SPOT #5
Money/wealth is not spiritual.

AWAKENED ABUNDANCE TRUTH #5
Wealth is an attribute of spirit/truth/God.

The money blind spot has hurt so many heart-centered people. As we discussed in chapter 1, one of the early culprits that led to this was the saying/philosophy, "The love of money is the root of all evil" (often misquoted as, "Money is the root of all evil"). But money and the things it can buy—and really, *all* things—are only *symbols of abundance*, not abundance itself. (Just as the fruit on a tree isn't the real abundance of a tree; it's the outer evidence of it.) The real meaning of this saying is that the love of the *symbols* of abundance and the attachment to them is the actual "root of all evil" or negative consequences.

Once we know the source of supply is spiritual, invisible, and within us, we begin to lose our attachment to the outer symbols. Once we know that the fruits will keep appearing as long as we nurture the roots, we have less need to hoard our fruits in barns, where they rot and do little good for us or anyone. This frees us up to enjoy the fruits, to savor them, to have them in abundance without guilt, and to share them freely without fear.

But this blind spot goes much deeper. It's one of the core reasons why the world is largely run by more materially-minded people, with values that don't necessarily lend themselves to love, community, service, and the true betterment of the planet and humanity. Meanwhile, the deeply spiritual, heart-centered, and creative people are the servants of these masters and structures. To be fair, there are many conscious, conscientious, wonderful people with a lot of money; and they're doing great works in the world. This is not at all meant to be an antirich commentary. It can also be said that some of the greatest acts of global innovation, evolution, and value-adding impact have come from some of the richest, most successful—but not necessarily most enlightened—beings.

The development of the steel industry, railroads, computers, the internet, and many other major inventions or industries, though sometimes created by ego-driven, greedy, or megalomaniacal people, have nevertheless led to some of the greatest advantages on the planet—including reduced crime, violence, war, and poverty, and increased access to food, water, housing, education, and opportunity. Such is the nature of divine love and grace: it finds a way to serve the world, even through individuals who might have other ideas in mind, including selfish purposes. In the biblical story of Joseph, his brothers sell him into slavery out of jealousy over the vision God gave him. It sends Joseph on a long journey full of challenges and setbacks but ultimately leads to fulfilling his vision: to become the second-most powerful man in the land—the right hand of the pharaoh. When his brothers were eventually brought before him to be judged, Joseph spared them, stating in Genesis 50:20, "You intended to harm me, but God intended it for good to accomplish what is now being done, the saving of many lives." He saw that everything was conspiring to fulfill a higher purpose—even what appeared to be bad. He saw that the ever-expanding expression of good/Source is the only real activity in the universe.

Still, so many good people with amazing talents, gifts, and abilities remain in the background, in the dark corners of the world, struggling to make ends meet and dying with their music still in them—often because they had too much baggage around money, wealth, sales, and success. If the most creative, conscious, heart-centered people are going to rise into positions of prominence and power, and have the resources to fund their visions and the greater visions of the planet, helping both to evolve to a whole new level, we need to heal this. In a sense, that is the purpose of this book—to dramatically and permanently change the conversation and the consciousness around wealth and abundance for this group of people.

So where does this set of false beliefs that create this money blind spot come from? In large part, it comes from religion. First, because religion has had a long history of declaring that sacrifice, suffering, and deprivation are the only means to salvation. Second, religion has conditioned people to believe that Earth is something less than sacred and divine, and that we should ultimately forsake it for our piece of real estate beyond the pearly gates. And third, because the whole idea of sacrifice has been misunderstood. The Latin root for the word *sacrifice* is "holy," or to make something sacred, but through incorrect usage, it has been twisted into meaning something very different.

Even so, the psychological reason why so many heart-centered people struggle with this goes deeper than just money or material gain; its roots are in our core wounds. Most people who have turned to a spiritual path; sought an inward journey of greater self-actualization; or have just devoted themselves to being better, kinder, more loving people did so because they experienced trauma or great pain and wounding around this world, specifically around the areas of personal power. Their relationship to power, authority figures, and especially the consequences of being a powerful person is negative and fraught with ambivalence. To be specific, most people on the heart-centered path were judged, attacked, shamed, blamed, dominated, or controlled by the people in positions of power and authority.

Maybe they watched as authority figures (including their parents) did "bad" things, hurt others, or hurt themselves—often in connection to power, money, work, or success. Or they saw others in the world or in their own neighborhood suffering at the hands of the rich and powerful. This wound made it almost unbearable to live in this world and drove them to find someplace where they could be free, feel safe, and find some meaning and purpose to it all. In the worst cases, this leads to violent neurotic patterns; but in most cases, it causes people to seek a spiritual or creative path, embrace nature and animals, try to become better people or even do-gooders—all as a means of escaping the world and its harsh, cruel power structures.

Is it any wonder then that the idea of selling yourself or your work, or having a lot of money and success, would bring up fear, doubt, guilt, shame, or just an unconscious, unnamable resistance? If you're one of these people, the good news is that this rejection of the world and its material ways led to you develop some truly important talents, gifts, and abilities. It led you to develop your heart, mind, and creative capacities and set you on a journey of awakening. There have been no mistakes; it's all been conspiring for your evolution and ultimate destiny. But now, in order to fulfill that purpose, you must embrace the dark side of wealth, power, and success. What is the dark side? It's everything you've been running from, trying to ignore, hide, heal, fix, get rid of, judge, or deny!

The key takeaway for now is to understand that the idea that money or wealth is not spiritual is a coping mechanism born from this core wound. The truth is that it's impossible for anything to be unspiritual in the absolute sense, since spirit is the substance of all that is. God is in everything, and everything is in God (and by God, I am not referring to a man in the sky but the intelligence, principle, and power behind all creation). That doesn't mean we see things correctly and are experiencing them in their true divine nature—often we're not. But everything, in its true essence, is a divine, perfect idea, whether it's money, the body, sex, business, art, commerce, or any other area of human life.

We don't want to reject *any* part of our humanity, including money. We want to understand money's true nature and its correct application, so that it can find its rightful, constructive expression in the world. Money is an expression of divine energy, consciousness, even love. When we earn it, grow it, and circulate it consciously, we supply the resources for more good to manifest for all. We don't think it's wrong to have an endless supply of health, love, peace, joy, or creativity. When you understand that wealth and its expression as money (or any form of abundance) is just another spiritual quality, you realize it's just as holy to have and express as much of it as you desire!

Please don't brush over this point: wealth and abundance in all its forms is really a spiritual idea, quality, or activity as sacred and divine as love, peace, joy, beauty, or any other spiritual quality. There is no division, no separation in the mind of God. There is no spot where God is not, which means there is no spot where all the qualities of ultimate good are not. When you judge or reject any part of creation, including wealth in its many forms, you are rejecting a part of God—a part of your true self. And to that extent, life, love, and abundance can't express through you and manifest in your experience. This appears as various forms of lack, which can often come across as circumstances out of your control—the loss of a job, unexpected bills, a lack of opportunity or ideas for new opportunities, a stagnation around your creativity, and conflict with others in the area of wealth or finances (the number-one cause of marital conflict).

But rather than recognizing that this is a direct result of your rejection of wealth and abundance, it will look and feel like you're being victimized, and further confirm why abundance is such a bad thing, entrenching you even deeper in this limited belief. This becomes a vicious cycle, a downward spiral that creates a failure pattern difficult to get out of. In fact, it's impossible to overcome until you realize that you and your fear, judgment, and rejection of wealth are at the root of it.

You're not doing anyone any favors by staying broke, having little cash flow, or lacking in the various forms of abundance that allow you to be all you were created to be and contribute. You don't help others become more abundant by staying in lack. Your unconscious vow of poverty doesn't leave more of the pie for those less fortunate—in fact, it's the opposite. When you shrink your capacity to receive and generate abundance, you shrink the pie for everyone connected to you—unless they're more conscious than you. But when you're willing to be a bigger channel of abundance, you *increase* the amount of supply available for everyone involved. This is possible because *wealth is spiritual, and spirit is infinite.*

Think of it like a radio broadcast: if you tune in to radio station "K-Rich" and play the music, does that limit the music for others tuning in? If millions more tune in, does that music run out? If everyone turns up the volume to full blast, does the volume run out? Of course not. Even better, with all the volumes turned up, the music would amplify and create a more powerful, collective sound wave. Likewise, wealth is a broadcast—a frequency—and the more you tune in to it, turn up the volume on it, and express it in the world, the more there is for everyone. So let's start dancing to the beat of abundance!

What are the signs that you've been caught in the money blind spot?

- You believe money and spirituality are incompatible, or that having too much wealth or success could slow or stop your spiritual progress and take away from others.
- You're broke, living paycheck to paycheck, barely making ends meet—or only just getting by. A more extreme version of this is that you actually justify this state of lack by believing you are somehow more holy or spiritual because of it!
- You judge others who are wealthy or successful, especially those who are very rich and successful.
- You feel guilty charging high prices for your services—or for charging anything.
- You don't like talking about money and even feel guilty, nervous, or ashamed around the topic.
- You take a strange pride in how much you give away for free, how you don't charge much when you do charge, how little you have, or how you're not part of that capitalist culture. You may also feel guilt around admitting that you have made a lot or have a lot.
- You can't keep what you earn because you feel guilty or ashamed for having more than others. You have to spend your money or give it away. (This is often not conscious, but you know it's happening if money burns a hole in your pocket or goes out the door as fast as it comes in!)
- You crumple your money up or stuff it in your wallet or purse like some contraband you don't want anyone to see—versus having it nicely folded or laid out, the way you would treat clothing you cared about. (Money is like a person: if you judge, condemn, or reject it, it will find the quickest path out of your life. Treat it well.)
- You might feel guilty or shy about selling or marketing yourself, or about discussing your talents and abilities in a confident way. You tend to play down your strengths and assets, and feel those who play up theirs are arrogant or self-centered. (This isn't directly

about money; it's about abundance and self-worth, which are closely connected to how much you allow yourself to have. Net worth doesn't equal self-worth, but self-worth often determines net worth.)

How do you remove this abundance blind spot? Hopefully, this section has illuminated the error of this kind of thinking. That alone can create mental and emotional momentum, making you a candidate for new insights and inspiration around this area. But this one is pernicious and must be consciously addressed on a regular basis. Every time you have an opportunity to ask for what you really need, charge what you're really worth, and go for what you really want, remember that having less doesn't help anyone and having more doesn't hurt anyone. Everyone is connected to the same Source, making their ability to manifest abundance equal to anyone else—it is ultimately up to them to activate it.

This can be controversial, but it's the truth (albeit a bitter one sometimes): nobody is poor because someone else made him or her that way. That's not how life works—not even in the poorest part of the world. I'm not saying we shouldn't do everything we can to raise the world out of poverty (that's a big part of why I'm writing this book), but it can't happen long term without a change in consciousness. As lottery winners have proven, you can give a poor person millions of dollars, and in a few years, they'll not only be broke again but often in worse debt. Why? *Because they haven't had a shift in consciousness.* This has also been shown in the transfer of companies or other assets to family members. If they don't have or develop the consciousness that built that company or earned that asset, they can end up running the company into the ground, losing much of what they've inherited.

It's all about consciousness. If someone doesn't have financial abundance in consciousness, no matter how much you give them, they'll never truly have it. Conversely, if someone *does* have it in consciousness, no matter what is taken from them, they'll rebuild and replenish it.

I can hear some of you saying, "But what about children born in poverty or people whose lives are devastated by corrupt government, disasters, or other major calamities beyond their control?" As much as it breaks my heart to see this, and as much as it compels me to do everything I can to change it, the principle is still the same: nothing can enter our experience unless it's some part of our consciousness. Remember that a baby isn't just starting their life; they may be in a little body, but they are a big soul with a history that began before they got here.

We don't know what karmic propensities a person arrives with. We don't know what curriculum their soul has signed up for, and how their challenges are serving their growth and evolution. We really can't judge by appearances. Maybe you don't believe in all of that and this feels like "blame the victim." I can assure you there is no blame or judgment here; just an understanding of spiritual principle. And again, this doesn't mean we don't do everything we can to help, heal, feed, house, and raise people to a higher level. But we also have to address the root cause: consciousness.

Manifest Abundance Now!

Claiming Your Abundance Consciousness

- As you practice asking and receiving, remind yourself of this principle: everything comes to you and to everyone else *by right of consciousness*. If you feel fear, guilt, or shame rising up in you—a sensation of tightness in your chest, butterflies in your stomach, or anxiety—breathe and release this energy. Then take another breath and graciously receive the abundance that comes to you, with gratitude and celebration.

Wealth can never separate you from your spirit; it can never make you anything you aren't already. Wealth *magnifies* your character. So if you're a good person, wealth will expand your sense of goodness and make you an even bigger giver. If you love God and people, the more you'll have, the more you'll serve, and the deeper your connection with your heart and humanity will become. That is your prayer—your intention—as you expand to receive all of the opulence life has to offer.

• As you engage in activities or conversations around wealth, notice your urge to talk yourself out of a sale, to downplay yourself, to judge or condemn people who strive for wealth and success—and when you do, *just keep quiet!* When you're selling something and someone asks how much it costs, don't do a long disclaimer, trying to convince them of your good intentions, or that you or your service is worth it. Just say the price and be quiet. If they balk at it, don't backpedal and become a used-car salesman, reducing your price until they say yes. This erodes your price integrity and your integrity in general. That doesn't mean you can't have other options or other price points, but you must take a stand for your value.

People treat you the way you train them. People don't pay you what they think you're worth; they pay you what you think you're worth. Don't let your fear or guilt drive your conversation or actions.

• When you're talking with others about money, the economy, success, or any related subject, become especially vigilant for those thoughts, words, or phrases that are limiting; and refuse to accept or give expression to them. If someone says, "The rich are taking over this country and we need to stop them! The economy is terrible, and there aren't enough jobs! Money corrupts everything," don't agree with that. You don't have to launch into a lecture about why they need to embrace their inner rich person, or how this is limiting them and everyone else. Just say, "Oh, interesting." (Think of the "oh" as a big circle that their comments pass through and keep going, not finding any place to stick in you.) And if you find yourself about to speak something limiting, ask yourself, *If what I am about to say were to become my reality, would I want that reality?* If not, don't say it! You can also notice how your body feels: if it's constricted, it's a good indicator that you're coming from fear and lack; if it's expanded, it's from love and power.

- Be proactive about this practice. Look at the areas where you have limited yourself because of this belief. If you aren't charging for your work, *start*. If you aren't charging what you truly need or want, *raise your prices*. If you're feeling ready for a raise, *ask for one*. If you are wanting more in your family, in your relationships, or in any area of your life, *ask for it without shame, blame, or apology!*

- Include a life of wealth and abundance in your big vision by creating a real plan for attaining it—then go for it. As you do, all the reasons why you didn't do this before will invariably come up— the fears, doubts, judgments, limiting emotional patterns. Be sure to include the work to address them in your plan and as part of your daily practice of healing, integrating, and awakening to your next best self.

Living with Eyes Wide Open

Seeing through these blindspots and activating more abundance in your life is a process—a journey. It's hard to walk our path powerfully when there are so many limited perceptions preventing us from seeing what's really here. What's worse, these beliefs often hypnotize us into seeing many things that aren't true at all. But if we remain alert, we can open our eyes, rub the sleep from them, gain a wider view, and make real progress. It rarely happens overnight; however, you can experience some significant shifts rapidly if you're willing to dive in and do the work.

That means it can't just be an exercise here and there. If you want lasting results, you must create new habits, and redesign your life around these organizing principles of abundance. As Confucius said, "All people are alike; only their habits differ." So, just as you might commit to new healthy habits, also commit to new wealthy habits.

And get help—you don't have to do this alone. Doing this work in groups, with consciousness coaches or mentors who will hold you accountable, and in structures that ensure you will actually keep moving—all of this is essential when you're developing a new Awakened Abundance mind-set. Otherwise, your unconscious coping mechanisms and survival strategies will take over, trick you into believing in lack and limitation, and cause you to give up. *Don't let that happen.* Value yourself enough to get what you need to finally master wealth and abundance. It will positively impact and accelerate every area of your life.

Life wants you to be abundant so that you have all the resources you need to give your gifts, make your difference, enjoy this incarnation, and put all that is awesome about the universe on display. Everything is conspiring for your success—everything is on your side! Now is the time to be on your own side fully. As you move forward with your own abundance project, keep that foremost in your mind and heart. Be kind and gentle with yourself. Be your biggest champion. Take a stand for you, and all of life will stand with you too.

THE SEVEN GIFTS THAT GIVE YOU EVERYTHING

We make a living by what we get. We make a life by what we give.
—WINSTON CHURCHILL

It's summer as I write this. Looking out at the freshly cut grass, hearing the *chk-chk-chk* of a sprinkler fanning out its cascade of water beads, a fond memory overtakes me: During the hot August days when I was a kid, parched from hours of climbing trees and throwing walnuts, my buddies and I would suddenly drop from the branches like monkeys, run up the driveway, grab the garden hose, and drink straight from the end like our lives depended on it. I can still taste and smell the warm, metallic-flavored water as it streamed from the semi-rusted, slightly crimped nozzle. I didn't mind it all—in fact, it was like the nectar of the gods to my dehydrated little body.

But there was another phenomenon I often experienced: the hose would get so twisted up after all the use that it would be hard to get much of a water flow. I would turn up the pressure, then turn it up some more, and finally, try to flip and twist the hose to unkink it—until *whoosh!* The water exploded out of the nozzle in my face! Again, I didn't mind. I would just turn it on my friends and commence a glorious water fight.

Maybe you didn't have that experience as a kid; but if you've ever done much watering of your yard, you know the frustrating experience of trying to get any consistent water pressure out of a crimped nozzle. You turn the water higher and higher, hoping you won't have to bother with all the kinks in the hose. And when that doesn't work, you twist and flip and kick the defiant rubber snake, trying to straighten it, only to make the existing kinks worse as you create new ones. Finally, when you relent and manually untwist each part of the hose, there's an exhilarating rush as the current is unleashed. The hose straightens and the pressure blasts through that tube, giving you an awesome stream that can strip any surface of whatever substance has been baked into it! There are few things in a homeowner's weekend that are more exciting. (Or maybe it's just me.)

But as I sit here, contemplating the importance of "flow" in the creation of abundance, the analogy of the kinked hose is a good one. Once you understand the real source and nature of wealth—this infinite, invisible energy within you—and see that whatever is missing is what *you* are not giving, the natural question arises: *How do I start generating more of this energy of abundance in my life?* In other words, how do you increase the current (which comes from the same root as "currency")?

Like that hose, this energy has to move through various channels in us before it can express itself. And I've found there to be seven core channels for this expression. These aren't channels like those in Chinese medicine or other energy practices; they're channels of consciousness.

Unfortunately, after years of living an outside-in model of the world, spending our days trying to get, attract, achieve, or otherwise draw things to us, these channels—designed to open *out* to allow more to flow *from* us—have atrophied until all we get is a dribble. They've weakened, corroded, crimped, or collapsed to the point that very little energy can flow into our life. (This is also akin to what happens to the arteries when we don't exercise the circulatory system.) The result is that the vital life force of our being, which is meant to flow into our experience and nourish our growth, has instead become stagnated until our energy system is more like a swamp, where very little can grow. This requires us to push harder (like the heart does), struggle more often, and develop more complex coping and manipulation strategies to try and get what we seem to be lacking. This is unsustainable and eventually leads to a breakdown of the different tributaries in our life—health, wealth, work, relationships, spiritual connections, creativity, purpose, and fulfillment.

But what if there was a practical way to open these channels again—to take all the kinks out of them so that this trapped energy could start circulating in our life the way it was meant to? Even better news: What if all the efforts we've put into improving our lives (prayer, affirmations, visualizations, intentions, sincere desires, and actions) have actually accumulated in us—like the pressure in a twisted-up hose as you keep turning up the water? And what if we only need to straighten it out again to experience a virtual *flood* of this life-giving energy in our everyday experience?

Well, there is a way, and it is the core framework of the Awakened Abundance principle: the Seven Gifts that Give You Everything. These are seven practical strategies that, when done regularly, clear away the cobwebs, rub away the rust, open up the blockages, and create a clear pathway for all that stuck life force within you to rush into your experience and become available for creating the life of your dreams.

Here are the Seven Gifts, also known as the Seven Abundance Activators:

1. Giving Out
2. Giving Away

3. Giving Up
4. Giving In
5. Giving Thanks
6. Giving to Yourself
7. Forgiving

These different ways of giving or gifting are like the pumps that prime "the core" channels through which we generate and circulate our life force. As I hope you are beginning to see, the secret to creating a life of abundance is represented by one word: *giving*. Remember, everything is within us. Therefore, if we want more of any quality to come into our life, we have to let more of that quality come out of us. And once you master these forms of giving, you'll crank up production within your divine power plant and generate a mighty flow—a flow that doesn't originate in the external world to begin with, so the world can never take it away.

Let's start mastering the art of giving!

Giving Out

In general, this is about giving of ourselves in whatever way we can—giving our love (in all its forms), our support, our service, and our abilities. In the business world, it's about "adding value" wherever you go, in whatever project or capacity you're working. For the purpose of this section, we'll focus on three key areas of giving out that can give you significant leverage in generating more of the energy of abundance: your time, your talent, and your treasure.

Time is especially important if you've fallen into the trap of waiting for the right moment, opportunity, or windfall to start expressing yourself in some area. The lie is that you can't fully show up and be who you really are or want to be until some condition changes. The truth is that *now* is the only time you can start generating this energy—now is the only time you can do or become anything! This gift is about finding immediate ways to serve, to share your talents, and to give of your substance, usually in the form of tithing or charity.

Do you want to be a beneficial presence in your family, your community, the world? Do you desire to make a bigger impact in some way, to help others, or to serve some cause? If so, are you doing it as fully as you can, giving your all *now*? Or do you tell yourself, *Someday, when I have enough time, I'll start [fill in the blank].*

This is outside-in living—the opposite of how life actually works. There's a reason that this desire is here now: it's seeking to emerge in you now, not in the future. In fact, the future is just a fantasy—it doesn't exist and never will. You can't do or be anything "then"—whatever you're waiting for you're actually waiting *with* and *weighing down*. So, as I like to say in *Emergence*, it's time to lose all the wait!

If the desire, the impulse, the urge is in you now, it's meant to express now. That doesn't mean you should drop everything and go work for a soup kitchen, or move to Calcutta and follow in Mother Teresa's footsteps. It doesn't even mean you should devote time to it every day. But if you want to have a more abundant, fulfilled life, you must let this energy find some outlet. Otherwise, it will stagnate and start to create a swamp in that channel of your life—and eventually, in others as well.

That desire is literally the *thing itself*—a divine idea, the next stage of your evolution in that area—seeking to be born through you. It's like the kick of a baby in the mother's womb, letting her know, "Hey, I'm in here!" If the mother felt that kick and said to herself, *Oh, that means that someday, when I have the time, when I can get around to it, when it's convenient, I'm going to maybe have a baby. I'll wait and see how things go . . .* If that were her attitude, she would go on eating, drinking, and acting as if she weren't pregnant, which could then lead to all kinds of complications with the developing baby, possibly even ending its life. Instead, she begins to nurture that child, change her environment, and organize her life around the fact that she's pregnant and will give birth to a whole new being.

Maybe you think this is a silly illustration, but the idea that we're "pregnant" with potential is very real and follows along many of the same principles of abundance development. So when we feel the kick of our desire and ignore this emerging impulse, or put it on hold until conditions are right, we don't nurture the developing energies; and this often leads to greater urgency and more restricted conditions in our life, because the energy is unable to express itself. If we continue to ignore or delay this "urgency of emergence," it becomes an emergency, forcing us to pay attention to what's trying to unfold through "symptoms" like depression, accidents, or any manner of breakdown in various life structures—health, wealth, work, relationships, spiritual connections, and so on. In fact, if you're already experiencing these kinds of challenges, especially in a chronic way, it's often a sign that you've been trying to survive in a world that is smaller than the one trying to emerge—the one you've already activated.

It's all about the flow of the energy. If it isn't expressed, it gets depressed. If it doesn't flow out, it implodes. Worse, like a wild animal locked in a cage, it begins to wreak havoc. If you have a desire to express yourself in a certain way—to cultivate certain talents, gifts, or abilities— but you're waiting to be good enough or to have the right opportunity, right audience, right timing, or right condition, you are blocking the evolutionary impulse within you, the next stage of your potential trying to be born. This unexpressed energy then becomes corrupted and turns into addiction, anxiety, depression, lack, and limitation. And because the universe is perfectly efficient and is all about expressing itself in an ever-expanding way, it will reallocate its resources to something or someone that is willing to let this energy unfold.

What does a gardener do to a branch that isn't bearing fruit? She prunes it from the tree so that the energy flows into the other branches and they can flourish. If you don't let life fully express—if you don't say yes to your yes and bear the fruit of your nature—it will eventually start the pruning process. The result is that your life will become increasingly barren, devoid of meaning, purpose, and passion. I know this sounds harsh, but life is purposeful—it exists to express its infinite abundance—and if you aren't willing to let it do so through you, you're not fulfilling your function in this life experience. And life, being perfectly ordered and efficient, will make room for the people and circumstances that *will* allow life to fully express.

Maybe you're thinking, *But I don't even know what my gifts are.* If that's the case, that's okay—as long as you're focused and committed to discovering them. Life is not saying, "You better get this right *today*," or "You better do good, go big, or go home"; it's saying that you need to *allow* the emerging impulse in you to come out, in whatever way it's trying at this moment. It's not about the quantity of action and achievement; it's about a quality of being, of allowing, of saying yes. It's about living your life as an exclamation point instead of a question mark—or worse, a period. If you don't know what your gifts are, then one of the top priorities of your life needs to be finding out. Not tomorrow; not in some future when it's comfortable and convenient, and you have enough time and money to go on that journey of introspection and discovery. But *today, and continuously.*

Finally, in this gift of giving out, we have your *treasure.* This speaks specifically to money and your willingness to give it to your place of inspiration. Another name for this is tithing, which means "ten" and is traditionally about giving ten percent of your earnings back to God, or wherever you get spiritually fed. The deeper esoteric purpose of this is, in truth, that your treasure doesn't belong to you in the first place; it belongs to God, Source, the universe, the world—just as your talents in the truest sense don't belong to you but to the community. This has also been called "giving your first fruits to God." (There's that fruit analogy again.) The reason for this principle is that everyone and everything is an instrument of life—a way through which life shares and circulates its good.

It's like a blood vessel in your body: its purpose is to carry, distribute, and deliver blood to the various organs of the body. But the blood doesn't belong to the vessel and doesn't even do it any good to hold on to it. In fact, holding on to it would damage the vessel. The same is true with the fruits on a tree: if the tree holds on to them, they rot, stagnate the tree, and prevent it from thriving and creating more fruits. Besides, what good are the fruits to the tree? The tree doesn't need them; the rest of the ecosystem does. And when all the flora and fauna in the forest give of their fruits—the byproducts of their rightful living—everything else flourishes.

Are you starting to see the perfection of this system, and why the idea of getting what we have and holding on to it until some future conditions are "right" to share it is the opposite of how life is designed to thrive?

If you don't have a church or some spiritual teacher or organization to tithe to, you can look at where you do get inspired and fed spiritually, psychologically, or emotionally. In its absolute sense, tithing is not the same as giving to charity, although for the purposes of this gift of giving out, I include charitable giving. In other words, if you have the desire to be philanthropic, then you want to start circulating in that area, in whatever amount you can. It's not really about quantity but, as with all growth, about finding a level of giving that requires you to stretch, dig deeper, embody more of yourself, and evolve.

It's the same principle as in any area where you want to become a bigger, better, stronger version of yourself. If you can easily lift ten pounds but you want to get stronger, you need to do more reps or lift a heavier weight. So if giving a dollar is easy but giving five starts to feel a bit scary, that might be a good place to start. You want to stretch to the point where there's a little pain but not so far that you pull a muscle (or break your budget). If you hurt yourself, you won't be able to continue for a while and might give up on the whole thing.

With tithing, as with all these gifts, it's important to begin circulating in that area even if you don't feel like it or want to, because it's about activating a principle. But within any given area, if you *do* feel a desire to express there, that's a clue that something more is trying to emerge; and it's important to honor that. So if you have the desire to be philanthropic, that means you're supposed to begin being philanthropic now.

If your mind says, *I want to give millions, but I don't have much to give; so I'll wait until I have more and be a really big giver*, it's a stall tactic of the ego. Your ego knows that if you actually start the flow of giving in this area, you'll grow, which means change; and to the ego, change equals death! Don't buy in to these stall tactics. If all you can give is five dollars a month to the cause of your choice, begin there. As Goethe said, "Whatever you can do or dream you can, begin it. Boldness has genius, power, and magic in it."

I have proven the efficacy of giving this gift in these three areas over and over in my life. When I wanted to sing, I waited to feel good enough or have the ideal opportunity. But instead of getting it, I grew more frustrated. Then one day at a party, someone asked me what I did and I blurted out, almost in exasperation, "I'm a singer/songwriter!" The energy of it must have been forceful because they looked a little taken aback. Not in a negative way, more like, "Wow, you're really passionate about this!" They offered me a singing gig at a retirement home. It wasn't the concert hall I had hoped for, but I said yes.

As a result, I began to sing every week at this location. It was fraught with problems and challenges, but as I kept showing up and giving this gift, I became better, more confident; and I developed many skills. As that grew, I was given more opportunities. With each one, I continued to give fully, as if it were my dream job. And as I did, more opportunities to express my gifts emerged until I was singing three or more days a week at different places, and making some decent money doing it. From not having the courage to sing outside my shower to being booked to sing almost full-time—and all in less than a year—that's the power of giving your talents right where you are, however you can.

The same occurred with my treasure. I had always wanted to be a bigger giver philanthropically, but when I read about celebrities and business tycoons giving millions, I felt so far away from that that I kept postponing doing anything. I just felt so small, so lacking. Then one day, while reading one of these articles, I suddenly felt what I imagined the person giving millions felt. It was a beautiful feeling, but it wasn't all that different than the feeling I had when I gave the small amount I was able to give. A realization dawned: *it was all relative, having nothing to do with the quantity.* To that celebrity, giving millions felt like me giving hundreds. Of course, I didn't actually know what they felt like, but the insight was so powerful that it was enough for me to start the flow.

I began tithing and giving to various charities I cared about. I didn't realize it at first, but within a relatively short time, my income began to increase and, with it, so did my giving. As long as I was giving, it continued to grow—until I was giving thousands to my church and various causes. As a result, I was invited to special events for big donors and got to have a slice of the experience that I had imagined only a couple of short years before.

Now, this isn't about getting recognition. In fact, if you seek recognition, that's not real giving. It's about the inner experience. And sure enough, the feeling I had when I gave thousands was not that much different than when I gave my first five or ten. Maybe it was a little deeper, richer, more fully embodied; but at each new level, it became the new norm. I was just a bigger channel now, where more abundance could flow easily.

The area of giving of my time was also a big one—and is something I continue to work on. I still find myself wanting to do more, for more people, but I have to balance it with my current obligations. However, the more I've been asked or prompted to give more of my time, for nothing in return—whether it was praying for someone; visiting someone in the hospital or in prison; or coaching, teaching, or creating something as an act of service—the more productive, creative, efficient, and effective I've become. I've seen my position in the world expand so that I can impact more people with less effort and time. In other words, the more I give of my gift of time from this place, the more time I seem to have.

The universe is looking for willing channels so that it can claim more territory on Earth to fulfill its greater purpose. When you're willing to be that place of giving now, by not waiting and giving as best you can, life says. "We've got a live one! Let's pour more through them!"

Manifest Abundance Now!

The Giving-Out Practice

Before you move on, contemplate these three aspects of the gift of giving out—time, talent, and treasure—and choose one action you can take:

- Where can you give of your time, talent, and treasure starting now? Begin by looking at where you've already felt some impulse in these areas—some place where you already want to give more. That's the ripest, low-hanging fruit. Pick that and give of it first. Then see what emerges from there.

- To accelerate your growth, focus on an area where you're waiting for something to change before you give more. Even better, if it's an area where you are experiencing some pain because of a lack of circulation, start there. Don't wait until you feel safe, secure, or unafraid, as you won't actually overcome these feelings until you act in a new way and begin releasing this stuck energy.

Giving Away

This gift is about letting go of things you don't need or use anymore in order to keep the energy—in the form of stuff—moving. Everything is energy, and everything in your environment is an expression of *your* energy. As you evolve by activating the desire within you to be more, have more, and express more, this evolutionary principle acts on your whole environmental field. But if you keep your environment the same while trying to change, you'll create blockages. (Conversely, if you merely try to change your environment while remaining the same internally, that will also create resistance and blockage.) This gift is also about sharing— about keeping all things useful. If you're not using it, someone else can; one man's trash is another man's treasure. The billion-dollar resale industry started by eBay (and all the garage sales before) attest to this truth.

The things we hold on to represent moments in our life story when we stopped growing—it's all stuck energy. When we release these things, the part we're playing in this divine drama can move into the next act, and our character can evolve. This starts freeing up this stagnated energy so it can take new, more empowered, more elevated forms. The popular book *The Life-Changing Magic of Tidying Up* by Marie Kondo points to the almost mystical transformational experience of releasing the clutter, and this is exactly what happens when you start giving away *everything* you no longer need or use.

This stuck energy, in the form of our unnecessary stuff, is old emotional patterns, self-concepts, or beliefs about life that have become coagulated in the form of material things. As I said, our stuff is literally an old story that keeps playing itself out, like the stage set and props of a production that has long since closed; yet we're still standing there, reciting our lines to an empty theatre!

When we're continuously surrounded by stuff that represents aspects of our life that are old, worn out, or cluttered, we become mentally, emotionally, physically, and spiritually adapted to them and can't move to the next level of our growth. Think about that stack of magazines you just won't get rid of, even though you've never read them and never will. I repeat, *you are not going to read them!* But you still hold on to them. Why? Because it's not just a stack of magazines; it's a symbol of wasted money, wasted opportunity, procrastination, maybe even a part of you that you judge as impulsive or ignorant. And to get rid of the stack would be to admit that you made a mistake—that you failed in some way. What about those clothes you bought but never wear, or the clothes you used to fit into but don't anymore? You keep holding on to them, telling yourself you'll wear them, but it's been years; and they've become nothing more than food for moths! But they are not just clothes; they are an unhealed part of your psyche.

Those stuffed animals from when you were a child, the corsage from your prom, the garage full of mementos or things you bought in bulk because they were on sale—much of it is unresolved emotional material; a futile holding on to your lost youth and better days; an act of self-preservation for some future lack when you'll need those twenty boxes of sterile wipes you bought at the Dollar Store! It's also a form of control, a way to feel like you exist—a means of giving weight, literally, to your existence. And it's a buffer between you and the rest of the world, which is really a buffer between you and how you feel deep down about yourself and the world. To actually release this stuff would be to remove the barrier between you and this stuck energy of uninspected feelings and beliefs. Your ego knows this and knows it would cause real change—which is like a virus to the system software holding the ego intact—so it keeps up a constant round of denial, distraction, and excuses as to why you can't get around to cleaning it out or why you really should hold on to it "just in case." It's all a stall tactic of the mind to prevent real change.

But if you'll have the courage to start letting go of all the stuff you don't really need or use—in your car, closets, cupboards, and drawers— you'll start a circulation of the life-giving, life-enhancing energy that wants to take your life to a whole new level of possibility. That means emptying out the junk drawer too. I mean, really, why do we have a junk drawer? Isn't that just a horizontal trash can? Of course, it's much more than that; it's years of broken dreams, lost opportunities, misplaced priorities, and unfulfilled hopes. It's also a lot of powerful energy that wants to be set free so you can have the energy you need to create a life full of new dreams and possibilities.

So how do you address this gift? For some, they just need to dive into the deep end and perform a major exorcism of their clutter. For others, that would feel like ripping their insides out, and it could backfire—there's too much unresolved emotional energy there. In any case, you need a clear goal and a specific plan to achieve it.

Manifest Abundance Now!

The Giving-Away Practice

- Start with the area that is creating the most problems, like your office space—that cluttered desk, those overflowing file cabinets, that inbox that hasn't been sorted, and that mail that hasn't been opened *for months*. (It's amazing how many people find lost money and uncashed checks when they do this!)

- If it's a big project, it might help to get support—you don't have to do this alone. You could hire an organizer to come in and manage the process. Or if that's beyond your means (or too embarrassing), you could invite some friends or loved ones over for a cleaning party. Get some pizza and beer, wine and cheese, or (depending on the crowd) maybe some kale chips and kombucha, and make it fun. Try not to peel the Band-Aid off slowly if you can help it. Do it in nice chunks—get some real momentum!

- Once you tackle that first area, move on to the next. Give things to charity, to friends; sell stuff on eBay; or have a garage sale. Just be sure to make a real plan, put it on your calendar, and get this old energy moving, so you can make room for the new energy trying to emerge.

- As you do this, don't be surprised if resistance arises, including old, painful emotions and thoughts. This is not only normal, it's one of the main reasons you're doing it. *Let yourself feel the feelings fully.* Let yourself grieve the parts of your life you never did. Let yourself feel the pain of those mistakes, those wasteful purchases, those lost hopes and dreams. Don't get caught in or indulge in them, but allow yourself to feel them, so you can transmute that energy into something higher. If you deny, ignore, fight, or repress this energy, it'll just show up in other ways—maybe as more hoarding of things you don't need or more stalling around living your best life.

- If this process is particularly painful, reach out for support. Take advantage of all the help you can. And be kind, patient, and loving with yourself. (We have complimentary resources to guide you through this process at DerekRydall.com, as well as coaches who are trained in helping people release old, stagnant energy and heal or integrate unconscious patterns.)

Once you've cleared your clutter, don't be too quick to fill up the space with more stuff. Be willing to sit with the emptiness, the sparseness. This is symbolic of an open, spacious part of your consciousness, like the desert before the new world is built. There's a reason the Bible describes the promised land as a desert, because it's not filled up with a bunch of old stuff. It's pure potential, where anything is possible. As you have the courage to rest in that emptiness—that stillness and silence of the void, where something used to be—you create the conditions for what is truly meant to be there. And if you practice the principles in this book, as well as the other Emergence principles I teach, your new, more inspired, more abundant life will emerge. It must. Because it's not personal, it's principle!

Giving Up

This gift is about releasing the clutter in our inner household—the old habits, resentment, criticism, judgment, and complaints that are stuffed in our internal closets, drawers, nooks, and crannies. The concept of house esoterically or metaphysically refers to our mind or consciousness, because that's where we really live. It looks like we inhabit the outer world, but we really reside in consciousness. And the outer world and its structures represent this inner world.

Mystically speaking, we could say, "We aren't in the world; the world is in us." This is why feng shui, the Chinese practice of creating a harmonious balance between the energies of a person and their environment, can be so powerful. It helps a person understand what's going on in their inner life by assessing their outer spaces, and can even predict what their outer spaces are like based on their internal state of being.

Why do we need to release this inner clutter? Besides the obvious psychological benefits, *all real growth or healing is about letting go of something*, not adding anything. You're already a whole, complete, perfect idea of life; you can't—and don't need to—add anything. Everything you need in order to be all you were created to be is already embodied in your consciousness; it's just being obscured by limited mental and emotional patterns. The challenge is that we experience our perfection through our relative perceptions—through these filters of our mind. And over time, we've been conditioned to pay more attention to the perception and the projection in form rather than the perfect pattern behind it. This has atrophied our ability to see and express our deepest, truest nature, and our ability to access the ever-present flow of unlimited abundance.

But as we release the inner clutter, we make space for the next stage of our potential to emerge. Something more is always trying to be born, but we can't operate at a higher level if we're holding on to things that are weighing us down. These habits of mind, emotion, and action are preventing us from growing and expanding, and are creating resistance to the creative, life-giving energy trying to unfold. What's worse, when we remain stuck in them while also having a desire for a better, more abundant life, it's like the Zen statement about trying to ride two horses at the same time, going in different directions—impossible and painful.

This is one reason we suffer from chronic challenges. We've activated a larger life and called forth our greater potential, but we're still holding on to a lot of inner clutter that is constricting our channels of flow. The larger self is trying to emerge but it's bumping into all the resistance patterns of the mind, creating mental, emotional, and material turmoil. As we release this inner clutter and allow that repressed energy to circulate again, it appears as new opportunity, insight, creativity, and success—an abundance of good. But let's be honest: it's easier said than done to clean out our inner junk drawers! We grasp on to these things, afraid we might need them somewhere down the line and believing they're somehow adding value to our lives—or literally saving our lives.

The habits of resentment, criticism, judgment, and complaining are coping mechanisms that we've come to believe are protecting us, or that have become addictions for venting and avoiding feeling what we really feel. We hold on to resentment because of the illusion that it makes us more powerful, protects us from being hurt again, or somehow gets revenge on the person who did us wrong. But this is like drinking poison and believing it's going to hurt the other person!

We continue to criticize because it allows us to feel superior and avoid feeling our deeper sense of unworthiness. It's also a great way for us to avoid having to take bold, progressive action. We don't have to risk getting hurt, rejected, or failing; we can just sit on the sidelines and criticize others. This judgment of others is a projection of our own unhealed shadows; we make other people a proxy for the pain we're not willing to feel and the lies we're not willing to heal. And we complain because it's a cheap way to vent the angst and frustration of a life not fully lived. Like criticism, complaining fools us into thinking we're being proactive or productive in some way by pointing fingers and seeing flaws; but it's really just another avoidance strategy that keeps us from getting in the ring to take the hits ourselves!

Another area of clutter that is talked about less often is our opinions and preferences—our black-and-white beliefs that some things are good and some things are bad. This is a slightly more advanced area of clearing, since much of our identity is made up of our perceptions of right and wrong, good and bad, what should and shouldn't be. People kill, die, and go to war for their beliefs as much as—and sometimes *more* than—they do for name, fame, or fortune. But our opinions, perceptions, and beliefs are not truth; and as we continue to grow, they can become more clutter. This is especially true because we are infinite beings unfolding an eternal idea. So, no matter how bad or how good something seems, there's always more trying to emerge. If we get locked into any point of view, we are, by definition, blocking the real flow of the moment. There is a stream of new life, substance, and inspiration always pouring forth; but to access it, we can't hold any idea, thought, or opinion we had the day before—or even the moment before—as being too precious.

All of these mental and emotional habits keep us stuck in a stale inner environment that eventually becomes like that swamp I spoke about earlier, where very little can grow. These habits are the armor that we wear as we go out into the fray each day. But the armor not only blocks more of life from getting in; it also prevents more of us from coming out. Like that gadget, widget, or gizmo you bought years ago to fulfill some task, the armor has long since outlived its usefulness. Though these inner habits had a purpose once—they might have actually served you for a moment—they're just broken pieces and leftover parts cluttering up your interior. It's time to clean house and take out the trash!

To begin working with this gift, you must become aware of when and where you hold on to your opinion—your point of view—and when and where you engage in one of the limiting habits of resentment, criticism, judgment, and complaint. That doesn't mean you can't have a point of view and express it, but you want to hold it lightly, in a more spacious context that allows room for something new to unfold.

As you notice these places where you're gripping or justifying negative habits, take a pause, take a breath, and consciously let it go. Notice the impulse to judge, complain, or criticize. See it. *Witness it without trying to do anything about it.* Then release it. As you do this, feel into the *energy* of it. That's really all it is—energy that has formed into a loop, a pattern, and is cycling around. You'll even start to notice that these patterns become predictable because they operate in cycles. This will allow you to be even more mindful of them and less likely to get caught in them unconsciously.

Manifest Abundance Now!

The Giving-Up Practice

- Practice releasing one opinion or preference a day. That doesn't mean giving up chocolate ice cream or watching football if you like them. But each day, as you do your spiritual practice—whether it's some form of meditation, prayer, yoga, or journaling—consciously offer up all your opinions, preferences, and agendas to be purified, released, and replaced with a deeper knowing of who and what you really are and why you're truly alive.

- Reserve your opinion and instead say: "God [or whatever your concept of a higher intelligence is], I don't really know what I'm looking at or experiencing. I don't really know what's best in this situation. Please interpret this for me. Open my eyes that I may see what's really here and be an even purer instrument of love, life, truth, beauty and abundance." Then rest in that for a moment, letting go of all attachments.

- You might feel a breath, a release, even a sense of peace wash over you. You can meditate on it for a while, journal about what comes up, or simply go on with your day. But now you've created space; and life will flow new energy and insight into that opening.

As this becomes a practice and then a subjective habit, you'll find yourself gripping things more lightly or not at all. You won't find the need to prove yourself as much, to be right, or to make someone else wrong. You won't push as much; and you might even start to experience real divine flow and true grace, where things unfold that you couldn't have thought of yourself, that you didn't study or learn, that you didn't even earn. You've become a clearer space for the perfection of your being to flow into expression and experience. Your world evolves gracefully, with ease and dignity, instead of strain and struggle. And the natural abundance of the universe is an organic part of your life.

Giving In

This gift is about surrendering to what is but also, more importantly, to what is trying to emerge. This is about yielding to the emerging impulse and letting go of our will, opening ourselves to a higher vision. This is not acquiescing to circumstance or limitation; it's letting go of control, of ego agendas, of the struggle to make things happen instead of making them welcome. It's resigning as manager of the universe and becoming an employee. Our spiritual destiny, including our divine inheritance, is already here, but it's infinite and, therefore, always unfolding. Surrendering to it—yielding to it—is a powerful practice for allowing our next evolutionary stage to express in any area.

The key distinction here is that surrender, in this context, is not about giving in to the circumstance; it's about letting go of the protective, defensive, self-preservation response and allowing the flow of new energy to manifest through you. It's like the acorn yielding to the oak of its being: If the acorn had self-consciousness, it might try to hold on to its protective shell and its acorn identity; it might even call up some healers to repair its shell when it starts cracking! And if it succeeded in this, the most it could hope for is to become the best nut in the forest; but it would never fulfill its true potential.

What is the significance of this in terms of generating more abundance? Remember that abundance isn't something "out there" that you need to get, achieve, or attract; it's something already within you. *So if you're not letting the next stage of your potential emerge, you're blocking the next stage of abundance that comes with it.*

If the acorn stays an acorn, its level of abundance is very small. If it surrenders to the oak of its being and lets that emerge, it brings with it massive abundance so that it can fulfill its destiny as an oak. Life fulfills the real demand made on it, and the real demand is made based on the level of expression. If you create a small life—a life of self-preservation, comfort, and convenience—you'll only activate enough abundance to fulfill that vision. If you yield to the larger life trying to emerge as you, however, you'll begin to activate the level of supply needed to form *that* vision. The abundance you're seeking is a component of the next stage of your growth. If you don't let go of the protective shell of your old identity and give in to this larger life trying to happen, you block all the supply that comes with it.

You can't solve the critical problems or achieve the core purpose of your life at your current level because you don't have access to the abundance of energy, intelligence, supply, and wisdom needed to create the next level. You must expand beyond the circle of your current self-concepts and stretch the channel through which life flows to and through you. This is one reason why people stay stuck and why many of the major issues in our world remain unsolved, despite all the efforts to the contrary.

We're trying to solve these problems at the level of the problems. We're trying to access oak-level abundance while remaining at the level of acorn consciousness. It's not only an impossible approach, it's an inefficient one, because you're asking for more than you're willing to become. And the universe is nothing if not efficient! It will give you an unlimited level of abundance if you're willing to live an unlimited life that serves others. But it won't give you more than you need or more than you're willing to use.

This is why the great spiritual masters often talked about the need to sacrifice the self—to lose our little life—for the sake of the larger self. Jesus said that if you try to save your life, you'll lose it. This is like saying that if you try to remain an acorn, you'll cut yourself off from the evolutionary life force trying to emerge as an oak (and eventually get eaten by a squirrel!). He also said, "but whoever loses their life for me [the sake of the Higher Self, or the Divine Pattern] will find it" (Matthew 16:25). In other words, if you're willing to let go of self-preservation and attachment to self-concepts, you'll experience a never-ending, ever-expanding expression of life, abundance, and potential.

This is not a religious statement; it's a statement of universal principle. But we have largely misunderstood these teachings, believing that "dying daily," or sacrificing, means losing something important or literally dying. It doesn't mean that at all; it means letting go of attachment and control, and yielding to the greater potential. It means realizing that what we identify as our life is really just a relative concept of who we are. In fact, "death" is nothing more than the release of these limited, material concepts—that's all that can ever die. But to the ego, real change *feels* like dying, so it works overtime, trying to prevent us from really changing—from surrendering to our current paradigm and giving in to the emerging vision.

Where are you currently struggling against some impending change? Where have you prayed, affirmed, or desired great change but aren't experiencing the results you want? Most likely, there's some old idea, self-concept, or protective pattern that you're holding on to. You're trying to change the world but stay the same. You're trying to be more abundant while holding on to the old mental, emotional, or physical habits that are based on a belief in lack and limitation.

It's like the man who exclaims that there are not enough good women out there (constantly talking about it and acting accordingly) at the same time that he's praying or affirming that he's in a relationship with his ideal mate. Finding her will never happen! You can't make a demand on life that exceeds your belief about it. You can't create more abundance of anything while also holding on to a belief—and all the associated habits—that there isn't enough. When you try to serve two masters, you become "a house divided." And a house divided can't stand—it has no structural integrity.

If you want more abundance—more of anything in any area— you have to let go of the concepts, feelings, and habits that contradict abundance, and embrace the ideas and actions that are congruent with it. This brings us to one of the most important pieces about giving in, or surrender: it's not just about letting go or yielding to something emerging, it's about *embracing something*. You can actively surrender by consciously and strategically moving toward the next level at which you want to live.

Let's say you're trying to activate more abundance in the area of work, but you're afraid of letting go of your current mode of making a living. In order to achieve this, you can't just passively surrender to the higher vision and "let go and let God"; you also have to proactively move toward the vision of the work you want to do and the person you want to be. You have to create a daily practice that is about generating the thoughts, feelings, and overall vibration *as if you're already living the life you desire*. Doing this allows you to bridge the gap—the fear—and make this transition more gracefully.

Manifest Abundance Now!

The Giving-In Practice

- Identify an area where you're resisting surrender—where you're holding on to the old way of being while also praying, affirming, asking, or pushing for something new. Get clear on what your new life would look like in this area and ask yourself: *If I was living this, who would I be, how would I feel, what would I do or stop doing?*

- Next, create what I call a "Quantum Plan" to move in that direction, which means both the external actions and the internal daily practice for becoming mentally, emotionally, spiritually, and vibrationally aligned with that new vision. As the fear, doubt, or other forms of resistance and old habits arise, breathe and release them; then put your attention on the new vibration you're embodying.

- Practice focusing on this new vibration until it becomes a subjective habit, and you'll find that *giving in* to the next level of your life is no longer a problem to be solved; it's an adventure to be lived!

Giving Thanks

An attitude of gratitude is the foundation of abundance—an affirmation that the gift has already been given, that we *already have something to be grateful for.* And it's the truth—we *do* already have everything. So building a state of gratitude is the fundamental condition for this truth to emerge in our lives.

What you appreciate *appreciates*—it grows. We've been given all of infinity; nothing more can be added. But even though we have it all, it must be activated. Gratitude is not just a nice idea, a good moral value, or a virtue; it's literally the corresponding frequency that tunes us in to the flow of good and makes us a channel for it. But in this section, we want to take gratitude a little further than traditional explorations on the subject.

You see, it's easy to be grateful for good things—that doesn't require much character. Even some of the most despicable people are grateful for things they like. But the true practice of giving thanks includes all the seemingly bad things too. In fact, that's the most powerful way to grow this spiritual muscle and build what I call "soul stamina," which is the capacity to be a beneficial presence in the midst of even the most challenging conditions.

Gratitude in the face of challenges—in all things, in all ways, for always—is not an easy path for sure. It's hard to be grateful when your bank balance goes negative. It's hard to give thanks when your body breaks down. It's hard to appreciate your life when nothing is going your way. But if we want to open the treasure house of good locked within us, we must practice gratitude until it becomes a habit. And the magical thing about this gift is that the more we live in a state of gratitude, the more reasons life gives us to be grateful. This happens because, as we've already touched upon, life works inside out, not outside in.

Our core feelings are not an emergent property of our conditions. Despite appearances, what we feel isn't caused by our outer experiences; rather, our outer experiences are an emergent property of our core feelings. This is why we can't wait for conditions to change before we allow ourselves to feel the way we want to; we must choose the expansive feeling first, step into it, activate it, express it, and live it— then the experience changes to match it.

The arc of this practice of gratitude looks like this:

- We begin with no reason to be grateful.
- We find something to be grateful for.
- We grow to be grateful for everything.
- We finally become grateful for no reason.

In other words, gratitude becomes an unconditional state of our being. Can you imagine what that would be like? What kind of power could you have if you lived in a constant state of gratitude? This doesn't mean you wouldn't have ups and downs, hard times, and even what you might call negative (contracted) emotions. But what if you could feel grateful even in the midst of feeling sad? It's not a contradiction; it's a real possibility. Emotions are just energy in motion. They're like clouds that pass through the sky—they're not permanent. But gratitude (and other spiritual qualities) are the very fabric of the sky of our being. They don't come and go; they're forever. Our awareness of them ebbs and flows, but like the sun, they're always shining in our soul.

To practice this gift, start where you are and find something—anything—to be grateful for. It doesn't have to be big. In fact, it's important to have levels of gratitude, finding appreciation in the smallest or simplest things; otherwise, you might condition yourself only to be grateful when big things happen. Maybe it's just the wind on your face, the sun on your skin, the smile of your child, or how that person held the door open for you. There is so much to be grateful for; we just get out of gratitude practice because we become accustomed to what we have.

One way to tap into how blessed you are is to imagine that a person from a developing country, with little to nothing, has suddenly inhabited your life and body, and has all your resources, opportunities, health, energy, intelligence, relationships, and abundance, regardless of how good or bad you think your life or its various elements are. As you sink into that imagined experience, what would that person be grateful for?

This can be especially powerful in areas where you're feeling a lack or limitation. For example, maybe your body is less than perfect or has some physical challenges that make you feel lacking in some way. But if you were to imagine that someone with a disability or a disease has suddenly inhabited your body, how would they feel? Maybe you have a hard time being grateful for your financial situation because you have debt and unpaid bills; or you are living paycheck to paycheck, on someone's couch, or even out of your car. But if you imagine someone living on the streets of some poor city suddenly inhabiting your life and your financial situation, you quickly see that they would feel rich indeed! Even if all they had was your car to live out of, that would be a cause for celebration. If you have indoor plumbing, some food every day, paved roads, clean water, access to basic resources, and friends and family who care about you, you have more than a large majority of people on the planet. It's all relative—all a matter of perspective.

That doesn't mean your challenges don't hurt. This isn't meant to diminish your pain or suffering. If you break your leg, it may not be as bad as someone who breaks their back, but it still hurts badly. However, getting some perspective on your life compared to others can be a powerful strategy for activating gratitude and a consciousness of abundance—of having. This is one area where comparing yourself to others is a good thing! You can even make this a journaling exercise, going through your various life structures (health, wealth, work, relationships, spirituality, personal development) and listing all the things you're grateful for. Then each day, upon arising, take a few moments to mentally list several things to be grateful for, until this becomes a new habit. That's the key with all of this—that it becomes a habit. Habits are what build our character, and character is what determines our destiny. So this is a worthy investment of your time and energy.

The next level is to consciously give thanks for the areas that you're struggling in. Maybe you pick one area to practice on—one that is challenging but perhaps not critically so. To work on this area, you start by methodically blessing it and expressing gratitude for it, without knowing why. Try to generate some level of positive feeling—even a pinprick of it will do. But even if you don't *feel* the gratitude, keep doing it anyway. Then dig a little deeper with the following practice.

THE SEVEN GIFTS THAT GIVE YOU EVERYTHING

Manifest Abundance Now!

The Giving-Thanks Practice

To begin activating this unconditional gratitude, ask yourself these questions about something that is currently challenging you:

- How might this situation be serving me?
- What is the blessing or lesson in this?
- How might this be helping me become or achieve what I deeply desire?
- How might this be making me a better, stronger, wiser instrument of service in my family or on the planet?
- Contemplate these questions and journal about them. As you tap into new insights, new awareness, and aha moments, give thanks for that. And as you feel a sense of gratitude, consciously radiate it into this challenging experience.
- If you're having trouble tapping into the feeling of gratitude, imagine something that makes you feel grateful—perhaps a past experience or something you'd like to experience. Visualize yourself in it, focusing on whatever makes you feel good. Breathe and expand that feeling until it fills your body. Then radiate that energy into this difficult situation. This is a form of alchemy—the taking of energy from one area that feels good and expanding it to envelope another, until the problem area in your consciousness begins to vibrate at the higher level.

You can stop periodically and just tap into the feeling of gratitude on its own, for no reason, attached to no object. Gratitude isn't conditional—it doesn't need an object; gratitude simply *is*. As you practice activating this feeling without any object, you train yourself to feel it unconditionally, eventually finding it bubbling up in your awareness unprompted, for no reason at all.

When this happens, it's one of the most wonderful gifts to receive, but it can be a bit strange at first. You may find yourself looking around for the cause of it: *What just happened? Did I get some good news? Did someone do something nice for me? Did that check finally arrive?* And then, with delight, it will dawn on you: *Oh, wait, I'm just grateful, because that's my nature!*

Giving to Yourself

This gift is one of the most overlooked elements of activating our inner wealth-creating mechanism, especially for heart-centered, spiritually minded people who have shadows around being needy, greedy, or selfish. To truly give themselves everything they've been seeking from others can seem almost blasphemous. But the key takeaway here is that unless you give to yourself in the same way you give to others, you can never have what you really want or need. A common analogy for this is being in an airplane when the oxygen masks fall: you have to put the oxygen mask on yourself *first*, before helping anyone else, or you'll pass out and be of no use to anyone.

Taking the analogy of breathing a little further, the full cycle of the breath amplifies this. If all you do is breathe out, you'll expire. You must first breathe in before you can breathe out; you must first fill yourself up before you have anything real to give. A lack of practicing this principle leads to burnout, resentment, having less to give, and in some cases, much more destructive actions. Mastering this gift allows you to be a stronger conduit for giving more than ever before and helps you to realize a level of true inner freedom.

Remember, it's all in you. The things you're trying to get from someone or are waiting for them to give you are a projection of *your* unexpressed power and potential—and they're blocking the flow trying to come *out* of you. Life doesn't happen to you; it happens *through* you. If you want more to come into your life, you have to let more life come out of you. If you want more love, you have to activate more love by giving it to yourself first. The same goes for any quality you're waiting for or are wanting more of. People treat you the way you train them, and you train them by how you treat yourself. So if you want the world to see you, hold you, and give you more, you have to treat yourself in kind!

Where are you looking to someone else to meet your needs, waiting for them to give you something; or have you given up on ever getting it? Are you looking to your partner to give you appreciation, validation, or respect? How about your boss, your colleagues, your family, your friends, your kids? Wherever you're doing that, you're blocking the natural flow by creating extra pressure in the relationship, which often backfires, because you're making someone else responsible for something they can't give you. This doesn't mean you can't ask for things—that you can't say to your partner or your boss that you would like to be more respected or to ask for what you need. But in your mind, you need to know that they're not the source of this; they're a channel at best. This allows you to ask but also to take "no" graciously. Meanwhile, you're not waiting for them to fill you up, because you're already filling yourself up.

Manifest Abundance Now!

The Giving-to-Yourself Practice

- To practice giving to yourself, begin by asking the following: *If I loved myself completely [or whatever quality you're trying to have], how would I treat myself?* You can augment this sentence so it's time, location, or relationship specific. For example, *If I loved myself completely, how would I treat myself today / this week / on the job / in my marriage?* Then listen to what arises in consciousness. You can journal or use freewriting to explore whatever starts to come up. (You may not get a crystal-clear message right away; or you might just get a flash of insight, a fragmented image, or a feeling.)

- If the answer is vague, like "take better care of yourself," ask questions to make it more specific and concrete (like *What would it look like to take better care of myself?*). Do this until you get something that is doable. And once you become aware of something, *act on it.* Guidance without action is just information—or as the Bible puts it, "In the same way, faith by itself, if it is not accompanied by action is dead" (James 2:17). Worse, it can lead to becoming energetically congested and create other problems in your life.

- If the thing you're waiting for or trying to get is something material, like money, a job, and so on, ask, *What does this represent to me?* In other words, what does money mean to you, what qualities does it stand for, how does it make you feel? Articulate this, then give *that* to yourself.

- Now ask, *What would I be able to do or how would I start to be if I had this material thing?* For example, if you had more money, would you take more time on your creative pursuits or take better care of yourself? In that case, you would make a plan to start living into this reality regardless of having the money; you would start designing a life that has time for self-care and creativity. There's always some way you can give yourself what you really need. And this action opens the channel, starts the flow, and leads to the next logical step in your progression.

- Take a moment to focus on one area where you're either looking to someone to give you something, waiting for something to change, or feeling hopeless that you'll never receive what you want. Identify the quality or the material condition you want more of (money, job, and so on). Ask yourself how you can give that quality to yourself and how you would begin to show up for yourself if you had the material condition you want.

- Create a simple plan that allows you to work with this every day for at least the next week, including whatever actions you need to take, then put it on your calendar. A vision without a plan is a fantasy, and a plan without a schedule is wishful thinking. You don't want a wishbone; you want a backbone. So make the plan real, make it a priority, and this will make it welcome.

Forgiving

This is obviously a powerful gift, but the deeper meaning and potential of practicing forgiveness goes much further than most people know. We understand on some level that forgiving is about loving our enemies; praying for those who hurt us; returning love for hate; and releasing everyone from karmic, emotional, and maybe even financial debt—so that, in our heart, nobody owes us anything and vice versa. The magic is in the word itself: *for-giving*. It's about giving, not getting; and it's about extending yourself, not withholding.

There's a profound connection between a lack of forgiveness and the creation of lack and stagnation conditions. When you don't forgive yourself, you're saying, "I owe myself"; when you don't forgive another, you're saying, "You owe me." Both are states of mental/emotional/energetic debt that create lack and stagnation in your life. As with all of these gifts, it helps to think of your life as a pool of water with inlets and outlets: When you aren't willing to give, you block the outlets. When you aren't willing to receive—from within or without—you block the inlets. The result: your life becomes a swamp in which the energy isn't flowing. And in a swamp, very little can live or be nourished. This stagnant energy then manifests as limited experiences due to a limited or nonexistent current.

Remember, *currency* is a derivative of a Latin root that means "to run," or a condition of flow. So when your flow, or current, becomes stagnant, it can manifest as a lack of currency (sometimes literally, as money); and that often creates the condition of debt. So behind most experiences of chronic lack—and probably all financial lack—there is a story of unforgiveness. When this is healed, that energy is freed up, and the current starts to flow again.

This is simple enough to understand, but the real challenge is the practice of forgiveness. At the first level, it's difficult because we feel we've been done wrong or that we've done wrong; and it doesn't appear that there's any remedy to that feeling without an actual reversal of that condition. Fortunately, it has nothing to do with the condition; you can fully forgive or be forgiven even if the past condition never changes, because it's mostly an inside job. This doesn't mean there isn't a benefit to taking specific actions to make amends or reparations for our past deeds—in fact, taking certain steps can hasten our feeling of forgiveness. But in the event that no particular action is possible—say, because the person is no longer living—forgiveness can still happen.

One of the initial stages of forgiving someone is realizing that withholding your forgiveness doesn't hurt them; it hurts you. As I mentioned earlier, holding on to resentment and believing it's going to harm the other person is like drinking poison and expecting *them* to get sick—you're only poisoning yourself. But there is another level to this, which is often misunderstood until you realize the emergent nature of energy—that *all of life flows from you, not to you.* So if you withhold love or any positive quality toward another, you're actually blocking that quality from expressing fully in your life. Life never withholds itself from us, but we can withhold ourselves from life; and the result is having less of what we want and need to create real abundance.

It doesn't matter why you're withholding or how wrong you think the grievance is against you. If you withhold love (or any spiritual quality) *for any reason*, you're blocking the full expression of that quality in your life. That's why it's often been said that forgiveness is not for the other person; it's for the one forgiving. When you realize this, it becomes easier to forgive—you realize that you're not doing it to be a good person but to free yourself, and increase the flow of energy in your life. The other person may never benefit from your forgiveness, but *you always will.*

The other benefit of practicing forgiveness is that you start to realize that sharing, shining, and circulating your life, love, and all the divine qualities—toward everyone—is a good idea. You no longer need a reason to love, serve, or bless; you just want to circulate your life force so it can expand, intensify, and manifest in your own life. The result is that everyone is blessed, because you've decided to be an unconditional blessing. This is the deeper meaning behind the biblical statement that "I now realize how true it is that God does not show favoritism" (Acts 10:34)—He shines His light on the saint and sinner equally, and pours His rain on the just and unjust alike.

It's beyond the scope of this book to give a complete course on forgiveness, but it's helpful to understand the different levels. On the first level, forgiveness is very much a tool of the ego and sounds like, "Well, you did me wrong, but I'm above that now and I'll forgive you—but I won't forget!" While it's certainly better than holding on to terrible resentment, this level of forgiveness puffs up the ego and becomes a source of pride, arrogance, or superiority, which limits one's growth. It also still holds the perpetrator in a negative light, seeing them as a "bad person" on some level, and certainly doesn't want any good to come to them.

The next level of forgiveness is a little better, though it's still an activity of the ego. This level sounds like, "I'll forgive them and let it go, but I hope they learn from it and move on themselves." At this stage, there's a bit more release and even a slight desire for the perpetrator to have a better life too.

As we start to open up our hearts and develop compassion, we begin to understand that people are always doing their best, even when they do bad things; because in their conditioning, they've justified their actions out of a sense of fear or separation. It doesn't mean we have to condone bad behavior, but we understand where people are coming from. This higher level of understanding usually comes from our own introspection—from working with our shadows and flaws, and developing compassion for ourselves. It allows us to say, "I forgive you because I understand that you're coming from your own unconscious fears. I don't condone the action, but I don't condemn the actor; and I truly want the best for you." At this level, forgiveness comes more from our spirit than our ego. It's a real movement of the heart—of divine love. Even so, it's often hijacked by the ego at some point and can create a sort of spiritual arrogance ("Look at how spiritual I am"). Nevertheless, it's this third level that leads to real healing and transformation beyond just you.

But there are two more levels, which take us down the rabbit hole. The first is when we come to realize that there are no accidents in a perfect universe—that we actually created soul contracts for our own growth before we were born. In other words, we all signed up for a divine play that we cocreated and cast for the evolution of our soul. Sometimes we play the good guy, and other times we play the bad guy; sometimes we are a walk-on role, and other times we are a costar—and all in the same lifetime. Think of the common rules and roles in many of the great stories throughout history: the hero can only be as good as the villain is bad. If the villain doesn't do his thing, the hero can't become a hero. If there's no conflict, the characters can't grow.

As in the Bible, if Judas hadn't done what he did, Jesus couldn't have done what he did. Some of our most significant times of growth came because someone else "did us wrong." Again, this doesn't condone bad or destructive behavior, but it does put it all in the proper context. When you really understand this, you can begin to reframe your whole life story so that you are no longer the victim or a prop in some random production; instead, you become the star of a powerful show! This level of forgiveness allows you to not only have compassion for others caught in and acting out their own darkness but to actually be *grateful* for the part they've played in your divine drama.

The final level of forgiveness is when you understand that, in Ultimate Reality, there is only One Life and One Power, and its nature is love. So there isn't any life to hurt or be hurt, or any power to do anything to anyone. There has never been an accident or error, never been a victim or victimizer; nobody has ever done you wrong, and nobody has ever been hurt. When you pierce the veil of appearances, you see that no mistake has ever been made, and all is truly well. In fact, it is this consciousness of wholeness that can heal *anything* (or, more accurately, it *reveals* the intrinsic wholeness that was always there). When you come to this level, there is nothing to forgive; there is just an awareness of the perfection of all life. That doesn't mean you don't interact and do things to bring more order, harmony, and justice to this world. Our human journey, with all its seeming contrasts, opposites, and polarities, is designed so we can create, express, and embody our infinite nature—but from this level there is no more effort or struggle in the process, and things tend to unfold more by grace.

Manifest Abundance Now!

The Forgiving Practice

There are many ways to practice forgiveness and on many levels. To begin, identify the person you are forgiving—remembering that to withhold your forgiveness doesn't hurt them, it hurts you—and try these processes:

- Write a letter to them (for your eyes only), specifically forgiving them for every grievance you hold. For example, "I forgive you for lying to me. I forgive you for making me feel unworthy. I forgive you for criticizing me all the time . . ." It doesn't matter if your assessment of the situation is true; all that matters is that you willingly offer up forgiveness. You can do this multiple times, until you start to feel a release and a diminishment of negative energy around the person. You can also do this for self-forgiveness.

- Consciously desire the very best for them, and affirm that they have everything they could ever need. This is called "loving and praying for your enemies." Imagine them having the life of their dreams, being happy, whole, and free; want for them everything you want for yourself. If this brings up resistance, just notice it, send it love, and keep practicing. At some point, you will actually start enjoying the feeling of wanting the best for them. That's when you know you're making real progress!

- Secretly send them something. A gift. A love letter. Some money. Find a way to support them or add value to their life. This is considered an advanced practice. When you truly desire the best for this person and *want* to serve them in some way—when you love this person unconditionally—you have completed the process of forgiveness and have activated a whole new level of abundance in your life.

Giving Is the New Getting

The Seven Gifts are a core framework for activating your inner storehouse of riches—the infinite supply that's always available. It's a very practical, methodical way to generate the energy of abundance in every area of your life, regardless of conditions. But the biggest takeaway here is that giving is the real secret of life.

Remember, all of life is emergent. So the only way to have an ever-expanding experience of the riches of life is to be a giver, a generator. Because of this truth, there is no true joy or happiness if you aren't growing and allowing more to flow from you. As the old saying goes, "If you're not living, you're dying." Another way to say this is, "If you're not *giving*, you're stagnating."

So give. Live. Share. And watch all the good in your life multiply!

4

THE LAW OF CIRCULATION

> Let us take our bloated nothingness
> out of the paths of the divine circuits.
> —RALPH WALDO EMERSON

"No matter what I do, he doesn't make time for me; he doesn't appreciate me," my new client Susan said, on the verge of tears. Actually, she seemed more like she had run out of tears—like someone who had cried so much that there was no more water in the tank. She was dry. And so was her life. It was a cracked riverbed that hadn't seen rain in a long time. But I could feel a dam deep inside her, where the pressure was building up. If we could just put a chink in it, we might get that river flowing again.

"Well, what have you done?" I asked.

In truth, I already knew what was happening. After thousands of hours of listening to people, I can usually sense the patterns of their life within minutes instead of months—sort of like that old TV show *Name That Tune*, when only a couple notes are played to identify a song.

"What do you mean, 'what have I done'?" she asked, a little defensively.

I knew this would trigger her. I already sensed that the message she got from her husband was the same message she had been

121

hearing most her life—that she wasn't doing enough, being enough; that she simply *wasn't* enough, period. The result was a coping mechanism with which she had become focused on trying to do more, be more, and give more to everyone else—so that someday, she would be "enough," and become lovable and acceptable again. Then she could finally breathe easy.

"You said, 'no matter what you do,' so I'm wondering, what have you done?"

She was silent. But the silence was so loud, so full of all the years she had tried to prove herself. Then she breathed wearily and answered, "Everything."

"Really? Did you ever take him to the beach and hire a skywriter to write your needs in the air above him? That would be cool."

This was a strategic pattern interrupt. There's always the chance it can backfire, especially when someone's so heavily invested in her story, but I could feel an opening.

"*What?*" She sounded like she didn't know if she should laugh or spit.

"It was a joke."

She let out a sigh of relief and half chuckled. The spell had been slightly broken.

"Okay, maybe not *everything*."

"The stories we tell ourselves are like autosuggestions that hypnotize us and make it impossible to see that there are more possibilities," I said. "But that's not your biggest problem, Susan. Your biggest problem is that you need to embrace your inner diva bitch."

She laughed so hard she literally let out a cackle.

"*I . . . I, I . . . what?!*"

She kept laughing, half in shock, but also clearly liking the idea.

"You've spent most of your life giving to other people, being the good girl, the caretaker, the people pleaser, right?"

"Oh yeah," she admitted, letting out a sigh of relief as if she was being seen for the first time in a long time. Then she took a slow breath, like she was finally savoring the oxygen.

"Aren't you exhausted?"

"*So* exhausted."

She took another breath, getting more much-needed air.

"Early in your life, you got the message that it wasn't okay to want what you wanted and really meet your needs. In fact, you got the message that you were bad or selfish for wanting so much, right?"

"Totally. My mom was so self-involved that she made everything about her; and my dad was like another child. *God.*"

I could hear some of the power starting to come back online, like someone finally got her.

"And to survive, you created a coping mechanism of being more giving, more helpful, unconsciously believing that someday, if you gave enough, you would finally be taken care of. For a while, this strategy might have helped, or at least kept you out of trouble. But that 'someday' never came. And you've spent your life saying yes to everyone else's 'yes' and no to yourself. That's the story of your marriage, isn't it?"

"You got me pegged," she said, a little lighter, and took another breath.

"The problem is, you can't give anything to anyone if you don't already have that thing yourself—at least not without draining yourself, running on empty, and becoming incredibly resentful. That's what you've been doing. You also can't get anything from anyone that you aren't giving to yourself. Even if they give it to you, if you don't already have it to some extent, you won't be able to receive it."

I let that soak in; it was a lot to comprehend.

"I think I know what you mean," she said, feeling the truth of it.

"You can't breathe out until you first breathe in, and you can't keep breathing unless you breathe out—you can't sustain the breath unless you receive the next one back in and release the next one back out. It's a complete cycle. You've been spending most of your life breathing out, and you're gasping for air. He can't give it to you—nobody can—at least, not permanently. Only you can breathe for yourself. That love and appreciation you've been trying to *get* from him has to first come from you—you have to give it to *yourself*. Only then will you have something to give. Because of your upbringing, when you got such a strong message that it was wrong or selfish to give yourself what you really needed, you stopped. And that's why your life and passion and marriage have dried up."

"Wow," she said, like an inner breaker had just been flipped on and the dusty dashboard was starting to light up. "It makes total sense. There have been so many times when I've wanted to do something or get something or go somewhere, but I was afraid my kids would think I was a bad mom and my husband would complain or give me 'that look.' And even the couple times I did, that's exactly what happened."

"Yeah, they don't like the inner diva bitch," I said.

She laughed out loud again.

"Because she has healthy boundaries, she takes care of herself, and she knows how to say no when the line is crossed. They're used to getting their way."

"That's *so* true—ugh!"

"You can totally reverse this. It won't be easy—you'll get some pushback. But what choice do you have? You can't go on this way; it's literally killing you. That's what only breathing out tends to do."

"I know you're right . . . I'm scared, but I know you're right. I have to start taking my power back. What kind of role model am I showing my kids? It's not helping anybody."

She took a deep breath—really took it in—and I could feel the circulation starting to flow again.

"I think you got it," I said, reassuringly. "This is where it starts. So let's talk about how to put it into practice . . ."

● ● ● ● ● ● ●

The Law of Circulation is a foundational principle in all areas of life. Without it, life stagnates, degrades, and ultimately, dies. As we've discussed, a body of water that has no inlet or outlet—no circulation— becomes a swamp, where very little can grow. If electricity doesn't circulate, it's a broken circuit and can't power anything. If oxygen, blood, or any major bodily substance doesn't circulate, disease or death occurs. If life doesn't circulate in nature, amongst all the flora and fauna, things begin to die. This same principle applies to every quality in our lives: if love, joy, intelligence, or abundance doesn't circulate, it diminishes and dries up. This is why living by only one or two elements of circulation always results in lack and limitation.

You can't just store things up, you can't just give things away, you can't just receive, and you can't just take. You need a complete circuit—the true circle of life—in order to live, thrive, and prosper. And then you need to increase the volume and velocity of the energy circulating, which creates an unending flow of abundance in your life. Remember, the word *affluence*, which is often identified with someone who is wealthy, comes from a root that means "flow"; and the word *current* comes from the same root as currency, which often references money. The more flow you have, the more circulation of life energy and wealth you will have too—in every area of life.

To understand and apply the Law of Circulation, you need to break down the three components of it:

1. You can't give what you don't have.
2. You can't keep what you don't give.

3. You can't sustain what you don't receive.

Put another way, you need to have, give, and receive in any area in which you want to generate circulation, abundance, and sustainable growth. As we touched upon with the giving-to-yourself gift, you have to start by giving yourself whatever you want more of or are trying to get from someone or something. That's where Susan was painfully lacking. But it doesn't stop there. If you just give to yourself, that's like taking an in breath and holding it: if all you do is breathe in, you'll die.

You can't keep what you don't give—it has to be circulated. You have to breathe out. This is the next step in the Law of Circulation—giving whatever appears missing or whatever you're trying to get. Finally, you must receive the breath back again to complete the cycle; you must allow life in, allow love in, and become more receptive. And you can never *stop* breathing for any period of time. It's an ongoing process, a way of life. So, too, is becoming a generator of abundance. You must practice this principle until it becomes, well, as natural as breathing.

The ramifications of understanding and living this law are nothing less than true freedom from the external trap of seeing people, places, and things as your Source. This is the practical fulfillment of the Big Betrayal principle. But as you apply the Law of Circulation, it will release you from the power struggles that are inevitable when we believe someone or something is our Source. No longer will you have to wait for people and conditions to change before you can step into your full power and begin generating true abundance. You'll become the supercharged trim tab we talked about in chapter 2 (author Stephen Covey's concept)—someone who can have great influence and impact no matter where they are in the hierarchy of their personal or professional life. So, the activation of the Law of Circulation is a key component to Awakened Abundance—the ultimate wait-loss program.

Let's break this down even further...

You Can't Give What You Don't Have

It should seem logical that you can't give what you don't have. In a concrete or material situation, this would be an observable fact—something we couldn't deny. If you don't have chocolate, you can't give chocolate. If you don't have apples, you can't give apples. But when it comes to our mental, emotional, and spiritual life, we often act as if we can override this principle and escape the consequences. You give of your love, loyalty, and devotion to someone for years, rarely asking for anything in return, and even more rarely giving these qualities to yourself. And for a while, it seems to pay off. The one on the receiving end likes it and might even reward you, and you bask in the glow of being a good person. At times you feel tired, burnt out, unappreciated, even angry, but you find ways to rationalize, repress, or cope with it, buying you more time.

Eventually, though, the imbalance manifests, often in dramatic or destructive ways: depression, chronic fatigue, addiction, passive-aggressive or aggressive behavior, and ultimately, a breakdown in our bodies, business, bank account, relationships, or all of the above. By then, we rarely see or understand the real cause. Instead, we blame ourselves, someone else, the economy, the world, even God, which magnifies our feelings of being a victim and leads to either a further downward spiral or a swing of the pendulum to the other extreme. We may start taking and pursuing, trying to even the score and balance the scales from a place of anger, pain, and a sense of feeling cheated. But the truth is that it's nobody's fault outside of us—no condition is to blame, as life never cheated us; we've been cheating ourselves all along. Remember: from the Emergence paradigm, life doesn't happen *to* you, it happens *through* you; and whatever's missing is what you are not giving—and that especially includes what *you* are not giving *to yourself.*

This is one of the core reasons heart-centered, giving people experience overwhelm and burnout—they're constantly giving from a place of depletion. It's further exacerbated when the individual has a shadow around selfishness, which is very common among this type of person. They carry guilt, shame, and fear about being selfish. They don't understand that selfishness is a divine quality when it's understood and embraced.

Somewhere early in life, they got the message that asking for what they wanted, doing what brought them joy, or taking care of themselves in some way was a bad thing. It could've been that Mommy was always so busy and overwhelmed, because she suffered from the same issue; and when the child asked for more, it set Mommy off, causing her to say things like, "Don't you see how busy I am? Can't you see Mommy is tired?" The parent might not have directly said the child was being selfish, but the message was clear: "You're hurting me with your request." The child feels guilty or ashamed and is afraid of being rejected, so they start developing other ways to get their needs met; they decide that their needs don't really matter; or they find a new level of safety and self-worth in becoming Mommy's little helper, a caretaker, a do-gooder... And the cycle of self-rejection begins.

This is just one example of how this pattern starts, but there are many ways it can manifest. Another common way is via a parent or authority figure who forces a child to share before the child is organically ready to. There's a reason children don't want to share initially—they're still learning how to *have*. They're discovering what it means to possess something and are embodying the *feeling tone* of having. This is a critical developmental stage. If the child is forced to share before they're ready, it short circuits this stage, and mentally and emotionally gets them stuck at that level.

The result can go two ways, depending on the intensity or frequency of this experience: the child can learn that *having* is a bad thing—that they're a "bad" boy or girl for wanting to have and for not sharing—or the child can rebel and become even more possessive and stingy. In either case, they haven't learned and integrated the essential element of having; and they'll grow up with a sense of deprivation that will drive them to either give of themselves too much, from a place of emptiness, shame, and guilt, or withhold themselves due to emptiness, anger, and a fear of losing.

Developing a consciousness of having is so critical. Matthew 13:12 states, "Whoever has will be given more, and they will have abundance. Whoever does not have, even what they have will be taken from them." When Jesus taught people how to pray, he supposedly said, "Therefore I tell you, whatever you ask for in prayer, believe that you have received it, and it will be yours" (Mark 11:24). This wasn't a metaphysical trick to attract something; it was a mystical truth that *you already have it.* But it must be activated through your inner and outer work—you won't just accidently stumble upon a consciousness of having. You have to intentionally develop it.

When you pray, you need to pray *from* the belief that you have. When you say affirmations, you need to do "af-*from*-mations," not "af-for-mations." When you visualize your ideal life, you're not doing it to make something happen; you're doing it to activate the feeling tone of it *already happening.* When you go into the world to achieve something, first establish yourself in a mind-set that you already have the thing you're trying to create. And when you find yourself looking to someone else for a quality you desire because you feel this quality is lacking in your life, you must first give that quality to *yourself.* Love, value, respect, appreciate, praise, serve, and *fill up yourself first.*

In the previous chapter on the Seven Gifts, we talked about a practice you can do to embody the principle of *giving to yourself* (page 111), and I want to add another practice to further build that consciousness of having. It's a simple journaling exercise called "The

Night Pages." I shared this in my previous book, *Emergence*, but would like to include it here too, because it's a powerful way to develop the "have state" of being.

Manifest Abundance Now!

The Night Pages

This journaling exercise is best done at the end of the day, as an inventory of your progress. Writing down what you are noticing and experiencing helps you expand your consciousness of confidence, possibility, and overall abundance—and creates the inner conditions for greater insight, inspiration, and expansion. Don't be fooled by its simplicity or familiarity.

- Make four lists:

  1. I Have
  2. I Can / I Am Able
  3. I Have Achieved / Successes
  4. I Am Grateful For

- Under "I Have," write everything you have, inside and out—the qualities you are activating and expressing; your gifts, talents, and abilities; the people and things you value; whatever money you have (even if it seems too little to note). Include things to which you have *access* that you don't actually own. You might list paved roads, sewer systems, a public library, and the internet. All told, you probably have more wealth than some of the royalty from ancient times. Allow yourself to revel in all you have.

  If there's a particular area in your life where you've been looking for a breakthrough, pay special attention there, and be as thorough as you can in recording all that you actually have in that area. For example, if you want to start a business but need a million dollars in capital, your tendency might be to focus on what you don't have (the million dollars) and then react to that, which is likely to magnify the feeling of lack and create resistance. Instead, focus on what you do have, inside and out.

- Under "I Can / I Am Able," write about all the things you *can* and are *able* to do. This is especially important to do in areas where you feel stuck, victimized, lacking, or inadequate. Using the previous example of trying to start a business, think about what you *can* do in support of that goal. You can create a business plan; you can call everyone you know and offer them an investment; you can learn about people who have built businesses from nothing; you can do inner work on building the mind-set of a successful business owner—there's so much you *can* do.

- For the "I Have Achieved / Successes" list, write down all the things you've accomplished or achieved. Then, daily, write down at least five successes you had that day, even if you list "got out of bed" or "brushed my teeth"—there are many people who didn't achieve either of those. Again, pay attention to any area in which you're trying to have a breakthrough. If it's money, look for the things you've achieved in that area, including any money you've made, saved, invested, given, or found—even if it's just a penny! The universal intelligence doesn't know quantity, just quality.

- For "I'm Grateful," it's pretty obvious, but stretch yourself. Find things to be grateful for that you've taken for granted. Let yourself be surprised by what you find to be grateful for. Really allow thanksgiving to be activated ("I'm grateful for that person who opened the door for me," "I'm grateful for the sun activating my vitamin D," "I'm grateful for my ability to be grateful!"). Once again, pay particular attention to any area in which you're working for a breakthrough. What can you be grateful for there?

As you do this, you're not only developing a consciousness of having, you're creating conditions congruent to your bigger vision—conditions that are *welcoming*. Wealth can't come into a consciousness or experience that isn't already a vibration of wealth. Nor can love take up residence where anger, resentment, or blame are making their bed. The next level of your life that is trying to emerge is literally *made out of these qualities* you're activating.

As you practice this consistently, it becomes more than just a nightly exercise; it becomes a way of life—a way of seeing and being. As you go through your day, you start automatically seeing things in terms of what *is* instead of what isn't, what you have instead of what you don't, what is possible versus what isn't. You don't just see the glass as half full; you see it as *completely* full—half air, half liquid! Increasingly, the locus of power and potential is within you, and you're no longer on your way to something that will bring you fulfillment; *you are coming from fulfillment itself.*

You Can't Keep What You Don't Give

As you begin to live more in a state of having, you now have something to give. This doesn't mean you shouldn't give anything before you build a state of having, but embodying that state should be a top priority. The key, as in all of our actions, is the place we're *coming from*; the action itself is neutral. It's the reason we're taking the action that activates the laws of creation. If you're giving to someone to get, you are out of alignment—whether it's to get approval, applause, appreciation, respect, or love. If you're giving from an inner expectation (whether conscious or unconscious) that they will eventually give back to you and take care of you, you're off the beam. Truly, if you're giving for any reason other than just to give, unconditionally, then you're manipulating and creating a greater sense of lack and separation.

In the purest sense, this even includes your place of business or the clients you serve. Ultimately, you want to give your time, talent, and service unconditionally—meaning that, at least internally, you're not doing it for the name, fame, or fortune; you're doing it because that's your nature. A tree doesn't give of its fruits to get money or anything else; it gives them because that's what it was designed for. You are designed to give of your gifts, talents, capacities, and spiritual qualities as a divine offering to life. Spiritually speaking, none of these things belongs to you; they belong to life.

As I mentioned in the beginning, the word for "man" in Sanskrit means, "the dispenser of divine gifts." In a very real sense, you have been sent here to give of your whole life in service of the world—in whatever capacity you are called. This doesn't mean you don't charge for your services or don't make agreements with others that include some kind of mutual exchange. Absolutely, you do. But internally, you know that you're not looking to the world as your Source; you're anchored in the source within—in the have consciousness—and giving from that overflow. In this way, you are *in* the world but not *of* it. You're a free agent, a blessing, a beneficial presence that adds value wherever you go. And because you're giving from that state, the universe expands your channel and makes you an even bigger giver.

Conversely, if you withhold from life, life will be withhold from you—because it can only come into your experience *through* you. So if you want more to come into your life, you must continuously let more life come out of you. Whatever you're not letting out is something you don't get to have or experience. And eventually, that channel stagnates, dries up, and atrophies. It's like a tree not letting its fruits go. Eventually, they rot, block the flow of life in the tree, make it sick, and potentially kill it. At the very least, it would not be able to produce more fruit because the very channels through which the fruit blossoms would be blocked. The same is true for us: the more we let life flow through us to the world on every level, the more life sees us as a willing channel to fulfill its greater purpose. It gives us more opportunity, a bigger platform, and increasing abundance, without limits. The only limit is our willingness to keep giving and allowing this life to flow out from us—our willingness to enact the Law of Circulation.

This state of withholding shows up in a variety of ways, but always, it's some form of waiting for the right circumstances to give. If it's about giving money, we're waiting to have enough. If it's about giving our love, we're waiting to either feel comfortable sharing that part of us with someone or waiting for that someone to first give their love to us. We only want to give as good as we get, which seems logical enough. If someone is disrespectful to us or doesn't give us much respect, the last thing we would think to do—or want to do— is give them *more* respect. If someone is unkind to us or doesn't show us much caring, it feels odd to show them *more* love. If someone doesn't seem to acknowledge us, listen to us, or value us, it can feel like self-betrayal to seek a deeper understanding and acceptance of them.

If you haven't yet built a state of having, it can be detrimental to try and extend yourself in these areas where you're already suffering, because you'll often be doing it from a place of manipulation (to get something), and it will backfire—if not externally, certainly internally. But as you start giving these qualities to yourself, you're ready—and even spiritually obligated—to start giving them away, regardless of what others are doing. It can be awkward and uncomfortable at first; your ego may rebel, and layers of unresolved emotion may surface. In those cases, it's important to tend to those parts of you—to love them and give them what they need. But then you must return to the process of giving what you have, sharing your gifts, circulating your good, casting your bread upon the waters—because this is the only way more can show up in your life.

In intimate relationships, this might look like noticing your chronic complaints about your partner ("They never listen to me, they don't appreciate what I do, they don't value my interests . . .") and beginning to give them those things. For example, in conversation, instead of seeking to be heard, you seek first to listen and understand them; you give them the listening you've been trying to get. And only after they truly feel heard and understood do you ask to be heard in return. If you find yourself feeling like they don't appreciate what you do for them, you might stop and contemplate all the ways you don't appreciate what they're doing, and start openly giving that appreciation. If you crave their approval or interest in the things you care about, a good practice would be to consider the things they care about that you judge, dislike, or dismiss. Start looking for the value in these things so you can have some rapport around your partner's activities and interests. That doesn't mean you have to become a football fanatic, culinary connoisseur, or great outdoorsman because they're interested in these things; but it does mean you stop judging them for loving sports, watching cooking shows, and always wanting to be outside. Acknowledge their passion for the subject; or try to find what's interesting, creative, or inspiring in whatever they're passionate about, and engage with them in that activity on occasion. Who knows? You might just discover a whole new world of possibility for yourself.

The irony is that when you start really looking at this dynamic between the two of you, you'll often find that many of the things you're complaining about them not giving you are things you're simultaneously not giving them in some way. While you're criticizing them for being judgmental, you realize, *Oh wait, I'm judging them right now!* While you're complaining that they never listen to you, you suddenly see that in those moments where you're wanting them to listen, you're not listening to them. It's all a mirror, and it's all a projection of our consciousness. *As we clean up our side of the street, polishing the mirror of our perception, what gets reflected back to us becomes more harmonious and in alignment with our deepest desires.*

There are many areas of life where you can practice this step in the Law of Circulation. At work, it's very common to give only what you're paid for, to watch the clock, and make sure you don't give a minute more than you need to. Likewise, the standards might not be too high, and there may be a lot of mediocre levels of performance, which have become the norm. You might think, *Hey, everyone else is doing it. If nobody else cares that much, why should I?* Or you might tell yourself that the boss doesn't value or appreciate you, so why in the world would you give more of yourself? It can also be scary to begin giving more than expected because of the possible backlash of the other employees. I've heard many examples—and experienced them myself—where someone starts giving above and beyond, and the employees get mad for being made to look bad by comparison. This peer pressure is powerful, but it must be overcome if you are to grow, evolve, and activate your full potential. I was fired *three* times from a job because I continued to up my game by giving more and more. But when I eventually left, within a month I was hired in a job that met my deeper needs and paid me twenty times what I made before! That opportunity wasn't created in my future; it was created in the job where I was expanding my capacity to give unconditionally.

You can also practice this at home with your children. As parents, we often complain that our kids don't listen to us, don't respect us, or don't appreciate us. But when we look closer, we're usually doing the same to them. Sure, we love them, take care of them, and want the best for them, but do we *really* respect them as unique and perfect expressions of life? Do we *really* listen to and appreciate them—not from our paradigm of what should or shouldn't be but from *theirs*? Are we taking time to stand in their shoes and deeply understand life from their experience? You might be saying, "That's not my job as a parent.

I'm not there to be their friend or to get them to like me. I'm there to educate, discipline, and protect them." And that's true. But it's not the whole story.

These beings are as infinite, eternal, and divine as any adult, and are therefore deserving of just as much respect. Frequently—and unknowingly—we as parents become more like dictators, projecting our unresolved issues on our children and using them as proxies to work out our own stuff. It becomes a power trip: we finally get to control someone, to have power over someone, to get our way. Of course, that most often leads to frustration as our children rebel against our dictatorship. But when we begin to give them what we are seeking—and what they're often starving for—we not only begin to heal many of the conflicts we've struggled with but also start to fill *our children* up, so they can build a consciousness of having as a foundation for their life. Ultimately, that is the greatest work of a parent—to fill our children up with a sense of who, what, and why they exist, and how valuable and worthy they are. Even if they don't get all the right strategies for living, if we give them a consciousness of having, they have more than most.

There are many ways we can practice giving what we have or what we're trying to get. But the key is that we do it from the place of having. Any of the examples above could be practiced from a place of not having. In fact, they often are. As I described earlier, many people are giving and giving—to their spouses, children, work, and clients—but from a place of limitation or separation, a fear of loss, or a need to get something in return. It's often an attempt to manipulate—either to make you feel better, safer, more worthy or to make the other person feel these things—so that they'll take care of you in return, or at least not reject you. And this is not sustainable, because it leads to burnout, resentment, anger, and depression (which is often a lack of expression or repressed anger). As you practice this, remain mindful for those moments when you slip into giving to get—when your giving isn't coming from a place of abundance or fulfillment.

I'm not saying that giving has to be perfect, that you have to feel great every time, or that you should be analyzing every breath you take while you're giving something. You definitely want to allow this practice to become natural and easy, not some heady discipline that makes you even more stressed and afraid of making a mistake. But when you find yourself constricting, pushing, or withdrawing, take a moment to turn within and see where you're coming from, what you're feeling, and the story you're telling yourself. Then tend to those parts, give them what they need, and fill yourself back up.

Manifest Abundance Now!

Giving Away What You Want

- To begin practicing this, pick an area where you've felt something is missing or someone isn't giving you something, and create an intentional plan to start giving it to them (and to yourself, if you haven't already).
- Another way to work on this is to focus on an area where you're *waiting* to get something before you give—only giving as good as you get—and instead, begin giving it now. If you're waiting for more validation or payment at work before you give a higher level of excellence and service, start giving it now. If you're waiting for your partner to "do their part" before you'll be more loving, respectful, or appreciative, start treating them this way now. Give away whatever you want to have more of.
- Be specific, keep a journal of your progress, and stay vigilant for the times when you slip back into some form of agenda or manipulation. Remember, you're not doing it to get them to change,

give you something, or tell you how great you are; you're doing it to circulate more of your inner abundance, so that your life may expand and reveal more of your divine inheritance.

You Can't Sustain What You Don't Receive

Giving to yourself and to others isn't enough to fully activate the Law of Circulation; it's not a complete circuit until you allow yourself *to receive*. In a way, this is a version of giving to yourself: you are giving yourself the gift of *allowing* others and life to give to you. You're loving and valuing yourself enough to receive all the blessings around you. This can come in many ways—from the simplest things, like the unexpected compliment, to a person holding a door for you; or a smile from a stranger to someone offering to help you in some way, showing a deeper level of love, kindness, and support. You can also activate this by being humble enough to ask for help and then graciously receiving it.

But there are more opportunities to count your blessings and receive all that life is giving you. The sun on your skin; the wind in your hair; the flower blooming; the birds singing; the ground that holds you; the home that shelters you; all the elements, moments, and conditions of life that bring you value—all of it is *life loving you*. But if you don't acknowledge and breathe it in, you don't embody just how much life loves and supports you; and you don't fully complete the circuit.

Again, we have the analogy of the breath: you breathe in (giving to yourself), you breathe out (giving to others), and you receive the breath back in again. It might sound like receiving is the same as giving to yourself, but it can be quite different in practice. For example, it might come easy to start taking better care of yourself and honor yourself in different ways, but when someone else tries to give to you, it triggers unresolved guilt or shame. It somehow feels awkward or wrong for someone to see you and meet your needs—sometimes before you know the need yourself. So even when you've learned to give to yourself and others, this piece can become the stumbling block that prevents your full demonstration of circulation. In fact, for some, this can be the hardest step in the whole process. It's one thing to give to yourself, especially if you can do it somewhat in private; but to be publicly loved, honored, respected, complimented, or noticed in any positive way can bring out a lot of unhealed stuff!

We can be clever with how we block this part of the process. Someone compliments us, and we deflect it with something like, "Oh, this old dress. I just threw it on!" Or "What—*this* hair? I barely spent any time on it." Or we immediately compliment them back, to take the heat off of us. We also block it by not letting people help us when they offer or by not asking for help when we need it. These blocks not only rob us of the gift and a healthy circuit, but they rob the giver of their ability to give, interrupting their circulation as well. In a very real sense, it's selfish to not let others give to us.

Other, subtler blocks to receiving: When we become so busy we can't "stop and smell the roses," we are preventing ourselves from seeing and receiving the blessings around us. We miss that moment of beauty, we take for granted that helping hand, we're blind to that smile—or we misinterpret it as something negative: *Why are they smiling? What do they want from me? What are they up to?*

In order to truly receive the gift from everything and everyone around us, we need to slow down and cultivate a life of contemplation and deeper observation. It's like the analogy of someone rushing through his or her day "out of breath." They might even say, "I'm so busy, I can't catch my breath," which is the receiving part of breathing. We can't always be doing; we have to allow for being—for that pause after the doing, that pause that lets life in, that silence between the notes that makes the music (without it, it's just noise). If our life is too crowded, inside or out, there's no room for anything or anyone to get in. But when we create the space to listen, to see, to just be, life flows in effortlessly—just like the breath does on the in breath.

There are many ways to develop this inflow. Besides smelling the roses, you can smell the aroma of your coffee or food before and while you eat. When you're bathing, you can feel the water cascading over you or soaking you. When you're with someone, you can practice taking your attention off yourself and taking them in. Instead of preparing your response while they're talking, you could just listen and see what happens—what a concept!

Even moments that might otherwise seem mundane, boring, or tedious (like waiting in line at the bank or the DMV) can become transformational. Just breathe in and notice all the unique beings around you, feel the connection you have, and be grateful for the service the place provides. As this becomes a subjective habit in you, your capacity to see and receive the abundance *all around you* will become virtually unlimited. Every moment, every day, every person, and every place will team with a vitality, a beauty, and a potential that feeds your heart and soul.

Keeping the Circuit Connected

As with many aspects of the Awakened Abundance model, this isn't about just strategies and tactics for solving problems or achieving specific solutions; this is about building habits that transform your character and become a way of life. Positive habits aren't easy to build, and changing your character for the better is even harder. That's why most people don't do it. But your habits and, ultimately, your character determine your destiny—not the conditions you face—so it's a worthwhile endeavor to pursue. Remember: it's not about perfection; it's about practice. Daily. Consistently. Regardless of whether or not you feel like it.

At first, take it slow. Don't try to pile on ten new habits and master all of this in a week. Not only will it most likely fail (and potentially create a downward failure pattern), but it's not necessary. Small changes, over time, can change the world.

It's like golfing: You start out with a tiny ball that you're supposed to navigate far down the green into a tiny hole you can't even see. If you've never done it before or aren't a very good player, it can feel virtually impossible. Still, you begin with your first shot. The hole is way off, but you adjust, take aim, and hit the ball again. It overcompensates and goes into the bushes . . . but you're actually a little closer to the hole. You do this over and over—maybe it takes you a dozen or even one hundred shots—but little by little, you actually hone in on the target, and eventually get the ball in the hole. Anyone can do this; it just might take longer for some. The key is sticking with it, continuously readjusting, and trying again, until you get the desired result.

The same is true with Awakened Abundance. So take it easy, take the shot, and keep moving.

5

EVERYONE IS YOUR CHANNEL; NOBODY IS YOUR SOURCE

Most powerful is he who has himself in his own power.

—SENECA

When we bought our first dream home, it felt like we were living in a resort. It was summer; and every day, we'd walk up the street as a family and swim in the community's beautiful pool, then come home and snuggle up on the coach for a fun night of "must see TV." Life was good. But inside, I was afraid. Afraid it would all go away like it did when I was a kid. Afraid I was living on borrowed time, borrowed money, borrowed faith (mostly my wife's faith).

She didn't seem to be concerned at all; she believed we could afford this new life. I, on the other hand, was struggling to grow my writing and consulting business, and living from project to project, with no real security. I was doing the inner work to tap into my true abundance and feel the assurance that all was well, but it was harder than ever with the new everyday pressure of a mortgage payment and our second child. I had to do a lot of praying, meditating, and affirming just to stay above water.

The blessing of this challenging new stage of life was that it forced me to begin apprenticing under the principles of wealth and

143

prosperity—something I hadn't really done; partly because I had rejected a lot of worldly materialism as an artist, but mostly because I never had the need to provide so much. Now, staring at a budget that had more than doubled, I had to dig much deeper than before. And as winter came, I spent many nights by the fireplace, reading, journaling, praying, and affirming the highest truth I could touch, often falling asleep on top of the books.

Meanwhile, my wife had her own spiritual practice and, perhaps because she didn't have the same kind of pressure around money, she was having powerful openings. She began to be convinced of how abundant we could be and how it would all be taken care of. I remember thinking, *That's easy for you to say. You don't have to pay the mortgage every month.* At the time, she had a job and earned a nice piece of the pie, but I was increasingly responsible for more of it as her dream shifted to being a homeschooling mom for our two kids.

One day, she came to me exhilarated, exclaiming that she had caught a vision of my success and how abundant we would be. The energy of her enthusiasm was palpable and catchy—it lifted my spirits and gave me a vibrational touchstone to lean on. But I still didn't have the level of faith she possessed; and I believed that, without it, I was never going to have my big break.

Then something strange happened. Soon after her big declaration, I started getting more work. And within a short time, I landed my biggest client ever. I couldn't believe it, but I was definitely willing to receive it! Suddenly, we were flush with cash—and had the prospects of much more to come. I was riding high. But my wife wasn't all that surprised.

At first, I felt a little dismissed. Here I was, making a big move and bringing home some serious bacon, and she was like, "Yep, that's what I thought."

Then it hit me . . .

She was *already living there* before it showed up. She was already riding that wave of abundant energy, and I was just catching up. I had to paddle pretty fast to get ahead of that wave, but I finally caught it. And one day, while I was meditating, I realized that the abundance that was flowing into our life was not just coming from me—it was also flowing from *her* consciousness. Sure, I was doing good inner and outer work, and had embodied a lot; but she had definitely helped to kick this demonstration into high gear.

I thought, *But if some of this is coming from her, why didn't it manifest for her?* And the answer came back: "It did. She's enjoying the fruits of this new level of abundance!"

For a moment, I thought, *Well that's not fair. I'm doing all the work and she's enjoying the fruits!* But that quickly passed as I realized that, while her consciousness might have been, in part, the source of the demonstration, I was the *channel* through which it came. It was a mind-expanding awareness. As a stay-at-home mom, it appeared as if her options were limited. But that would only be true if she were the only channel in her life. What I saw instead was that everyone and everything around her was a channel for her good—and I was the perfect channel for this expression.

I could see that no matter what position we're in, as long as we make that connection and have the realization that we're abundantly taken care of, it will show up—somewhere, somehow, through someone or something. We could be dropped on a desert island, but if we realized our oneness with life and abundance, we would be fed, clothed, and taken care of—even if birds had to bring us food like the ravens did to the prophets of the Bible, or if manna had to fall from the sky, or if gold had to appear in a fish's mouth!

This changed the whole game. I not only began to see how nobody was ever limited by their circumstances but how everyone and everything in life is a potential channel for our good. All I had to do was keep making that contact within—keep opening my heart and mind to let more life flow out—and it would find the perfect channel to express my fulfillment. I also began to be freed from the old baggage of seeing people as victims, and feeling guilt or shame when I asked them for something or charged them for my work—thinking that somehow I was taking from them, causing them to have less. As I would discover, this shift was critical in my ability to turn transactional relationships into transformational ones, and to eventually grow a thriving business in which I was making a great living and having a major impact doing what I loved.

The Law of the Channel

This master teaching can be one of the most liberating ones for heart-centered, spiritually minded people; or for those who have shadows around being selfish or greedy (which we'll address in chapter 6). You know the type (or maybe *are* the type): they're kind and giving, often have wonderful talents to share, and are usually caretakers of one kind or another; but they feel bad asking for what they really want or need, charging what they're worth for their work (if they even charge at all), and keeping what they have (because they unconsciously have to give it all away out of guilt).

The core misunderstanding for people like this is that when they ask for something, it takes something away from the other person— whether it's time, energy, or money. This is a fundamentally *false* belief based on a Newtonian, materialistic view of the world; and it has led to a zero-sum, consumption-based economy. The truth, as this chapter will explore, is that people are not our Source but a channel (as is *everything else* in creation); and we are all connected to the one Source like branches of the same tree, which is infinite and inexhaustible. When we're willing to make a big demand of life and ask for what we need from others, we don't limit what's available; we expand the possibilities. We don't take a slice out of a small pie; we expand the size of the pie for everyone.

This is a very different way of looking at the world. From the relative level of our senses, it looks like everything is interacting, one thing causing another. But from the quantum, spiritual, or invisible level, that's not what's happening. There is no cause and affect, no interaction; there is only omniaction and emergence. Nothing is causing anything. Things are creating certain conditions that are congruent to certain seeds—like the pattern of an oak is already in the acorn, and when the condition matches the seed pattern, its potential emerges. As this potential emerges in time and space, in the world of duality and opposites, it *appears* as if one thing is causing another. But really, it's an emergence of the one as the many—again, like the branches of one tree.

In this realization, we discover that we're not just separate people; we are "places in the field"—openings, channels, or centers in the One Mind. And as we connect with that part within that is one with everything and everyone, it emerges into expression—but not always through our individual bodies (the "branch" we represent); sometimes it emerges through a different branch of the one tree. My story about my wife illustrates that. She touched the deeper truth of abundance within her—at the center of her being, which is the same center as mine— and as that potential emerged, it found the channel where it could most easily and quickly manifest, which happened to be my client and me.

One Source, Many Channels

There is one Source but there are many channels. As we begin living in this new, more expanded paradigm, we have to adopt a new way of being. We have to let go of the idea that we, as individuals, have to get everything done or be the solitary instrument for everything in our lives. Just as a single branch isn't managing the whole tree—or even a small fraction of it—we have to let go of the idea that we are the managers of our universe. We also have to let go of needing to know how something will get done or show up, or who and where it will come from. The Divine Mind is aware of all possibilities simultaneously—something we, in our human mind, can't begin to understand. So when we try to use our limited mind and limited set of experiences to determine the best way something is to show up, we are profoundly limiting what's possible.

The only thing we can focus on is the *what*: *what* do we want, *what* do we sense is trying to emerge in our life, *what* are we committed to. At the same time, we must realize that our best guess at the what is still clouded and filtered by our conditioned ideas of what *should* be, what *has* to be, what *can* be, *who* we think we are, and *why* we think we're here. That's why, when we use manifestation tools like creative visualization, we have to remember that the pictures we come up with are not necessarily the way things will appear when they manifest. It's okay to use those tools, especially if we use them to activate the *feeling* of the vision (you can never go wrong with the feeling); but we shouldn't hold on to the picture, because that might not be what we really need in order to take our life to the next level.

Our role starts to become more simplified. Our job is just to tap into the vision as best we can, activate the feeling and connection with it so that it becomes real within us, and then take compelling action in the direction of it. How it shows up, where it comes from, and when are not really up to us. As we become comfortable with this new way of living, we release the resistance to the natural, abundant flow of life; more channels begin to open up to us; and our good flows to, through, and around us, at a whole new level.

Infinite Organizing Power

One key principle to understand is that life doesn't have only one or two or ten ways to fulfill itself—it has *infinite possibilities*. If a door closes, a window opens. If all the doors and windows are closed, there will be a skylight to go through—or life will just move a whole wall out of the way! An idea realized in consciousness must find fulfillment. When you are in tune with your true potential, your inexhaustible abundance will find a way to manifest in your life. Even if the only person who can fulfill your need is on the other side of the world, they'll find their way to your front door, or you'll be guided to theirs. Life will not be mocked, blocked, or denied—and it has an unlimited variety of means and tactics to meet your needs.

This is such an important principle to embody, because the default of the human mind is to determine what is possible by what it can see, hear, touch, taste, or imagine. But many of the most important innovations, breakthroughs, and leaps in progress—whether individually or collectively—are outside of our current concepts and paradigms. My story of getting that commercial when I was at the end of my financial rope illustrates how sometimes the quickest, most effective way to achieve a result is beyond what you can imagine. I would never have visualized, affirmed, prayed, or even taken action toward that outcome because it was outside of my self-concept at the time. The channels I was looking to were very different than what the universe had in mind for fulfilling my needs. If I had continued to go along my chosen route, trying to make something happen based on my ideas of where my good should come from, I might have ended up on the street and never had that powerful demonstration.

So if you want to experience the greatest level of abundance in the most graceful way, you have to let go of your ideas of how it should happen, where it should come from, and who it should come through. If you've decided that the only way you can know true love is if Bob or Sally loves you back, you might be alone for a long time, never finding the true love of your life. If you're convinced that the only way you'll become a successful author is if Oprah interviews you, you may be working that regular job for the rest of your life and miss all the other ways your dream could be fulfilled. If you think the only solution to your financial problems is if you get a raise, get a loan from your parents, or win the lottery, you might just end up in bankruptcy court!

I'm not saying this to make you afraid; I'm saying it to motivate you to let go of how you think anything should happen and who you think it should come from, so that the infinite organizing power of the universe can find the shortest, easiest route for you. We must get out of our own way—out of the way of the universe—and let the intelligence that creates and governs everything take care of itself.

At first, this can seem like a scary proposition—letting go of control always is. But as we acclimate to this new way of living and begin to see that things still get accomplished—and in increasingly easier, more creative, or just plain better ways than we could have humanly imagined—we start feeling a sense of relief. It's like believing you have to control your breathing all day long, experiencing all the worry and stress that would induce, and then one day, being relieved of that duty. At first you wouldn't trust it, but eventually, you would start breathing a lot easier!

Imagine the possibilities if you never again had to decide the how, who, or where but only had to focus on the what. How much more energy would you have for creating the life you desire? In fact, when you release the constricting elements of who, where, and how, you increase the volume and velocity of your energy, which increase the flow—the affluence—in your life.

Give Specifically, Receive Universally

So everyone is your channel and nobody is your Source; your only job is to tap into the "what" and live as if it's already true. But there's one other pitfall to practicing this principle. As we work with the Law of Circulation, filling ourselves up and circulating the good we have, it's a common experience to expect our reward to come from the place from which we have been giving. If we do a great job at work, bringing excellence and giving more than is required, we often expect to get a raise, a promotion, or some other clear response to our generosity.

When this doesn't happen, we feel cheated and betrayed, and either retaliate or withdraw our level of circulation. That begins to constrict our flow and creates a downward spiral that can erase all the progress we made, making a good situation bad and a bad situation worse. The same is true in relationships. We love, value, respect, and appreciate someone yet get little to no goodies in return. This hurts and angers us; we stop giving at that level; we start giving as good as we get; and we even lash out, leading to a stagnation, degradation, and ultimately, the destruction of that relationship.

There are several reasons why a particular channel doesn't return the energy we've circulated to it. First, this person may not be able, for whatever reason. That place of employment simply might not have the money in their budget or another position to promote you to. The person you're in relationship with may be dealing with some deep issues that make it too hard for them to reciprocate (although, with time, they may grow into it if they're open), or they may not be willing to reciprocate. It's also possible that your boss, spouse, partner, friend, or colleague may misinterpret your actions, believe you have a hidden agenda, or even harbor some unhealed resentment or jealousy, thereby resisting the flow trying to emerge through them. Another possibility: You may have some unconscious issues that need to be healed or a latent potential that can only be activated through some situation that causes you to dig deeper. The lack of reciprocity could be exactly what you need to search within yourself and discover a whole new level of self-love and self-support. Finally, it just may be the wrong channel for the result that would serve you best; but in your limited human thinking, you can't yet see that.

For all these reasons, you never want to limit your demonstration to any channel you're circulating to. You want to give unconditionally, letting your giving be fulfillment in and of itself. A gift isn't a gift if it has conditions; conditions make it a contract. Anytime our giving has an agenda, it's not real giving; it's manipulating or controlling to get the specific result we believe we should get. That kind of giving rarely activates the flow—in fact, it often impedes it, because the other person feels the pressure and closes their channel.

Ultimately, we want to give, serve, and circulate our life and all our capacities unconditionally, seeking nothing in return. This is the way all of nature gives and the reason why nature is a perfect system of flow, renewal, and expansion. When we are able to give like that, shining our light like the sun—not caring whether people appreciate it, reciprocate it, or close their shades and block it—we will become an ever-expanding channel of the infinite good of life. The universe will see us as a worthy, welcome place to put itself on display in all of its brightness.

As I explained before, giving, sharing, and circulating unconditionally doesn't mean we don't have agreements and contracts that we must hold ourselves and others accountable to. In a way, we have to live on two levels: the human and the spiritual. So while we may have an agreement on the outside that says we do a certain job and our employer pays us a certain fee for it, we are still giving without an agenda on the inside, giving unconditionally and not seeing them as our Source. But this doesn't mean that you can't make a request for more or for a different behavior in a relationship. If you are loving, respecting, and valuing your significant other in an intimate partnership or marriage but they're not treating you equally, it's perfectly legitimate to ask them to. Asking is an activator of the channel. That's why it is said, "Ask and it will be given to you" (Matthew 7:7)—it opens the universal channels (or the channel you're asking) to begin circulating, and it opens your channel to receive.

Sometimes, you may need to press the issue, have difficult conversations, and hold your ground for the kind of relationship you stand for—with a very clear boundary of what is and isn't acceptable. This is an act of self-love and an act of love for your partner, as it calls them to a higher level. Of course, this assumes you are also doing the inner work and showing up in the same way you want them to show up. If you're not, then it's a projection and manipulation, and is doomed to fail.

As you do this kind of work in relationship, it's rarely easy. Deeper issues are often being worked out that require a period of discovery, integration, and unfolding. The key, as with all of these examples, is that you maintain the awareness that this person isn't your Source; they're a channel. The love, respect, or whatever quality you're seeking isn't coming *from* them; it's coming *through* them. That's the larger context in which you live and operate. And if that's embodied, then you can interact in a very human way without getting caught in the realm of secondary causation (the belief that you can't get what you want or need unless it comes from them).

This can also occur in professional relationships—with a boss, with a colleague, in a partnership, even with workers you are in a position to manage—where you must hold the other party accountable for the agreement you're in. If your coworkers are not doing their part, it may require asking them to show up more and standing your ground in order to open their channel and start the flow. Likewise, the process of doing that might be exactly what you need to build some inner muscles of your own—perhaps greater confidence, self-worth, trust, or other forms of personal power.

In the early stages of my business, I hired a small team to support me, and while it was helpful to have this extra backup at first, I soon found myself having to do a lot more hand-holding and micromanaging to get some of the team members to do the job they were hired for. I figured this was part of leadership and management, and did my best to coach and train these individuals. But soon, it became apparent I had created a codependent relationship that wasn't serving anyone; and I needed to hold them accountable to their initial performance agreements. The problem: I was afraid that if I called them out on their substandard work and required them to improve their performance, they would quit; and I would be stranded with a lot of work and no team to support me.

This experience brought up old shadows around being the "bad guy"—something I never wanted anyone to see me as. So I tried to avoid the confrontation by providing more coaching, more support, and always giving them the benefit of the doubt. The result: I started feeing stressed, overwhelmed, and resentful. Finally, I realized I had made them my Source and needed to stand on principle, holding them accountable, come what may. To do anything less would be to live out of integrity with myself. So I confronted two of the core team members, and stated very clearly the problem and what I needed for us to continue working together.

My worst fear came to pass: the team melted down; and I found myself having to fire the main employees, and handle all the customer support and project management myself. It was the nightmare scenario! But as I continued to do this work and strengthen my inner conviction that I was truly supported by life, I quickly brought in a new team that more accurately reflected where I was now coming from. And the level of support, productivity, and revenue *doubled* that year—then doubled *again*!

The small print on this universal contract states that it doesn't always work out the way you want at first. In the short term, it is possible that, as you hold your place in this expanded space, living in the larger context of truth that other people are not your Source while acting at the human level of the issue, the partnership might dissolve, the marriage might end, you might be fired from the job (or compelled to quit), or your current business might end up in crisis mode. In this particular moment, it probably won't feel good or feel like a success, it might even feel like you've failed or that God has forsaken you. Hold on to what you know to be true, because if you've been truly doing the work, and you stay the course, that new level of consciousness you've developed will find the right channels for its expression; and your life will manifest the next stage of your emergence.

Your Projection Determines Your Potential

There's another very important element to turning transactional relationships into transformational ones, where you know they're not your Source but a channel, and the flow is able to circulate unimpeded. It's summed up in this statement:

How you hold or see someone determines how big or how small a channel they can become for you.

For example, if you see a client as not having a lot of money and, therefore, being limited in their ability to invest in their growth or education, you're creating a box around them that they can't exceed—unless they're more conscious of their abundance than you are. How you view a person—as a channel of infinite abundance, brilliance, and potential or as merely a person with finite resources and limited abilities—will determine whether or not your interaction leaves them with more, leaves you with more, or diminishes both of your resources.

One example that illustrates this principle is a study in which three teachers were given a set of students—all pulled from the general population of kids. One teacher was told the students were high achievers; the second teacher was told the students were below average; and the third teacher was told nothing, which became the control group. The result at the end of the study: the class in which the teacher believed she had above-average kids had some of the highest test scores in the district; the class in which the teacher believed they were below average scored some of the lowest, and the control group was consistent with the average scores.[2]

What was the difference? The expectation of the teacher. How the teacher *held* the student, either in a big box or a small one, determined whether the students would rise to fill that space or shrink to fit it. The same is true with all of our interactions. When we see our partner, family member, client, colleague, child, or boss as a channel of infinite good and ask for what we need, we not only increase our chances of receiving it but create the condition for that person to expand. Their act of giving not only adds to our life but makes *them* bigger as well, available to more abundance then before. From this new framework, we actually look forward to giving more people the opportunity to give to us—and more people seem eager to do just that!

This doesn't just apply to asking for something; it also applies to any expectation you have of someone. As in the teacher study, whatever perception you hold someone in determines, to a great extent, which side of themselves they'll show you. One of the most powerful and satisfying parts of my work is watching a client come into my program filled with self-doubt about their abilities and their future prospects, and, as I continue to see them for who they really are in potential and hold that space no matter what story they tell, witnessing them blossoming in miraculous ways.

I remember Mary coming to me, seeking to transition out of her corporate job and create a private consulting business. It was an impossible dream to her. She didn't believe she had anything truly worthy to offer and didn't think anyone would be crazy enough to pay for her services. On every coaching call, she would bring her stories of what wasn't working, her pain, and her challenges; and I would listen, allowing her the space to vent but never buying the story. Instead, I was always on the lookout for evidence of the greatness, genius, and abundance I knew was in her and trying to get out.

Little by little, I would bring her attention to those areas that were working and the talents that did have value until she had a vision for her life that inspired her. As she began to live into the vision and bump into other layers of limited programming and seeming inadequacies, I continued to hold her in a larger box of possibility, opening her up to see it for herself. And within less than a year, she had her own consulting practice, making a living doing what she loved—and loving her life and herself at a whole new level. This isn't a fluke; it's a common occurrence when you master the art of seeing the potential in people.

Take a moment to think about this. Look at the people in your life and the experience you have of them, especially the ones that are falling short of your expectations or desires. Now look at what you think about them and their capacities. Be honest: What do you believe about them; what's your judgment about them? Do you see them as being limited in this area? Do you see them as a victim in some way? If you see them as anything less than infinite expressions of unlimited power and potential, your interactions hold them back and diminish their capacity to give more to you. Now of course, most of us aren't capable of seeing people at that level, so don't judge yourself if this is a difficult task. Just try to establish an understanding of what's operating at an expanded level.

The fact is, you can't make a demand on anyone that exceeds your belief about them. If you believe there are no good men or women out there because all the good ones are taken, you can't expect the person you're interacting with to be "one of the good ones." Even if they are, they probably won't be available to you. Unless they're more enlightened and empowered than you, people can't meet you at a higher level than where you've put them. And if they are at a higher level, they're less likely to lower themselves to meet you; so you won't get what you need anyway. That's one reason why you see someone showing one side to one person and a totally different side to another—it has a lot to do with how they're being seen and held by the people they're interacting with.

It also has to do with how people are seeing and holding themselves. People treat us the way we train them—based on how we're seeing and treating ourselves. Just as you can't expect more of life than you believe about it, you can't expect more of yourself than your belief about yourself. If you think you're not worthy of wealth or capable of creating it, you'll have quite a struggle on your hands when you go out and try to make it happen. More than likely, you won't be able to move the needle much. But even if you do manage to willfully manipulate circumstances to get what you want, you'll have to use all your energy to hold on to it, because you aren't congruent with it. You don't own it; *it owns you*. It's like trying to hold a big beach ball underwater: you know if you relax, it's going to pop up and hit you in the face!

As you see how expectations determine outcomes, it gets harder to discern who is causing what. If how we see someone determines *his or her capacity to express* but how we hold ourselves determines how *someone else sees us*, who is determining what happens? The answer is both and neither. In truth, there is only One Mind, one consciousness, one self—individualizing as the many. When we elevate our consciousness so that we see ourselves or someone else in alignment with truth, that activity of our mind is really the activity of the One Mind operating through and as us—the center of that awareness is the same center in me as it is in you. So in the final analysis, whatever is the higher consciousness becomes the governing law of that relationship or interaction. This is the esoteric meaning of the statement by Jesus, "And I, when I am lifted up from the earth, will draw all people to myself" (John 12:32). That's a statement of quantum physics—that the higher vibrating attractor field draws all else unto it. Now that you know this, you're in a position to become a law of abundance, prosperity, and success to all who are in your circle.

Everything Coming to You Is Coming from You

We've touched on this several times already, but it's an important reminder in all this talk about receiving from others. Remember, *everything* that comes to you is coming *from you*. Not just the benefits your spouse or partner channels, like in my story earlier, but *everything* you benefit from in your life. Anything that shows up in your experience as a blessing or a benefit is an expression of *your consciousness*, even if it seems to come from all different people, places, and things, near and far. If you didn't have it as some activity in your consciousness, it couldn't appear in your experience.

That doesn't mean you don't appreciate everyone and everything for being a channel; it means you remain aware that abundance is really coming from you. And if, for whatever reason, someone stops being a channel, another one will show up—because they were never the Source; *you* were. This is an empowering realization, especially if you were in a position where you believed you were limited by where you live, what you're physically capable of, your current job, or what your spouse or partner could earn.

All the good you experience—your home, indoor plumbing, paved roads, public libraries, schools, clean running water, the internet, and so on—is all coming from your consciousness. If it's in your life, impacting you, it's an activity of your consciousness. That's principle. That's law. In a very real way, you are the creator of your entire universe from your perspective. You aren't really in the world; the whole world is in you, in your consciousness, and you are expressing and experiencing your unique interpretation of it. So everyone and everything that comes within your field of awareness begins to output *your* idea of who they are; what they're capable of; what's true, false, good, bad, or indifferent.

This, again, creates what appears to be a riddle, a conundrum: if this shared reality is coming from your consciousness but also from the person next to you, *who is creating what? Who is creating who? Are you a product of their consciousness or are they a product of yours? Are you in their universe or are they in yours?* Oy vey!

As already stated, the answer is neither and both. The entire universe from your perspective is a creation of your consciousness, and the entire universe from their perspective is a creation of their consciousness—but it's really just two different perspectives of the One Mind; as if God is an artist painting the same scene in different ways to see how many possibilities there are!

There's only one consciousness, one being, one "I Am"; and we are all unique centers and perspectives in it—unique ways Source is knowing and experiencing Itself. You don't have to go that far down the rabbit hole to understand and activate this principle, but it's fun to contemplate it. The key takeaway here is to begin to acknowledge that you are creating your universe out of your consciousness, though it appears as other people, places, and conditions—as channels to express; as branches on the tree all bearing witness to the invisible life that flows through it, and produces all the flowers and fruit.

Ask for What You Want

Now that you understand everyone is a channel but are living in the context that you are the Source, you can begin to ask for what you want—without shame, blame, or apology. Remember, asking is the mechanism by which you open your channel to receive and open other channels to begin circulating your blessings. That doesn't mean things can't circulate without asking, but asking is a powerful tool to activate this circulation at will. The more you ask, the more you receive. The bigger demand you make on life, the bigger result you can achieve. Life never withholds anything from us; we withhold ourselves from life by not giving or asking in abundant ways. Are you ready to be as bold in your asking as you are in your giving?

When we think of asking for what we want—especially the things that matter most—it often brings up fear, nervousness, and issues of low self-worth and low self-esteem. We're afraid of being attacked, dismissed, or rejected; and we don't want to feel the burning shame or guilt that it causes. It's a coping mechanism that is typically developed early in life when we *did* ask for what we wanted, and got judged or punished for it. It made us believe it was dangerous to ask—that we could lose safety, security, and love. So we decided the world we lived in wasn't hospitable to asking for what we wanted, we designed a map of the world to match this belief (including neuropathways that mirror it), then we created a survival kit to make it through. The problem is our map isn't true anymore—and maybe never was—but we're still moving through life as if it's an accurate depiction of the terrain. It's like trying to navigate through a major city with a map from a century ago—you're going to get pretty lost, confused, and frustrated!

The other challenge is that we often wait to feel safe, comfortable, or at least, not so afraid before we ask for what we want. But that doesn't work, because life happens in reverse of that. We have to step into the new life—the new state of being—and act like the person we want to be; then we activate that potential within us. That means working on our inner and outer life by having some kind of practice that keeps us connected to our heart, our spirit, and our deepest goal or vision; then we take outer action that is congruent with that. As you do this, you'll bring up anything that is in the way—the unexpressed emotions, the repressed shadows, the hidden values conflicts—and this is a good thing. Those patterns are lurking in the dark already, siphoning off your energy and eating away at your life structures like psychological termites. It's better to uncover them sooner rather than later, so you can do the work to heal, release, or integrate them. (We'll talk more about that in the next chapter.)

Manifest Abundance Now!

The Ask Plan

- Reflect on your various life structures—health, wealth, work, relationships, spirituality, personal development—and take an inventory of the different things you would like to ask for. Things you would like to ask of yourself; of God; of your spouse, partner, kids, family, boss, colleagues, friends, or clients. Make a list, and get it all out.
- Scan over that list and find a couple of easy asks, and then the most difficult one. Create a real plan to make these requests. Set an appointment with the person, if necessary, and put it on your calendar.

- Do the easy ones first, over the next few days or so, then do the difficult one. Practice asking on a regular basis, until it becomes a habit.

Remember, asking from the Awakened Abundance paradigm is not about trying to get something you don't already have; it's a way of opening and activating the channels in your life (as well as in yourself) to allow more flow of the infinite abundance. When you do it from that space, it doesn't take anything from anyone—*it expands the good for everyone.* And as this principle and practice becomes embodied, you'll start to feel a greater current of confidence and power, which will lead to new and better opportunities to express your deeper potential. So ask away!

Ask for What You Really Want and as Much as You Want

Asking for what you want can be difficult enough—for some people, excruciatingly so—but to ask for *as much as you want* in your personal and your professional life can feel almost criminal to a heart-centered, spiritually-minded person. This is particularly true if you're asking for something that seems excessive or outside of the norms of your community, family, culture, or societal conditioning.

When it comes to business, charging what you're worth can be incredibly difficult, especially if you're charging for things society believes should be free or inexpensive: creative endeavors, spiritual teaching (or any teaching), helping the poor and downtrodden, supporting children or the elderly, working at a church or temple, and the many forms of counseling and advice-giving services. That doesn't mean you can't or shouldn't give service for free—unconditional service is a cornerstone of Awakened Abundance (as described in the first of the Seven Gifts, on page 84). But if working with people in these capacities is your primary source of living, charging a fee or receiving other forms of remuneration is not only okay, it's necessary.

The other area in which this limited belief can crop up is creative pursuits. Charging for your art—and charging well—can seem like a scary or even embarrassing proposition. You might find yourself thinking, *Who am I to charge for my art? I'm not famous or special. Why would anyone pay for this—or pay this much?* I've known many brilliant artists that charge less than a checkout clerk at a grocery store for their art. When you consider the amount of hours it might take to master a craft, then the hours it takes to paint, sculpt, or build a work of art, it really adds up. I've seen many artists spend a dozen or more hours on a piece, then charge a few hundred dollars for it—amounting to about $20 an hour. Add in the materials and resources it took to be able to create that piece (electricity, rent for a studio, paint, canvas, and so on), and the pay is barely minimum wage.

I've also watched as, even at that low rate, the artist still feels awkward when it comes time to tell the patron how much the piece costs, and sometimes even lets the patron haggle them lower! The same is true in the healing arts, where counselors, alternative-health providers, spiritual practitioners, energy workers, and massage therapists feel bad or scared about charging and then backpedal when the customer balks at their already reasonable (or insultingly low) rates. They don't mind paying other people for these services, but when it comes to them, it's a different deal.

Scratch the surface of many of these people, however, and you discover that they harbor judgment about people charging a lot or making a lot in these professions (let alone any profession); or they had potent moments growing up where they were shamed or scared by some message around asking for what they wanted, asking for too much, or being perceived as selfish. They might have experienced pain because their parents were like that; or their parents talked badly about people who charged a lot, made a lot, or had a lot. Or their religious leaders indoctrinated them into a belief that having great abundance in any area was sinful and having less was holy. Bottom line: it just feels bad—even evil—to ask for as much as you want or to charge what you're truly worth. And when this is unconscious and in conflict with what a person consciously wants—namely, more abundance or success—it creates an internal battle that weighs them down and burns them out.

But this doesn't stop with the heart-centered, spiritually-minded, and artistic crowds. Asking for what you *really want*, asking for *as much as* you want, and charging what you're *really worth* can be extremely hard for just about anyone, including people in business, government, politics, and beyond. When it comes to asking a loved one—especially a significant other—for what you *really* want, fear of judgment, rejection, and even abandonment can come up, tempting you to back down. This often leads to convincing yourself that you don't really need what you wanted (more time, love, appreciation, support), or that you need to work harder to be more and do more in order to earn what you need. This is a reenactment of core childhood wounds and, when left unhealed, can cause resentment, burnout, blowups, and the breakdown of relationships.

When it comes to business, the idea of stating your fee, expected salary, or asking for a much-deserved raise can cause you to acquiesce to veiled (or not-so-veiled) acts of intimidation, to shrinking in fear of being fired or losing a client, and to just accepting what you're given. The cause of this is often an issue of self-worth; a lack of seeing your value in your area of expression; or a shadow around being too needy, selfish, or demanding. This unconscious pattern can hobble you, robbing you of the courage to stand for what you're worth and making it more difficult to articulate *why* you're worth it, *what* you've done to earn it, the *cost* of not having your service, and the long-term *value* of keeping it. So when it comes to asking for that raise, asking for more time with a spouse, or asking someone to treat you better, you feel you have a weak case or no case at all for your request, and your value isn't conveyed in a compelling enough way to win the reward.

The good news is that you don't have to live like this anymore.

At this point, you're beginning to understand that nobody is your Source—you don't take anything from anyone by asking or charging because doing so expands the possibilities for everyone—and no matter what anyone says, thinks, or does, they can never take away your abundance once you have it *in consciousness*. They can threaten you, judge you, attack you, fire you, or leave you, but the most they can ever do is close off that *one channel*. You are the Source—not them, that job, that project, or that relationship—and there is *infinite organizing power* in the universe that can find another perfect channel for whatever you need, no matter how many are unwilling or unable to let your abundance flow through them.

Consider the implications of this: It means that you're safe and free to stand in your power; ask for what you want; charge what you're worth; and honor and respect all the channels in your life without projecting limitation, guilt, or fear onto them. And if these channels say no, you can receive that graciously and move on to the next willing channel. Nobody has to lose—it's not a zero-sum game and an infinitely expanding pie. And the more you play at this level, the bigger the pie gets for you and everyone involved.

Manifest Abundance Now!

The Big Ask

To help you ask for what you really want and as much as you want, follow this simple guideline:

- **Step 1: Establish Your Baseline**

  In whatever area you want to ask for more, what are you currently asking for and getting? For example, if you want more time with your spouse, how much time are you currently asking for and getting that feels normal or nonthreatening? Maybe you're spending no time with them and feel guilty asking for any time; or maybe you even feel like a pet begging at the dinner table for whatever leftovers you can get. Be honest about your feelings and your desires. In the area of business, what is your current salary or your current fee that feels normal or nonthreatening? Maybe you're volunteering, working well below your market value or giving away services for free. Maybe you even feel like you should be paying the other person for the privilege to serve them! You can also think in terms of fair market value or basic norms for the relationship you're in, although that might already feel too high.

- **Step 2: Raise Your Ask until It Feels Crazy High**

  If you feel comfortable charging $20 an hour (or $100 for a piece of art) or asking for a 10 percent raise, incrementally raise it—to $25 an hour, then $30, then $50—until you start to feel like it's too ridiculous to consider. If you feel comfortable asking your spouse to spend a few hours a week together, raise that number until you're sure he or she will think you're crazy or desperately needy! Whatever the ask is, raise it until the idea of asking for that much money, love, appreciation, support, time, and so on seems like a total nonstarter.

- **Step 3: Lower It until It Feels Too Low**

  Once you have that high number or crazy ask, start lowering it again until it feels too low, not enough, depressing to imagine. The amount is not the issue; the feeling is what's important. That's what's telling you where your current set-point is—your mental equivalent around how much you feel you're worth or how much you believe you can ask for and get.

- **Step 4: Raise It Again, until It Starts to Feel Like a Stretch**
  Once your ask begins to feel painfully low, raise it again; but this time, sense into the amount or request that starts to feel scary or makes you sweat a little. You don't want it to be such a stretch that you're going to pull a muscle—just right on the edge of feeling both exciting and anxiety producing. This is the sweet spot.

- **Step 5: Develop Your Offering until It Feels "Worth It" Inside of You**
  Once you have that bigger ask or higher price, begin to play with your offering. This is easier to imagine if you're trying to sell a product, service, or particular role as an employee. But when you're selling the idea of someone supporting you in other ways—spending more time with you; or giving you more love, appreciation, or respect—it gets a little trickier.

It might be enough to just be honest and vulnerable with them, sharing from your heart what you really want or need—that can be a powerful way to open them up. But sometimes you have to make an offer they can't refuse. Merely saying "we're married, so you *should* spend more time with me" isn't good enough. Who says they should? Where is that written? That's an entitled mind-set that is taking them for granted, making a demand instead of a request, and coming from a wounded or limited place—an approach that is unlikely to open their channels or yours. You need to think about all the value you bring to your time together, all the possibilities of sharing and exploring and playing together—and it has to be things that have value to *them*, not just you. That means you have to understand *their* needs, not just yours. The more legitimate ways you can add more value to their life, the better.

When it comes to your professional life, think about all the education and experience that allows you to deliver the value you do, and put a value on that. If you studied for years, put a value on the hours you invested—as well as the actual money you invested—and add it up. If you bought other programs or invested in other ways, consider the monetary costs, the opportunity costs, the sacrifices (the things you missed out on because you focused on this area). Really feel the investment of time, money, and energy you've put in. Then look at the specifics of what you offer—the product, service, or employment role—and ask, *What else could I offer that brings more unique and added value to this but doesn't necessarily cost me more or take more time?* Stack more value on your side of the equation without adding more time and investment.

Look at *all* the possible elements you can add that would have real value to the client, customer, or company—elements that you've possibly taken for granted. For example, maybe you're coaching business owners on how to build a business—something you've done yourself. And maybe, over the years, you've created certain SOPs (standard operating procedures) around important business functions, like team building, sales, marketing, social media, and so on. They serve your business and help you run a more streamlined organization, adding value to *your* bottom line.

It might have taken you months or years and hundreds or thousands of dollars to create these systems and templates, but now they're just documents and habits that you don't perceive as having independent value. However, they could be tremendously valuable to someone who's building their business *now*. These templates and systems could save them months or years of experimentation, and a lot of money and headaches—benefits that have real, tangible, monetary value to them. If you estimate that it cost you $5,000 to create these systems, you can put a $5,000 value on them. You can also account for inflation—what was $5,000 when you started may cost $6,000 now. Take the time to do a little research into the current pricing to see if anything has changed to your benefit.

You might have other assets too, like books, eBooks, research, articles, audio or video recordings, and programs you've made or have the right to distribute—and these may be great supplements or complements to what you're offering. This is called a value stack because you're stacking various kinds of valuable assets to your core offering. The more you flesh this out, the more things you might discover you could add. And if you don't have these assets or enough of them, *you can create them*. It's easier than ever to write a book, shoot a quality video training, or record an audio program. You could interview your potential or existing clients, customers, and boss to find out what else would be of value to them and then build it! Once you have it, you can give it over and over again, without having to create it on demand. Now it's an asset that has ongoing residual value.

Can you begin to see—and even feel—how you *can* put together a package or offering that makes your higher rate or your raise seem like a no-brainer?

One word of caution: Be careful not to go overboard. If you stack too much, it might start to look ridiculous or too good to be true. And even if it really *is* that good, the impression that it's "too good" can cause someone to distrust you and back away. Also, make sure that what you're stacking actually adds supplementary or complementary value to the core offer, and is something you can actually fulfill. If you're asking your spouse for regular weekly dates and adding the bonus of washing his car every week, it could make you appear somewhat needy (and ultimately, make you resentful when you're outside, drenched in suds, and he's relaxing on the couch inside, watching the football game). If you're asking your family to support your college education or business venture, promising to work for the family business for free or to join the

Peace Corps upon graduation, if that's not what you truly want, it will ultimately backfire.

At the end of the day, just use your common sense. If you're coaching someone on how to build their business, adding a program that helps them get more dates won't make much sense. And if you work for a company doing sales, throwing in free massages may not inspire them to give you a raise. (Then again, it just might!) Bottom line: create an "integrated offering," where each piece makes the core offering more valuable or the core goal more attainable in less time, with less effort, and with less cost overall. Saving money can be an important part of your request with a significant other as well. If you show them that going on more dates won't cost as much as they think, that just might clinch the deal.

Remember, whatever's missing is what you're not giving. If you want something more to come into your life, you need to let something more come out of you. The universe has infinite ways you can achieve this—especially if you're willing to put these principles to work; be creative, innovative, and industrious; and *ask for what you want*. Potential is all around you—in your marriage, your industry, your community, your business, your relationships with clients (current and past), your family, your job, and the world at large. There are unlimited opportunities for you to share, serve, create, contribute, *and* receive an abundance of good things. What it requires of you is to stay alert to what you truly want and to what others really need, then taking your talents, gifts, and abilities to create an offering that meets the needs of both sides.

The more value you can offer, the more abundance you will create. There's no limit to how much value you can offer; therefore, there's no limit to how much abundance you can have.

Even when you've done all of this and feel good about your offering, you might still bump into the ego thresholds, shadows, and values conflicts when you actually speak your request or offering out loud. We'll address these in the next chapter; but for now, remember that you don't have to let your feelings determine your actions, and you don't have to believe it to achieve it. Keep asking, moving, and creating; and some of that inner turmoil will be burned up in the sheer momentum and expansion of going for it. What remains, you can work out in your daily healing and integration practices.

Where are you wanting to make that big ask in your life? Where are there more opportunities for adding value in your current relationships, your business, or your job? Make a list of these areas, including all the possible things you could offer as well as the things you could add to make these offerings more valuable. Once you have that list, pick something you can implement over the next week, and find someone to support you and hold you accountable. Then develop your pitch, and go ask for what you really want, as much as you want, and make them an offer they can't refuse!

Fortune favors the bold. So be bold!

6

HEALING ABUNDANCE SHADOWS AND VALUES CONFLICTS

> Man stands in his own shadow and wonders why it's dark.
> —ZEN PROVERB

Even when we are armed with deep knowledge about the true nature of wealth, even when we have awakened from the core abundance blind spots and have a practice for activating our true potential, we can still find ourselves sabotaging our efforts, becoming stuck, and failing to create real abundance. The reason is that limited personal patterns are still operating unconsciously, driving our compulsive behaviors. I call these "Abundance Shadows and Values Conflicts," and in this chapter, we'll dive into this subterranean world to uncover, heal, and integrate them.

The goal: to not only release internal resistance but to unleash the creative energy that has heretofore been used to battle these suppressed, denied, or disowned parts of ourselves.

You can have shadows in any area of life, but wealth and abundance is a particularly interesting arena to explore. Most people think wealth is just wealth, money is just money, and the issues that relate to these are material. But wealth or money issues are more often about power, safety, security, self-worth, confidence, personal identity, fulfillment, and values—and all of our baggage about these concepts. To understand what money, wealth, or having real abundance actually means to us, we have to look deeper at why we want it and what we really want.

When we investigate what we truly want, there's oftentimes something we want to feel, which we believe having abundance will bring us. Other times, it's about something we want to avoid feeling, which we believe will happen if we don't have an abundance (if we have a lack) of whatever it is we want. Bottom line: there's some mental-emotional state we're ultimately seeking that comes from having or not having abundance. However, most of us are not conscious of this fact. Instead, we're caught up in the belief that the outward symbols of abundance are all we need; we think we have to *purchase* the desired state of being through some kind of outer activity, change in condition, or transaction.

It's like the Zen story of the man who went to a farmer (who also happened to be a Zen master) and asked if he could have a job, to which the master replied, "I'll give you a job, but I won't pay you. What do you really want?"

The man thought for a moment, then said, "Well, I need the money, not the job."

The Zen master replied, "I'll give you the money, but you can't spend it. What do you really want?"

The man turned his head sideways, not understanding where the master was going.

"I want to buy food," the man said.

"Okay, I'll give you food, but you can't eat it," the Zen master said. "What do you really want?"

The man took a breath, frustrated and confused, then sat down and contemplated more deeply. Finally, he looked back at the master with a newfound level of awareness.

"If I had a full stomach, I could finally relax, feel safe, feel good about myself, and just enjoy my life," the man said. "So I guess what I really want is self-worth and peace."

"Ah," the Zen master said, nodding in agreement. "Unfortunately, I can't give you that, because you already have it within you."

The real reason we're seeking abundance or avoiding it is to activate a positive state of being or to avoid a perceived negative one. The real issue in all of our conflict and struggle around abundance— whether it's with a partner, family member, boss, or ourselves—is some internal need to feel a certain way about ourselves and life. Only when we understand this can we stop the useless efforts to manipulate people, places, and things to get what they can never give us, and begin to address the root reasons and the areas of our being that can finally give us what we hunger for. Addressing our Abundance Shadows and Values Conflicts and all their related issues is a powerful step in the right direction.

All of our striving to get something or get rid of something is an effort to activate some state of being.

A Brief History of Our Shadows

A shadow, in this context, is some part of you that has been disowned. Somewhere along your life journey, usually early on in childhood, you had an experience that made you believe some part of you was unacceptable or dangerous. You might have acted in a certain way and were shamed, blamed, or punished for it. Or you might have been a victim of someone else's behavior, which made you decide you would never be like that. In both cases, that quality of your being, which was inherently good, became labeled as "bad." The result is that it was repressed, denied, and ignored; and its energy turned back upon itself until it became destructive in your life—by creating some internal pattern that harmed you, by projecting on or blaming others, or through attracting people into your life who carried that same shadow. In addition, when you repressed one part of you, you had to create a counterpoint to balance the energy, because the energy doesn't go away; you had to keep it pushed down and out of your consciousness.

Remember the example of holding a beach ball underwater? To prevent it from flying up and hitting you in the face, you need some kind of counterforce to keep it submerged. Likewise, when you repress a part of yourself, you create another facet of your personality to push it down. Depending on how much energy is contained in the shadow (due to the intensity of the original trauma that created it), your efforts to counteract that shadow can become compulsive and obsessive.

Initially, this kind of motivation to be different or better can develop some great qualities and capacities—in fact, many of the things we like about ourselves are the product of this compulsive need to *not* be something hidden in our shadow side. But at some point, the utility of this wears out; and the thing that used to be an asset becomes a liability. It no longer works as well—or not at all. We start to feel burned out, frustrated, angry, or depressed in an area where we used to feel empowered. Usually, we try harder, push ourselves to outrun the shadow, or just give up. The real message, however, is that it's time to turn around, confront, and embrace the very thing we've been running from, hiding from, or denying about ourselves.

These shadows get created in many ways. Sometimes, it's a single powerful moment that makes a big enough impression to create a shadow; other times, it's a series of experiences that finally push you over the edge. You might have grown up in a family, school system, church, culture, or country with many shadows around abundance (i.e., limited beliefs, fear, guilt, and shame). It might have been overt; and you can remember your parents, relatives, teachers, or priest talking about those "bad, greedy, selfish rich people." Or there may have been such an atmosphere of guilt or shame around wanting more of something—time, attention, love, support, or opportunity—that you internalized a belief that it was wrong to have or want much of anything.

For example, if you have a strong shadow about greed or selfishness, it might be because, when you were younger, you asked for what you wanted—even demanded it—and were told you were selfish, or were guilt tripped by a tired parent or other authority figure. The result: you developed shame or fear around this part of you; and you drew a map of reality that said being "selfish"—wanting something and taking care of your true needs—was bad and scary, because it could result in being rejected by and losing the very people and things that sustained you.

To protect yourself, prevent being rejected, and survive in this world where selfishness could be dangerous, you created a coping mechanism of generosity, selflessness, people pleasing, or caretaking, and began saying yes to other people's needs (while saying no to your own). You gave away your time and treasure to others (while not meeting all your own needs), and even felt guilty when you had a lot or had more than someone else—sometimes to the extent that you would have to give it away, spend it, or sabotage your success to bring yourself back down to the level of others.

As you grew up and your desire to have more, do more, and be more grew stronger, you found yourself bumping up against this shadow every time you were about to take an important step. You probably didn't call it a shadow (it felt more like fear, anxiety, stress, or overwhelm—signals that you were in danger of losing something or getting hurt), and you most likely backed down from the challenge or opportunity. It may have shown up as sabotaging a business deal that would have made you wealthier, more successful, and better able to take care of yourself—all of which could trigger the shame, guilt, or fear of being judged as selfish, self-centered, or greedy. It could also show up as sabotaging a new job, a dream project, or an ideal relationship if, in your mind, it would equate to a new level of abundance, thereby triggering similar shadows that contain shame, guilt, and the fear of being judged as having or being too much.

From my own childhood, my experience of my father was that he became less available to our family the more successful he became in business. It seemed that the busier he got, the more his marriage to my mother declined, and the more dysfunctional our home was. My young artist heart didn't understand his world, and his business head didn't understand mine. As I used to joke, he thought Pearl Jam was something you put on toast, and I thought Dow Jones was his business partner! He told me artists lived below the poverty level, and I needed to go to college and get a real job. I know now he meant well—that he was trying to protect and prepare me for the world he perceived—but the result was that I had a very negative feeling around many qualities he represented. Things like discipline, control, money, business, and all they entailed became a shadow for me.

To compensate, I dove deeper into my mind, heart, and eventually, spirit. I focused on developing the right side of my brain, the feminine side of my being, the artist-mystic dimension of my soul. The positive result was a flowering of my talents, gifts, and abilities. The downside was that, as I grew up and had more responsibilities, I didn't have the inner and outer structures to support my bigger dreams. Luckily, I wanted what I wanted badly enough to start working on these underdeveloped—and even rejected—parts of me. This led to becoming more productive and disciplined; but because I hadn't actually embraced these shadows, it also led to me becoming more controlling and obsessive—to the point where I was scheduling every fifteen minutes of my life.

When I got married and had a family of my own, the energetic force of these shadows finally broke through with such power that it brought me to my proverbial knees. I suddenly realized that I wasn't equipped to raise a family and build a business because I only had access to half of me. I knew that if I didn't make a dramatic turn, I would never be able to fulfill my greater vision or take care of my wife and children. So I began to embrace these shadows of power and masculinity—the controller; the disciplinarian; and the greedy, selfish, aggressive parts of me. It wasn't easy, and it didn't shift overnight. But soon, I began to experience new levels of wisdom, guidance, and support emerging—like I had taken my foot off the brake and allowed all this suppressed energy to flow again.

What We Fight, We Fuel

Whatever we're trying *not* to be, we activate *more* of in our consciousness, either attracting it into our life or expressing it in uncontrollable outbreaks and eruptions of this repressed energy. What you resist, persists. As Debbie Ford, one of the leaders in shadow work, said, "What you can't be with won't let you be."[3] These shadows are actually a useful, valuable, and necessary part of you; they've just been misunderstood and rejected. Like dark, fertile soil, which is made up of everything that has died and decayed, this darkness within you is the very ground from which your life is meant to grow. A seed can't thrive without enough soil. Likewise, you can't fulfill your potential if you're trying to get rid of all your dirt!

When you embrace these shadows and integrate their wisdom and power, you don't become their negative version; you redeem and transmute their energy, revealing their true, constructive use and value—similar to what happens when the sun shines upon dark, dank soil and activates its life-giving nutrients. "A weed is just a plant whose virtues have not yet been discovered," said Ralph Waldo Emerson.[4] Similarly, these parts of you that have been judged as enemies are actually allies you don't understand yet. You are living in a universe that is totally on your side—all its power, substance, life, and law is working *for* you. But you can't experience that until you get on your own side. This means embracing, loving, and accepting *all of you*. As you do, you discover that there was never anything missing, lacking, or broken about you; everything you could ever need to fulfill your destiny has always been within you.

Take the selfish shadow. When integrated, it allows you to take greater care of yourself so that you're healthy, happy, and better able to serve another. The greedy shadow allows you to indulge unapologetically in the things that bring you the most joy and fulfillment, supporting you in learning, growing, healing, and mastering the areas of life that create the most success for you and those you interact with. The angry shadow (or what I called the "inner diva bitch" earlier) is actually your source of power when integrated, helping you create healthy boundaries that honor and respect your deepest needs. Every single "character flaw" you've been trying to get rid of, fix, heal, deny, or reject is carrying a seed of power and potential just waiting to be embraced and integrated.

I recall one example of how the greedy/selfish shadow played out for a client of mine—Cheryl. She was very generous, always willing to help others, but struggled to make ends meet, had a hard time charging clients what she was worth, and didn't take very good care of herself. She felt anxious, depressed, angry, and resentful about this— all of which were signs that she was repressing a deeper energy that had become destructive from lack of expression. As the Gospel of Thomas says, "If you bring forth what is within you, what you bring forth will save you. If you do not bring forth what is within you, what you do not bring forth will destroy you."[5]

By working with her shadow, she discovered that, because she came from a large family in which there was never enough time, money, or resources to go around, she had to learn to get along by not wanting much. She also remembered moments when she did ask for what she wanted, and the response was harsh and dismissive, sending the message that it was wrong and selfish to ask for more. She felt ashamed and afraid that even the little she had might get taken away if she didn't fall in line. So to get the love and security she needed to survive, she repressed this part of her and developed another dimension of her character: the good girl, the caretaker, and the helper.

The gift of her shadow was that she developed some qualities that definitely served her. She became a very loving, kind, and generous person. The problem was that she no longer had access to this other side of her—the selfish part that was able to ask for what she wanted without guilt or fear, and would keep asking until she got it. As we continued to work together and she integrated this shadow energy back into her psyche, this capacity became available again, resulting in acknowledging, asking, and receiving much more than had ever been possible—or even imagined—before. She didn't become an angry, greedy person; she became even more giving. But it was a generosity that no longer robbed her of the life she was meant to live, and it modeled for those around her a much more empowered path for success.

Even something like the bad-guy shadow, when integrated, can have very positive gifts. When you embody this side of you, you're able to break the rules that no longer serve the higher order—to be a rebel in areas where you're meant to innovate and lead a progressive movement (even if that movement is just in your family). Some might think you're evil or bad because they want to keep the status quo, or they feel threatened by real change. But you'll know and feel that you're on purpose, and the result of your efforts will activate the evolutionary impulse in you and in those you serve and lead.

Remember, everything about you is ultimately divine when it's understood, integrated, and authentically expressed. The areas you deny, reject, repress, and resist out of judgment are those that fragment into distorted, destructive ways.

The Gift of the Shadow

If we understand that everything is working for our highest good, that nothing is wasted, that there's nothing wrong or broken about us, then we can realize there's just a misinterpretation or misperception of some part of ourselves. The shadows are shadows because of this misperception, but their true nature is good—just as healthy, rich soil is made of everything that has died and decayed and rotted. And the more we have of it, the more abundance we can support. All those dark, seemingly dirty parts of us are the fertile soil within which our seed of potential can grow.

When we try to get rid of all our dirt, we're literally getting rid of the very ground of our being, which is needed for growth. Our shadows are actually very valuable parts of us, but they must be respected, tended, and integrated to reveal their goodness.

There's another level to the benefits of shadows that we rarely see. The shadow itself, in its seemingly dark expression, has actually been serving as an ally in your growth and evolution. If you hate or judge the selfish part of yourself, it often causes you to develop a more giving part of your character—like my client Cheryl's story—which can be a blessing. If you hate or reject the controlling or dominating part of yourself, you often develop a more flexible, flowing, diplomatic aspect to your character, which can add a lot of value to your life and work. It's like going to a gym and exercising: the weights provide resistance to work *against* the muscles (called resistance training), causing them to rebuild and tone in stronger and healthier ways.

The same is true for those parts you've been resisting. Since you grew up pushing against them, you've built muscles in other areas of your life. In this way, all these negative, bad, dark parts of you have been like your inner workout equipment or inner trainer, whipping you into better shape. If it weren't for these darknesses, you wouldn't have had anything to push against; and you would have remained "flabby" in those other areas. As you start to see that these dark parts of you have been here to support you, you release the judgment and begin to appreciate and value them in a whole new light—you realize that they've been gifts all along. This is the beginning of healing the internal rift and integrating this part of you back into your whole life again.

Manifest Abundance Now!

Identifying Your Abundance Shadows

There are several ways to identify your core abundance shadows, but a great place to start is by looking at the areas you're pushing, forcing, struggling with, or avoiding. In any area where there's a strong push or pull, there's often a shadow trying to get your attention. The following processes will help you to spot these shadows.

Once you know what shadow you're working with, you can integrate it with a free, guided audio process that I've created for my website. Go to DerekRydall.com/ShadowProcess to learn more.

Uncover Your Hidden Shadows

Below are some sentence stems divided into four different areas of abundance: money/wealth, success/fame, talent/ability, and relationship. Complete the sentences up to five times each to uncover the hidden shadows within each area of abundance. (Or feel free to create your own if these don't cover your areas of development.) Just don't overthink or second-guess the answers; try to let them arise organically and spontaneously.

Money/Wealth Abundance
- If I have/make a lot of money/wealth, I'm afraid that . . .
- If I have/make a lot of money/wealth, I'm afraid people will think I'm . . .
- If I strive for wealth or money, I'm afraid that . . .
- Really wealthy people are . . .

Success/Fame Abundance
- If I have a lot of success/fame/popularity, I'm afraid that . . .
- If I have a lot of success/fame/popularity, I'm afraid people will think I'm . . .
- If I strive for success/fame/popularity, I'm afraid that . . .
- People who are really successful/famous/popular are . . .

Talent/Ability Abundance
- If I'm really talented/skilled, I'm afraid that . . .
- If I'm really talented/skilled, I'm afraid people will think I'm . . .
- If I strive to become really talented/skilled, I'm afraid that . . .
- Really talented/skilled people are . . .

Relationship Abundance
- If I'm loved/valued by my partner/boss/parent, I'm afraid that . . .
- If I'm loved/valued by my partner/boss/parent, I'm afraid people will think . . .
- If I strive to be loved/valued by my partner/boss/parent, I'm afraid that . . .
- People who get a lot of love/appreciation are . . .

Identify the Shadow Judgment

Take the answers from each of the above sentence completions and consider what having each area of abundance would mean for you (*If this happens, I'm afraid I'll become/be . . .*). The idea is to uncover the hidden judgments (the second and fourth bullet points could provide some clues). For example, "If I have a lot of money, people will envy me or want a lot from me; and they'll think I'm *greedy, stingy, selfish*." Or "People with a lot of money are *greedy, selfish, self-centered, mean, insensitive, hurtful, abusive*." Or "If I'm really talented, I'm afraid people will judge, criticize, and attack me, and think I'm *arrogant, self-absorbed, strange*." Or "If I'm really loved by my partner, I'm afraid they'll expect too much of me, try to control me, or smother me; and they (or others) will think I'm *ungrateful, entitled, selfish*."

Do you see the judgments coming up in the adjectives?

Whatever your answers, if you're still having difficulty seeing a quality, ask: *What would being _____ make me? What would others think I am if I were _____? What would being _____ make me think about myself?*

You'll know you're touching upon it when it's a clear judgment. And you'll know you have a hold on an especially important shadow if it makes you cringe at the thought of being that; if it's hard to even think it, say it, or imagine being it; or if you find yourself denying or trying to convince yourself you're *not* it. Whenever you're defending yourself as not being something, that's a sure sign you're touching on a shadow.

Shadow Venting Sheet

Get into a state of remembering and feeling the most charged/upsetting experience you've had in some area of abundance. It could be money, a job, a project, or something that involved a person in these areas—like someone who had more money than you; a boss who fired you; or a family member who judged you for being too talented or too successful, or for going for your dreams. It could also be a situation when you were younger, like when your dad yelled at you about money or someone stole it from you; or a time when you were attacked or judged for being too good at something or for being too selfish.

Once you're in that state, write down all the judgments that come out about the specific topic you're working on (money, talent, success) *as if it were a person.* Or if you're focusing on a specific person, you can vent about them. Create a worksheet with these statements and blanks, such as:

- You are such a _____.
- I hate / it drives me crazy when you _____.
- I wish you would just _____.
- If you would only start / stop doing _____ then I could relax / love you / feel safe.
- The biggest problem with you is that you are such a / so _____ _____.
- The worst thing about you is _____.
- The thing I hate / dislike most about you is _____.
  The thing I wish you would change most is _____.

Now imagine someone else is doing a shadow venting worksheet about you after you get whatever it is that you want (name, fame, fortune, talent, attention, and so on). Pick someone whose judgment or opinion would be the most crushing or have the greatest impact, and complete the same list of statements with all the things that hurt you, anger you, break your heart, or make you cringe the most. When you do this, you're feeling into the worst thing you think they believe about you, the biggest judgment you've felt from them, or the specific judgment they've actually said to you out loud. For example, "You are such a *cheapskate*." "It drives me crazy when you talk about how *broke* you are." "You're so *arrogant*—you think you're better than everyone else." "You're so *needy, weak,* and *dependent*—you need so much attention."

Identify the Shadow Judgment

Like before, when you were exploring the shadow judgments in the "Uncover Your Hidden Shadows" practice (page 183), if the answers in your venting sheets are not direct judgments or labels but descriptions of actions or conditions, go back to the second sheet (the one about you) to discover what the specific shadow is. For example, if you get an answer like, "I hate it when you talk about how broke you are," follow that up by asking: What would being broke make me? *What would others think I am if I were broke? What would being broke make me think about myself?* If you hear, "It means I am a victim, a whiner, a complainer, a loser," that's a shadow you can work with.

Manifest Abundance Now!

Shadow-Mapping Your Childhood

For this section, you can do an exploration of your early years to locate the ideas that proliferated around the area of abundance you're working on. For example, what were your father's or mother's beliefs about money; success; relationships; the woman's or man's role in family, society, or the world? Did they fight about these issues or at least struggle with them? Did they gossip or judge others who had an abundance of wealth, success, talent, notoriety, and so on? What about at church, at school, at your friend's house?

Perhaps you heard things like: "Women are so needy—they always want more attention." "People with a lot of talent are so cocky, so full of themselves, so weird." "Rich people are cruel and heartless." "Money brings out the worst in people; money is the root of all evil." "You have to choose whether you're in it for the money or for the love/art/ service, but you can't have both." "It's either work or family—you have to choose. You have to make sacrifices. You can't have it all." "You can't make a living at that." "Women aren't good with money."

As you identify some of these core experiences that shaped your beliefs, ask yourself:

- What did I decide about [fill in the blank] and the people who have these things?
- What kind of people are they?
- What did I decide I would never become or be like?
- What am I afraid of becoming or being?
- What am I afraid my family or friends would think about me now if I was really wealthy, abundant, talented, successful, got a lot of attention?

Play with the information you're excavating to see if you can unearth some shadow judgments around these areas. You may start to notice more of the same shadows coming up, which is great because it means you're tapping into the core ones. Just keep writing, fleshing out this area of abundance, until you can see a picture of how your beliefs and judgments developed.

Manifest Abundance Now!

Cultural, Religious, and Gender Shadows

This process is about unpacking the beliefs or experiences that were part of your culture, religion, and gender identity growing up—or that might still be present now. You can start by journaling about your culture; the area you grew up in; your ethnic or religious background;

and your gender as it pertains to the area of abundance you're working on. What were the predominant beliefs, experiences, conversations, or media/entertainment messages around this area as it relates to your culture, religion, or gender?

For example, if you grew up as an immigrant or child of immigrants, was there a particular ethic around work and the value of a dollar? If you grew up in a Middle-Eastern, Asian, or European culture that values modesty, was there judgment around being big, bold, creative, or authentic? If you grew up as the child of Depression-era parents or grandparents, was there a sense of frugality or scarcity, where every tube of toothpaste had to be squeezed to the last drop? Or perhaps because of that experience of lack, were you instilled with a belief that family and people mattered more than anything else, creating a subtext that money, success, or any worldly accomplishment is potentially bad or at least not very important? In other words, was there a belief that you should learn to live with less, to get by with a little? Maybe it was even considered a badge of honor to have less.

Did you observe your mother or other women in your family or community as being empowered around things other than domestic duties? Was it mostly the men who controlled the cash and managed the finances? Was there a belief that women weren't good with money; they were just good at spending it? Or maybe it was the other way around—perhaps Mom managed the finances and clipped coupons, and Dad was the spender?

Maybe all of this created mixed emotions in you: on one hand, it was fun to experience the new toy or fun trip—to experience abundance—but on the other hand, it was painful to watch your parents fight over these issues. Perhaps it left you not knowing what was right, what you wanted, or whose side to be on. Did you go to church, temple, or synagogue and hear about how the meek shall inherit the Earth, that a rich man can't get into heaven, that the holiest people take a vow of poverty, and that you should give a lot of your money and time to the church or to charity, implying that having a lot of anything for yourself wasn't very godly?

To work on this area, just take some time to explore these different impressions in your journal or in contemplation. Use freewriting to learn more about them. Let the incidents and ideas flow. Pay particular attention to the moments or judgments that carry a painful emotional charge—making you sad, mad, or scared. Then move into the sentence completion below:

Money/Wealth Abundance
- When it comes to wealth/money, [fill in your ethnicity] people . . .
- When it comes to wealth/money, women are . . .
- When it comes to wealth/money, men are . . .
- When it comes to wealth/money, spiritual/religious people . . .

Success/Fame Abundance
- [Fill in your ethnicity] people who seek/have a lot of success/fame are . . .
- When it comes to success/fame, [your ethnicity] people . . .
- Women who seek/have a lot of success/fame are . . .
- When it comes to success/fame, women . . .
- Men who seek/have a lot of success/fame are . . .
- When it comes to success/fame, men . . .
- Spiritual/religious people who seek/have a lot of success/fame are . . .
- When it comes to success/fame, spiritual/religious people . . .

Talent/Ability Abundance
- [Fill in your ethnicity] people who strive for/have a lot of talent/ability are . . .

- When it comes to having a lot of talent/ability, [your ethnicity] people . . .
- Women who strive for/have a lot of talent/ability are . . .
- When it comes to having a lot of talent/ability, women . . .
- Men who strive for/have a lot of talent/ability are . . .
- When it comes to having a lot of talent/ability, men . . .
- Spiritual/religious people who strive for/have a lot of talent/ability are . . .
- When it comes to having a lot of talent/ability, spiritual/religious people . . .

Relationship Abundance
(Note: you can fill in whatever quality of relationship has the greatest charge for you.)

- [Fill in your ethnicity] people who seek love/validation/attention are . . .
- When it comes to intimate relationships, [your ethnicity] people . . .
- Women who seek love/validation/attention are . . .
- When it comes to intimate relationships, women . . .
- Men who seek love/validation/attention are . . .
- When it comes to intimate relationships, men . . .
- Spiritual/religious people who seek love/validation/attention are . . .
- When it comes to intimate relationships, spiritual/religious people . . .

Write out all the beliefs that resonate with you from society or your culture. Do the same work as before (in practices before this one) to uncover the shadow. It's not just the feeling or the belief we're after but the shadow judgment. For example: "When it comes to money, women are *incapable, incompetent, stupid, spendthrifts* (and so on)." "When it comes to money, men are *dominating, controlling, cheap, stingy* (and so on)." "Women who seek love, validation, and attention are *needy, weak,* and *clingy*." "Men who seek or have a lot of fame or success are *ambitious, power hungry, greedy,* and *dominating*." Or, as noted above, these qualities and genders could be swapped, depending on your experience.

If the statements or sentences you come up with are conditions, such as "Women are not wired to deal with money," "Men don't respect women when it comes to money," "Men are never satisfied," "Women always play down their abilities," "Minorities are taken advantage of," ask questions like: "And what does that mean about women/men/minorities?" or "What does that make women/men/minorities?" This should lead to some kind of judgment, which is the shadow.

Manifest Abundance Now!

The Shadow-Integration Process

Once you've created a nice page of shadows, go through them and underline all the ones that appear at least twice, circle those that appear at least three times, and put a star beside the one that appears the most. This is the one you'll start with in the Shadow-Integration Process. As you work with this one, you can go back to your list and work on the one that appears the second-most often. (If you have a tie, pick the one that has the strongest charge, and work down from there.) Alternatively, if you look at the page and a shadow that only appears once or twice has a particularly strong charge to you, you can also start there.

To get you started, let me take a moment to describe the core shadow questions that are part of the foundational integration process. If you've never done this before, I recommend that you go through (at least a few times) the free, guided audio process I created, so that you make a strong connection with your shadow (DerekRydall.com/ShadowProcess). As an alternative, use the following questions in journaling, freewriting, or just informally, as you talk to that shadow part of yourself.

If you're not using the guided audio process, begin by closing your eyes and imagining you're in a special place where you feel totally safe. It could be indoors or outdoors in nature, but it's a place where you are completely at home, protected, and at peace. Find a comfortable spot within this inner sanctuary to rest. Next, feel into the particular shadow you're working with and call it into this sanctuary. Allow it to appear in your mind's eye (ideally, some character that represents this part of you). Notice what this shadow looks like—how it's dressed; how it moves; its shape, size, color. As it approaches you, there is no sense of fear or danger, you sense that this is a wounded or disowned part of yourself and know that in this sacred space no harm can ever come to you. Once you feel established in this connection, ask these questions of your shadow:

1. **Where did you come from? What was the incident where I created you or rejected/repressed you? (Note: Sometimes this originating memory can be emotionally charged, a source of a trauma. In this space, however, you are separate from it and can't be hurt by it anymore. You can allow it to appear on a screen in front of you to create objectivity. What's important to know is that you do not need to re-experience the pain for this to be effective, that's not the purpose of shadow work—it is to rediscover this rejected part of you and realize its gift.)**
The aim of this first question is to remember the originating incident that triggered the fear, guilt, shame, or other pain around this aspect of you, and caused you to reject, repress, and

ultimately, deny that it existed. As you open to this question, allow images, fragments, thoughts, feelings, or other impressions to bubble up. You may not get a clear image or memory at first, but be patient. Allow your mind to wander and flow as it wants to, taking you back to a memory. Trust that it knows where it's going, even if the initial images or impressions—and even the memory you land on—don't seem to be connected to the shadow at first. It can be surprising what events had the greatest impact on us.

There are sometimes major events that played an obvious role in our early development. These are what we often go to first. If you don't easily land on something, however, it might be that you are expecting a big event, when in fact it was something seemingly small that left a big impression. It doesn't have to be an overtly traumatic or obvious wounding to create a shadow. There was one woman who had struggled to break through the glass ceiling in her business for years, until one day, during a regression meditation, she recalled a memory when her brother got an ice cream cone and she didn't (or maybe his was bigger). The result was a feeling of inadequacy, feeling less worthy than him, feeling like something was wrong with her. That was enough to drive a whole lifetime of compulsive behavior to prove that she *wasn't* less, which resulted in creating experiences that kept reflecting her shadow of unworthiness.

As you land on some memory, let it gel and formulate, until it reveals its emotional core. Feel into it—how you interpreted it; what decisions you made about life, about yourself; and what you decided you would change, become, or do as a way to overcome or compensate for this event. For example, if you have the selfish shadow, you might remember a moment when you asked for something from your father and he snapped at you, saying that he was busy and you were being a bad boy or girl for not respecting your daddy. Or maybe you wanted some money, a new toy, or new clothes for school, and your parents said you were only thinking of yourself—that if they got you something, they would have to get *all* the kids something. You needed to think of others, not just yourself.

If this event was strong enough, it could have left an indelible imprint in your mind and caused you to repress that part of yourself, creating a shadow around it. Or it could have been just the first in a string of experiences that ultimately confirmed for you that life wasn't fair, that you could never get what you really wanted or needed, or that it was just wrong to think about yourself before others. In either case, you then drew a map of the world based on this experience; created a survival kit to make it through; and decided that to survive you had to want less, ask for less, play smaller, and sacrifice your needs to make others happy, ensuring your safety and acceptance.

2. How have you been an ally in my growth and evolution all along?

Remember, the part of us we repress out of fear, shame, or any other judgment acts as a counterweight that we push against. As I suggested before, think of it like resistance training at the gym: in pushing against your shadow, you're building mental, emotional, and spiritual muscles. Our strong desire to deny, reject, or get rid of this part of us causes us to develop and strengthen the opposite part of us. If we rejected our selfish part, we most likely built up our selfless muscle by doing "reps" as a do-gooder, caretaker, people pleaser; or exercising our capacity to be a more generous, giving person. *This is the gift of the shadow.* And it's a gift that keeps on giving, adding value to our lives and the lives of those we touch. That is, until it becomes a liability because we haven't developed the other side of ourselves.

As you ask this question of your shadow, you're opening up to the blessings, lessons, advantages, skills, talents, and gifts you've received or developed as a result of the pressure this shadow exerted upon you. As you unpack the answers, it builds a greater bond with this part of you, because you start to see it as a blessing instead of a curse, an ally instead of an enemy. The more you see the value it brought you, the more you naturally appreciate it. And as a result, you begin to release the shame, blame, guilt, fear, or judgment of it. This is the beginning of reintegration.

Sometimes, it's hard to see the gift, but stick with it. Meditate on it, contemplate it, journal about it, and be patient and persistent in connecting with this shadow until it yields its deeper wisdom. Remember: this is about creating a relationship, as you would with a long-lost or estranged family member. It can take time to repair, gain trust, and get this part of you to open up. But is there anything more valuable than understanding, loving, accepting, and integrating yourself more deeply? That's the path to wholeness. I think it's worth the effort!

3. Why are you appearing now? What gift, lesson, or blessing do you have for me?
This question allows you to tap into the immediacy of this shadow. If it's still dogging you and causing problems, there's likely some message, lesson, or gift it has for you—something that will help you grow in your current conditions. This may come in the form of words or a symbolic gift that you don't understand right away. When the gift or lesson is coded like this, you can work with it

over time in your meditation or journaling, asking its meaning and watching what unfolds. Guidance doesn't always come in clear sentences that we can concretely act upon; sometimes it's more of an energy that begins to infuse and inform our inner and outer behavior. The deepest guidance doesn't come as information at all, but a journey that transforms us into the answer.

4. What do you need from me to feel loved, valued, and accepted— so you can take your rightful, constructive place in my life again?
This may be the most important question, as it leads to new actions that will activate and integrate the latent power and potential of this shadow. As you ask this question, you might, at first, get a general response like, "Love yourself more." That's not real, actionable guidance yet. In that case, ask questions that tease out specifics, such as, *What would it look like to "love myself more"? What would I do more of, less of, or differently?* As you ask this, you'll begin to get some impression of the new actions you need to take. It could sound like, "Exercise more," in which case you could ask, *What kind of exercise, how often . . . ?* Ask questions until you finally hear, "Take yoga three times a week. Drink eight glasses of water a day. Join a training group and run a marathon . . ." Now, you might not get anything clear—just a feeling, symbol, color, sound, or image fragment. Whatever comes, even if it seems like nothing, be patient and persistent. This is a growth process, not a one-and-done exercise.

Another important point to remember when doing this is that you're not asking, *What do you need from me so that you change?* You're not trying to figure out what to do to turn your selfish self into a more giving self, or your sad self into a happy self. You're not trying to "turn that frown upside down"; you're seeking to understand and integrate the power that the shadow contains. For example, if you just tried to turn your angry self into a happy self, you would miss the whole point: that angry self is actually your repressed *power source*. You don't want to throw cold water on that fire; you want to remove the judgment so you can fan the flames of your power and integrate it back into your life—the true purpose and potential of this shadow all along. There's nothing wrong with your angry self; *there was only something wrong with the judgment you had about it*. This is true with all shadows, all parts of you. There are no bad parts, no extra parts, no junky parts! There are just misunderstandings and misperceptions of what's really there, which have obscured your ability to see the value of including these things in your life and being.

5. **What will my life look like when I fully accept and embody you? What will the highest vision of my life be?**
This is a powerful question, because it opens you up to an inspired vision of your life, including the full activation and embodiment of this shadow. The value of this is that it creates new, positive associations with this dark part of you. When you see and feel that your life will be so much better as a result of integrating the selfish, stupid, needy, greedy parts of you, you'll release a lot of the resistance to accepting these parts and letting them take their rightful place in your life.

Shadow integration is a personal process. Big shifts can happen from a single encounter with your shadow, but more often, it's like a long-lost or estranged relationship with a family member: it takes time to rebuild and develop that connection. So be patient. Remember that the goal is not to change or remove your shadows, or to use them to get something you want; it's to build a deep, loving, compassionate relationship with these parts of you, so that you see their value and give them a seat at the table again.

Values Conflicts

The life we currently have is a result of what we most value. And depending on how much we value something, our life will change accordingly. For example, if we have a lot of money, it could mean the value of money is very high on our list. If we have a lot of rich, memorable experiences in our life and with our loved ones but don't have much money, it could be that we value experiences or connection more than money. If we have an abundance of creativity and creative works but don't have an abundance of relationships, we might value creativity or work more than people or connection. If we have a lot of open time and space in our life but not much success in our work, we probably value time, space, or freedom more than work, success, or wealth.

This is especially important to understand when we are struggling to have more abundance in one area and don't know why it's not showing up. For example, maybe we say we want to be more successful; but when we honestly evaluate our schedule, we see that we spend a lot more time hanging out with friends or family than we do investing in our work. This means people or relationships are higher on our value hierarchy than work or success. Conversely, we might say we value our family; but upon closer inspection, we see that we're spending most of our time working, which means we actually value money, success, work, or its byproducts (safety, security, self-worth, power) more than family. There's no judgment here—just a more expanded awareness of what we really value. Ultimately, the actions we take and the results we get are connected to this hierarchy of values.

This becomes particularly challenging when we value more than one thing almost equally, but our mind has been wired to pit these values against each other. In our belief system, to attain one value means we have to sacrifice the other one. It's like the heart-wrenching decision in the movie *Sophie's Choice*: we want both of them—even need both of them—but we don't want to sacrifice either. Regardless, our wiring tells us it's either/or, creating a push–pull, approach–avoidance, love–hate, yo-yo relationship with these values; and consequently, an up-and-down experience in our life. You've seen this in the person who makes strides, then loses their gains, then makes strides again—only to lose it all once more. The yo-yo diet; the serial relationships; the job opportunities that start out well but always end in quitting or being fired; or the sudden gain in money followed by a sudden expense, sending the money right back out the door, as fast as it came in!

For example, for years, I would strive for success; but just before I achieved real momentum, I would feel anxious, scared, guilty, or confused, and somehow sabotage my efforts. I would find relief and fulfillment by diving back into my art, spiritual practices, or family; but after a while, the anxiety and lack of fulfillment would return, making me feel the need to put my foot on the gas again—and the cycle would start all over. After multiple cycles of this, I started to sense that there was a clear pattern and a deeper reason behind it. As I investigated it further, I saw that I wanted wealth and success and I wanted a deeper connection to my art, my spirit, and my loved ones. The conflict: I felt like I couldn't have one without destroying the other. If I got too successful, I would end up losing my connection to my spirit, sell out my artistic values, or lose my family. If I forsook success for my art, heart, and spirit, I would end up broke, maybe homeless, and bring shame and pain upon my family.

Upon closer contemplation, I remembered that growing up, the more successful my father became, the more conflict there was in the family. (I talked about this earlier in the chapter.) As an increasingly busy businessman, he seemed to have less time for me and even less interest in or respect for my artistic ways. He would talk about how I should find a more professional path, and I was hurt by his lack of approval. Eventually, my parents divorced. As a result, I made a decision that I would never be like him. I would be a "good" man, a heartfelt man, an artist—I would not become the "business guy who only cares about money and success." This was mostly unconscious, but many of the things my dad represented became shadows for me.

After the divorce, I ended up living in my mom's friend's garage, sleeping on a mattress with my mom and sister. To say I was miserable is an understatement. Not because I didn't love my mom and sister, but because I was a teenage boy living in a garage on a mattress with my mom and sister! The result: I made a decision I would never live like *that* again. I would make my own way in the world, building a secure, successful life that ensured I always had a home and space and freedom.

You can see the problem: on one hand, I decided I would never be like my dad—a successful businessman—and on the other hand, I decided I would be successful so I could have a home and the financial security to support it. This created a "values conflict," where these opposing values became like fighting siblings in my mind, competing for my love and attention. And it was a fight I could never win, because I was fighting with myself. When I finally understood this, however, I was able to begin the process of rewiring these values together, so that they were on the same team, working toward the same goal: a successful, wealthy life of deep connection, art, and spirit.

Manifest Abundance Now!

Finding Your Abundance Values Conflicts

To begin identifying your values conflicts, use this simple sentence-completion exercise to see what you're afraid of losing or sacrificing (that's usually a key to discovering what the underlying opposing values are). Don't overthink your answer; just allow it to flow. For example: "If I'm really wealthy and successful, I'm afraid I'll lose / have to sacrifice my time, my family, my friends, my health, and so on."

- If I become wealthy, I'm afraid I'll lose/have to sacrifice . . .
- If I become really successful, I'm afraid I'll lose/have to sacrifice . . .
- If I work really hard toward my goals, I'm afraid I'll lose/have to sacrifice . . .
- If I come into a lot of money, I'm afraid I'll lose/have to sacrifice . . .
- If I really go for my dreams, I'm afraid I'll lose/have to sacrifice . . .
- If I really do what I want, I'm afraid I'll lose/have to sacrifice . . .
- If I fully express myself creatively, I'm afraid I'll lose/have to sacrifice . . .
- If I ask for what I really want, I'm afraid I'll lose/have to sacrifice . . .
- If I charge what I'm really worth, I'm afraid I'll lose/have to sacrifice . . .
- If I get everything I really want, I'm afraid I'll lose/have to sacrifice . . .
- If my family has a lot, I'm afraid I/we will lose/have to sacrifice . . .

Just seeing this values conflict and understanding it began to touch those wires and create a new spark. But creating what I call a "values affirmation" eventually connected those wires permanently.

Manifest Abundance Now!

Your Values Affirmation

To begin healing this values conflict, you need what I call a "values affirmation." A values affirmation is a statement that allows two or more seemingly opposing values to support each other, so that the attainment of one adds energy to the other and increases the odds of attaining it. For example, when I saw that I had the value of wealth and success fighting the values of art, spirit, and connection, I created a values affirmation that stated: "The more wealthy and successful I am, the more connected I am to my art, my spirit, and my loved ones. And the more I honor my connection to my art, spirit, and loved ones, the more inspired and empowered I am to be wealthy and successful in the world."

When I created this affirmation, I could feel the spark of connection. I could feel that I had hit on a truth of my being that had long been denied. It wasn't that I instantly believed it, but there was a release of energy that told me I was onto something. You'll feel this too when you hit upon your right values affirmation. There might be disbelief, fear, nervousness, or doubt that you can fulfill it, but there will also be this twinkling, this glow, this excitement—like you've tapped back into what could be possible.

You'll want to weave this statement so that it's simple to say, easy to remember, and the two opposing sides are serving each other. The following offers a few simple examples. (Don't take these as perfect models but as several possibilities.)

Opposing values: Wealth, Success vs. Time, Space, Freedom
Values affirmation: The more wealthy and successful I am, the *more* time, space, and freedom I have for myself. And the more I give myself enough time, space, and freedom, the more energized

and inspired I am to be wealthy and successful (to go for my big dreams).

Opposing values: Hard Work, Success vs. Good Parenting; Being Happy, Healthy

Values affirmation: The more I go for what I want and succeed, the happier and healthier I am, and the better parent I become. The more I take care of myself, do what makes me happy, and spend quality time with my children, the more empowered and energized I am to create the success I desire.

Once you find a statement that resonates with you, write it down, and speak it out loud—with passion—several times every day. You can look in a mirror and repeat it. Speak it in first, second, or third person to embed it on all the layers of the subconscious ("The more successful *I* am / *you* are / [*your name*] is . . .").

Consistency is important. It's usually not enough just to have the expanded awareness and recite this affirmation a few times. You've been telling yourself the opposite for years, so it's going to take time and effort to recondition your mind around the new pattern.

You can meditate on it like a mantra; you can journal about it or just write it on paper, over and over; you can think it or speak it while you're driving, bathing, walking, running, or working out. If you're jogging or walking, you can even synchronize it with your movements, to add an extra layer of embodiment.

It's a deceptively simple practice, but the implications can truly be life changing. Have fun and keep affirming it until it's second nature!

Remember: This is a journey of uncovering, transmuting, and redeeming these unconscious, often wounded or rejected parts of you.

Be kind, patient, and loving with yourself. Commit to working with these areas on a regular basis, just as you would if you were training for a physical competition or studying to take a big final exam.

Focus, repetition, and a willingness to keep going—even (and especially) when it's hard—is what builds new habits, develops true character, and determines your destiny. It creates real momentum, real success patterns. As your thinking hits that tipping point and goes beyond 50 percent subjective belief, you'll be on an upward spiral of growth; and many of the slings and arrows and limited beliefs of the world will no longer be able to touch you or take you down.

7

THE ABUNDANCE
BOOT CAMP

You'll never change your life until you change something you do
daily. The secret of your success is found in your daily routine.
—JOHN C. MAXWELL

Having a deep understanding of the Awakened Abundance Principle is a powerful beginning—and a necessary one. Without new knowledge, you can't create a new life or new results. But the key to sustainable, ever-increasing growth and success is designing *a way of life* with daily practices and outer structures that build new habits and create real momentum. Without that, the best we can hope for is short-term gains and momentary highs, because we'll inevitably be pulled back to our old, well-cut grooves in consciousness and familiar habits.

The life you're living right now is not designed to get you where you want to go; it's designed to keep you where you are. It's usually based on survival, coping, avoiding pain and loss, and seeking comfort and convenience. To get to the next level, you need to override this pattern, interrupt it, and recondition yourself.

That's what the rest of the book is about.

In this chapter, we're going to pull together all you've been learning into an actionable plan for creating lasting results, making you the abundance warrior you were meant to be. We're not just talking theory here; we're going to roll up our sleeves and change your life *for real*—in a way that's simple, step-by-step, and hopefully, a lot of fun.

Become an Awakened Abundance Warrior

In this context, "warrior" doesn't mean someone who is fighting others; it refers to the definition of "a person of courage, engaged in a struggle." In the purest sense, a warrior isn't someone who wants to fight—in fact, a true warrior does everything they can to avoid conflict. *A warrior is someone willing to face the seeming enemy and take a stand for true freedom.* And who is the "seeming enemy" we must face? Our own limited beliefs, perceptions, and habits. I say "seeming enemy" because those parts of us, like most enemies, are just doing what they believe is right and will preserve their way of life.

Most people, on all sides of a conflict, are good people who think their cause is just. Likewise, those parts of us we're fighting actually believe what they're doing is good. They're coping mechanisms designed to protect us; and when they were first developed, we may have actually needed them. But just as many of the weapons in our military's arsenal were built based on an outdated model of war and environment, similarly, many of the defense mechanisms we hold on to internally are artifacts of a world we no longer live in.

Being an abundance warrior in this sense is about building bridges instead of defending borders, opening doors instead of erecting walls. And that takes great courage. It can be scary to confront our darker shadow parts: neediness, greediness, selfishness, shame, guilt, and fear. Most people just want to be able to pay their bills, have a little fun, and stave off boredom until they die. Their whole life is based on safety, comfort, and convenience, not real growth and progress.

If you're still reading, you are not most people. You are someone who is answering a deeper call—someone who is ready to play a bigger game. And to do that, like a great athlete, you need to live a life of consistent practice and never-ending improvement. It requires time, energy, and focus. It requires you to be willing to change old habits and beliefs by reconditioning your mind so it's elastic, awake, and ready to tap into the flow and source of real abundance.

Most people never do this. Most people don't have a goal bigger than what they're going to eat and watch on TV tonight. Most people have TV screens bigger than the vision for their life! I'm not judging them—many people are so busy trying to survive that they don't have the mental, emotional, or physical capacity to engage in such lofty things as a life vision. And the rest have become hypnotized by a consumer-based, corporate-driven economy that conspires to keep us afraid and distracted enough that we keep buying stuff to dull the pain; we don't notice that the foundation of our rights and freedoms is eroding right under our feet. To be clear, this isn't a political statement; it's meant to inspire you to stay awake, to take back your power, to create a way of life that enables you to navigate this world and make it to your ultimate destination.

We must become strong, resilient, and bold if we want to create the life of our dreams and leave a lasting legacy for our loved ones. Yes, your bills will be paid; you'll have the money to go on vacation (maybe even enough to get your dream home and car); and you'll be able to generate an abundance of all the basic mental, emotional, and creative needs that make up a fulfilling life. But the real value of becoming an Awakened Abundance warrior is that, instead of being dependent on resources, you'll be connected to *the Source* of it all. You'll be tapped into the substance, power, and cause of *all* creation; so that no matter what obstacles you face, no matter what the state of the economy, no matter what anyone says you can or can't do or be, you'll have the ability to keep forging your own path and living your true destiny—and in a way that takes nothing from anyone but adds massive value to everyone you touch. Do you want to live that kind of life? If so, I welcome you to your Abundance Boot Camp!

Designing Your Abundance Blueprint

With the foundational chapters in this book, you've learned the core principles of abundance. And with the Seven Gifts and the chapters that followed, you were given powerful practices for activating and generating this substance of wealth into every area of your life. To organize it all into a way of life that leads to sustainable results—whether it's about having more wealth, health, creativity, love, or success—you need to work on these five core steps:

1. Discover your Abundance Mastery Goal.
2. Create your Abundance Breakthrough Goal.
3. Design your abundance lifestyle.
4. Develop your 40-day actionable plan to achieve it.
5. Commit to your goal with consistency and congruency (no matter what!).

The first thing to understand is that your past or present conditions don't determine your destiny—not your karma, astrology, numerology, or any "ology." What determines your destiny is your character; and your character is determined by your habits. As Confucius said, "All men are alike; it is their habits that separate them." Your habits are based on your consistent, focused actions. And what you do consistently is based on your commitment, which means doing what you said you would *no matter what.*

You can't create real momentum in any area if you aren't committed. Without commitment, you'll just dabble, play around the edges, kick the tires, maybe give it a test drive. And the moment it's hard, scary, or situations/people pop up to block you, you'll give up; get distracted; and work, shop, or eat to dull the pain.

Last but not at all least, as we've already discussed, you need to align all of this character and commitment with your most important goal or vision. Then you'll turn it into a real actionable plan and actually put it on your calendar!

Creating a way of life aligned with the Awakened Abundance Principle is a marathon, not a sprint. It doesn't come to those who are only interested in quick fixes and easy outs. As many people can attest, those who suddenly get an abundance of anything without having "earned it" in consciousness often experience more problems, not less: the dream job they're not prepared for that creates intense stress and ends in embarrassing failure; the overnight success that leads to excess, addiction, or worse; meeting your ideal mate in a whirlwind of romance only to end up re-creating old relationship conflicts that smother the spark before it becomes a flame. As the tortoise and the hare showed us, the race does not go to the swiftest or fleetest of foot but to the one who endures to the end.

There are all kinds of short-term gains you'll experience along the road to real abundance, but the greatest riches are only awarded to those who fall in love with the journey and begin to see that the whole road is paved with gold. At the end of a life, the most abundant person is not the one with the greatest possessions but the one who has the greatest possession of himself or herself. That is the true victory of a master of abundance.

So let's get started!

Step 1: Discover Your Abundance Mastery Goal

In this first part, you will articulate your Abundance Mastery Goal, seeing it as clearly as possible and putting it down on paper. This is the grand goal—the ideal life and lifestyle you want to live. Having a clear, honest vision of what you most want to achieve is an empowering act that will set the course for you to realize that dream. After all, if you don't know where you're going, every road will look interesting—and you'll get lost! The process of clarifying and breaking down this Abundance Mastery Goal will also help you figure out what strategies and benchmarks you'll need to put in place in order to live this ideal life of abundance with ease and grace.

This goal is about your highest vision. What is your grand vision of life and success? What is the ideal lifestyle you want? Not what you think you *should, could,* or *have to live,* but *what you deeply desire to be, do, have, create, and contribute* if you had all the abundance you needed to support it (time, health, wealth, wisdom, love, and so on).

Perhaps it's a vision of having your dream home, getting your PhD, traveling the world, funding your child's or grandchild's college education, or having the money to be a global philanthropist. Maybe it's about creating a beautiful family culture with such an abundance of love and joy in your life that it's contagious and leaves a lasting legacy. Or it could be about being a prolific creator, entrepreneur, or leader in some other capacity. It doesn't have to be grandiose, but it can be, if that's what inspires you to live your authentic and happiest life. Just remember: your highest vision is not about the world's idea of success; it's about living a life that gives you everything you need to express your full potential, fulfill your deepest purpose, and have an amazing time doing it!

It's beyond the scope of this book to do a complete vision workshop. Rather, the purpose here is to get a powerful snapshot of your ideal life/lifestyle so that you can get clear on the level of abundance it would require to live it. The following prompts will help you discover and define your big goal:

- Make a list of your heart's burning desires. Not just the superficial needs, like paying your rent or having a bigger TV. Give yourself permission to drop down into your body and feel into what would truly make for the most magnificent life and lifestyle. Where would you live, how would you live, who would you share it with, on whom would you make the biggest impact, what special or even priceless possessions would you have? If it takes your breath away, makes you blush, makes you think *That's crazy!* and is hard to admit to someone, that's the sweet spot.

- Make a list of the people whose life and lifestyle you admire the most throughout history and in the present day. They can be celebrities, thought leaders, artists, or your Uncle Joe (if he meets the criteria). Describe everything about their life and lifestyle that you love—not just the material elements but their character, their emotional state of being, their relationships, and their habits.

- Make a list of the greatest experiences you want to have in your life. Maybe it's regular family vacations, family reunions, building villages in Africa, camel racing between the pyramids, climbing Everest, taking a space flight. Have fun with this, letting your inner child out to play!

- Make a list of the greatest experiences you want to give to your loved ones. For example, maybe you want to send your parents on a worldwide cruise, let your children go to school abroad, build a recording studio for your brilliant child musician, or build a new center at your college. What brings us the greatest sense of joy and fulfillment is not just what we experience for ourselves but the life-changing experiences we can give others.

- What would you like to accomplish? You might have already touched on this in a previous question, but take a few moments to really drill down on this one. Imagine being at the end of your life and looking back fondly, knowing that you lived your full potential and purpose—that you gave your gifts, achieved your destiny, and left a lasting legacy. What were the most significant changes you made for yourself, for others, for the world? What were the biggest impacts you made in the life of your loved ones, in your area of work, or beyond?

- What else would this ideal life/lifestyle have that would make it complete—your 100 percent dream life? What would enable you to hold nothing back and leave nothing on the table mentally, emotionally, physically, financially, creatively, relationally, or spiritually?

At this point, you might be feeling overwhelmed; or your practical mind might be kicking in, telling you this is an irrational task (or even a waste of time) since it's never going to happen anyway—or at least, not for many years to come. This is just an ego stall tactic designed to prevent you from stretching and living a visionary life. The truth is, all of this and more is already here, now, within you; and it's waiting for the right conditions to emerge—conditions that you have control over.

Spiritually, there is no time or space, so there are no universal rules that say things have to take a long time. In fact, one powerful question for collapsing the time line and achieving the impossible comes from Peter Thiel, a prominent venture capitalist, who asks, "How can you achieve your ten-year plan in the next six months?"[6] When you engage your vision with this level of openness and a willingness to do the inner and outer work to make it real, you can begin living your life at a whole new level—a level beyond your imagination.

My story of going from living in an apartment, where my wife and I could never imagine affording our dream home, to moving into our dream home in about three months is an example of what's possible when you activate your inherent potential regardless of the appearances to the contrary. There's no guarantee that you'll get your perfect home in the next few months, make a million dollars in the next year, or achieve your ideal lifestyle in the next three years—it's not even necessary to have all those things to live a truly abundant life—but having a powerful, inspiring vision and beginning to activate the energy toward it *will* start moving things around to make it real.

What Is the Real Cost of Your Vision?

Once you've articulated your grand vision, take some time to figure out what the real cost is—what price you will have to pay—and not just monetarily but mentally, emotionally, creatively, and relationally. If you want to live in a particular kind of home in a specific area— even if you want your own private island—research it to find out some real numbers. If you want to have multiple vacations a year, talk to a travel agent and price out what it would cost.

If your goals are more relational and you want to have an abundance of friendship, family, and intimate companionship, study people who have achieved this, and identify what it really took to create it. What sacrifices and changes did they make in their lifestyle, what habits did they employ, what strategies did they use, what qualities of character did they develop? In other words, what price did they pay to have this abundant life of love and connection?

If your goals are more creative or entrepreneurial, investigate your role models in this area. What kind of investment in time and energy did it require for them to become masterful, successful artists or innovators? Where did they invest that time and energy—in books, workshops, mentors, coaches, schools, or other self-learning modalities? What regular habits did they develop? What kinds of people did they spend the most time with? What kind of lifestyle did they create to support their work?

As you do this research, you're achieving a few things. First, you're taking real action *as if* it's possible—don't underestimate the power of this. It begins to move the energy in the direction of your action. It also begins to unearth limited beliefs, fears, and habits that don't support this vision, so you can heal and release them. It's like a mental, emotional, and spiritual Roto-Rooter service.

It starts to make the vision real.

When I wanted to travel the world but couldn't even begin to know how I would afford it, I began researching the places I wanted to visit, creating an itinerary and pricing it out—and it totally opened my mind and heart to the possibilities. I was learning a lot, having fun, and starting to feel like a worldly, traveled person from all the research. It shifted my consciousness and seeped into my body, into my cells. Then things started changing around me. New opportunities began to show up, synchronicities began to happen; and one day, I received a "mysterious" email, seemingly out of the blue. It was a request for me to ghostwrite a book. The subject didn't immediately grab me, but there was something about it that felt compelling. I started a dialog with the potential client, and by the time I was done negotiating the job, it included an all-expenses-paid trip through multiple countries—not to mention a writing project that truly thrilled me!

This would never have happened if I hadn't been playing with world travel for a few months before, because it was the mention of a different country in the email that first caught my attention and made me consider responding. Then it kept me in the conversation when the initial project didn't excite me. This new internal drive to travel guided the conversation to a place where having me visit various locations to interview people *in person* became a real possibility. If it wasn't for that, I would never have suggested it; and I would have written it from my home office.

We see the world and what's possible through the filters of what we're interested and invested in. If you love clothes and spend time thinking and learning about them, you're going to see much more detail about clothing than the average person. You're also going to see the opportunities related to clothing; whereas, I might be completely blind to them even if they're right in front of me. This is the power of the reticular activator in your mind. And this is what gets turned on when you get involved in your big vision.

It Costs Less Than You Think

Another thing to understand is that the master vision you desire may not cost as much in time, energy, money, or other resources as you think. Maybe you don't have grand visions of owning a private island or a jet, or of living in a massive mansion on a hill, but you may be surprised to realize that even those things don't necessarily require as much as it might seem.

To make the point dramatically, let's look at that private island. To buy one could cost millions—tens of millions—and for most people, that puts it so far out of reach and in the very distant future that it's not even worth considering. But what if you rented it instead of owning it? The fact is, unless you lived there, odds are that you wouldn't spend more than a handful of weeks there every year.

So how much would it cost to rent an island for that space of time? Let's say it's $100,000 to rent a small island for a month, and that would be enough to satisfy your yearly needs. That's only a $100,000 added to your annual budget instead of many times more if you owned the island and managed all the upkeep regardless of how much time you actually spent there. At a 10 percent annual return, spending a month on this private island *as if* you owned it would require an asset worth about one million versus many millions. Sure, that's still a lot for most people, but right there, you've just cut your costs and time line to achieve this goal by a factor of three to ten times.

The same is true for a private jet. It would cost millions (often tens of millions) to own one (plus insurance, pilot, staff, upkeep), but you could rent one for $25,000 to $100,000 for international trips. So if you traveled every month, that's a quarter million to a million per year instead of $20 to $60 million to own.

And if you have the dream of having multiple homes around the country or the world, you could do the same math exercise: How much would it cost to buy them? How often would you spend time in them? Realistically, you might spend a few months a year between different homes. If you bought each one of these homes, it could cost you millions—and remember to add in all the insurance, utilities, taxes, and year-round upkeep. If you rented them for the same amount of time, it would cost you a tiny fraction of that. Again, how many years of earning—and *waiting*—did this simple exercise just shave off of your dream-life time line?

Most likely, your big dream doesn't include such extravagances. But by illustrating that living the lifestyle of the rich and famous is more within reach than you may have thought, you can apply the same strategies and mind-set to bring the lifestyle you desire closer to home—and in less time.

This same principle applies to the other areas of your dream life. You may have a belief that in order to really have a life rich in love, you need a lot of friends and family, or to spend every day with your significant other. But when you study the lives of those who experience the most love and connection, you find that it's mostly an inside job. If they have that inner connection to love—which anyone can create, starting wherever they are—they have a more abundant experience of love regardless of how many people or experiences are in their life. And when it comes to relationships, if they focus on the areas or activities that have the highest payoff, by understanding what their partner or family member really values, they can create an abundance of love without an abundance of effort, time, or expense.

In creative or entrepreneurial pursuits, while it often does take hard work to achieve significant goals, the ones that create success the quickest and sustain it over the long term usually aren't trying to do too much at once. It's not about writing ten books and hoping one breaks through; it's about writing the *one* book that deeply matters and then supporting it over a sustained period of time, until it creates its own momentum. In business, it's not necessarily about having multiple products, programs, or services to see what sticks; it's about finding the one path you can fully commit to and then staying the course until you get real-world results.

I don't want to bog you down with numbers and details. As I said, your ideal life may not include islands, jets, multiple homes, bestsellers, or a large family. The important thing to remember here is that living the life of your dreams doesn't have to cost nearly as much as you think—if you think creatively. With a creative approach, you'll likely see that you can afford to live this dream life with much less time, money, energy, or activity than you thought; and therefore, it can be achieved much sooner.

How does it feel to read this? Do you notice a shift in your consciousness—from feeling constricted around how hard it might be to have your ideal life to a more expanded sense of possibility? Remember, it's all about consciousness; so anything that makes you feel more expansive around your big vision is a valuable step in the right direction.

Take some time to unpack your big vision; the cost of living it; the price you might have to pay in terms of an investment of time and energy; and what types of assets, systems, or structures you might need to have in place to generate the abundance required. Then you can move on to the next step, where we'll lay out a process for activating this vision.

Step 2: Create Your Abundance Breakthrough Goal

Once you have your Abundance Mastery Goal, you want to reverse engineer it down to something you can really commit to and work toward. The idea is that if you can develop the skills, character, and habits of your mastery goal over the next forty days, you will be on track for creating the ideal life and lifestyle that you desire. To do this, you'll create a target goal that would cover your monthly needs, and a three- to six-month buffer.

Developing this cushion and the expanded feeling it brings is the first level we're shooting for. This is the state of having that leads to an experience of abundance.

Your Monthly Target Goal

To begin moving you in the direction of your ideal abundance lifestyle, take some time to figure out what you would need to achieve in the next year to be making real progress toward that. If your goal is big—say, a five-to-ten-year vision—just do your best to imagine where you would want to be in the next year in order to be on track. The fact is, we never really know how long or what it will take, or where life will take us—and that's okay. Your best guess is good enough. For example, if you realized that to fulfill your Abundance Mastery Goal you would need to be earning $250,000 a year, taking two big vacations a year, and producing a certain level of creative output (like writing a book a year), where do you feel you would need to be in the next twelve months to be on course for that?

Next, break down that one-year goal into four quarterly goals and then a monthly goal. Spend some time figuring out what it would actually take to cover all your monthly needs financially, creatively, emotionally, and so on. If you decide your yearly goal is $50,000, then your monthly goal would be a little over $4,000. If you're focusing on creating an abundance of love, you can decide on a number of "emotional deposits" in key relationships that will have you on course to fulfill your bigger yearly goal (for example, having the important conversations you've put off, being of greater service, spending more time together, or doing extra-special or long-overdue things that make a big investment in the relationship[s]).

You can do this for any quality you're trying to have in greater abundance. If you have a goal or deadline to write a book, get clear on how many pages you would need to write to be on track for that. This might also include structures and systems you put into place to ensure that you have the time and space you need to get the work done. In business, you might make an investment in developing new relationships that will give you ample opportunities for future contacts, contracts, or clients over the next year.

Your Abundance Buffer Account

If you want to accelerate your feeling of abundance, don't just focus on getting the month's work done; set a goal to create a three-to-six-month buffer. That means taking whatever your monthly goal is and multiplying it by the three to six months you're planning ahead for. When it comes to money, this is easy to understand (if you have $3,000 a month in bills, you would need $9,000 to $18,000 to create this buffer account). But you can apply this idea to other areas as well. For example, you can create a buffer account of extra time, so that if things don't go as planned, you can relax, knowing you have some breathing room.

If you're creating an abundance of love in your relationships, you'll want to make enough deposits that you have an emotional buffer account that can withstand problems that might arise or mistakes you might make—without bringing you below your basic level of love needs, or worse, putting you into emotional debt in that area. If it's in the area of creativity, you can bank a certain amount of work so that you have a cushion and don't feel so driven every day to get more done. That doesn't mean you won't keep working; it just means you won't be coming from a place of lack, but rather, a place of overflow.

This then becomes the audacious goal you're going for.

The fact that it might feel impossible is not only okay, it has the ability to pull out of you a whole new level of untapped potential that will catapult you forward through the year. Once you have this buffer, you have the first level of abundance freedom—but not for the reasons you may think or read in most books and programs on this subject. Most tell you to create this buffer (especially in the financial area) so you have a cushion, and that's fine—having the financial cushion (or any cushion) is important practically. But ultimately, real freedom is about a state of consciousness more than it's about how much you have or don't have. So in that context, the value of having this buffer is *the more expanded feeling of abundance* it gives you—whether financially, creatively, vocationally, or emotionally. And this expanded feeling of abundance is the very substance of abundance itself, which will begin to manifest as a more abundant life experience.

- Take a moment to imagine having this buffer of three-to-twelve month's worth of bills already covered (no matter what happens), enough feeling of love in your relationships that you know things will be solid regardless of the storms you might weather, and creative productivity or momentum that ensures you'll meet your goals and deadlines with ease. How does this feel?

  Imagine waking up in the morning and thinking about your life, knowing you have this buffer. Imagine going through your day and making decisions, knowing you have this buffer. Imagine going out with your spouse or family to enjoy a nice meal, a movie, or a vacation, knowing you have this buffer. Feel what it's like to have this space in your life—to know you're not living paycheck to paycheck, project to project, or in constant stress about the state of your relationships.

- Now ask, *What else might I do, knowing I have this buffer?* For instance, might you make time to take better care of yourself, exercise more, get a massage, or take a day or a weekend off more often? Would you spend more time with your loved ones or friends, doing the things that bring you real joy and fulfillment? Would you start that next book or entrepreneurial project, knowing that it doesn't have to bring you name, fame, or fortune anytime soon, because you have this buffer?

This more-expanded feeling, vision, and level of action is the real benefit of having this buffer—and this higher vibration of having creates the foundation for you to be even more conscious, creative, loving, giving, and powerful in every area of your life, allowing even more abundance to manifest.

Becoming Conscious of Your Abundance Level

One of the biggest stumbling blocks to mastering abundance in a real-world way is the lack of consciousness around how much you really have coming in and going out—what you're really spending, where, and why. This doesn't just apply to money; it can be applied to any area of abundance you want to grow. You first need to be conscious of what you currently have and how you're using it.

For example, maybe you're struggling to be more creative in some area, like writing a book that's been sitting half finished in a desk drawer or remodeling a bathroom that makes you cringe every time you walk by it. When you look at your calendar and see what you're actually spending on it and why, you'll get a clearer picture of what's stopping you from completing the project—namely, that you're not investing much or any time on it, or wasting the precious currency of your time on things that don't add a lot of value to your life. If you feel like your relationship isn't meeting your emotional needs or is even draining you, you might discover that you're spending a lot of your relationship capital doing non-nurturing things together, doing next to nothing together, or wasting it in chronic conflict. It might become apparent that you're making very few emotional deposits and a lot of withdrawals—and it's bankrupting your partnership.

This process is about lifting up the rocks, looking at what's been hiding underneath—the real facts, figures, and feelings—and healing whatever that brings up.

Now, at this point in reading, it's common to experience resistance. You might find yourself suddenly tired, distracted, or having an urge to put this book down! Maybe you're thinking, *I've got what I need; I'm good; I don't need to dig this deep.* If that describes you, I encourage you to stay with it. If you feel like this isn't very interesting or inspiring and you're just going to skip it or take a break for now, I can tell you, from all of my experience, that it's likely a "threshold response." That's what happens when we're on the verge of real change.

If you don't like looking at the numbers, doing the math, quantifying your feelings (so you can accurately track your progress), or getting honest with where you really are in the area you're most challenged with, that alone is a significant reason why you're struggling. It indicates an area of your consciousness that hasn't been purified, clarified, and strengthened—and I can relate. I don't like looking at facts and figures; I would much rather just keep moving and hope for the best. But as I continue to do what it takes to be a good steward of these aspects of my personal and professional life, the result is more abundance in many areas. So I get that this isn't always fun, but doing it is what allows you to have *more* fun!

Step 3: Design Your Abundance Lifestyle

Now that you know the Abundance Mastery Goals and Abundance Breakthrough Goals that would put you on track to begin living toward your grand vision, we're going to focus on creating a way of life that supports this. Your current life doesn't—if it did, you would already be there. So *we need to design a life that matches the vision.* As you do that, you'll activate these latent potentials and bring yourself into integrity with the life you really want to live.

To do this, we're going to excavate the core qualities of your big vision and engineer them into your everyday living, so that you're living into it as if it's a reality now rather than waiting for conditions to change before you show up fully for your life. This is the secret to creating progress and success regardless of conditions.

The Daily LIFT

Once you know your ideal abundance goal or vision (or have some sense of it), you can begin to cultivate the conditions that activate the feeling tone of that vision—the feelings you would have if you were *already* living it. The more you can live in the frequency of your vision, the more you're tuned in to the dimension of consciousness where that idea already exists. As I describe in my book *Emergence*, it's like tuning the dial of your radio to the station where your favorite music is playing: it's already broadcasting right where you are, but it doesn't manifest until your frequency (your dial) matches the frequency it's playing on. When that happens, you have a manifest-station! The beat of abundance and the symphony of success are already playing right where you are; and by doing the daily LIFT practice, you bring yourself into alignment with it.

To begin doing the LIFT practice (which stands for "Living In the Feeling Tone") of your vision, start with your Abundance Mastery

Goal—that vision of your dream life where all your needs are abundantly met—and enlist the familiar tool of visualization. However, you won't be using visualization to hold a picture in your mind and make it happen; you'll be using it to tap into the *feeling* of what it's like to live that vision. This is the most effective use of visualization. The old practice of using it to manipulate appearances has many negative byproducts, not the least of which is that your picture of how you think things should look might not be correct or in your best interest. (I've had to help people get out of situations they visualized themselves into—because once they got the thing they thought they wanted, it created more problems than they could handle. You don't want to suffer that same fate.)

When you use visualization to activate the "visionary vibration" without getting attached to the picture, you can never go wrong—because that feeling tone of expansion, abundance, power and joy is always true about you. When you use visualization to activate the "visionary vibration" (the feeling-tone of your vision realized) without getting attached to the picture, you don't try to bolt it down to your idea of what it *should* be, it shapes itself around your true purpose, your unique pattern, and your ultimate potential. And it often manifests better than you could imagine, because it fits you like a glove. It's not a manipulation of appearances; it's a natural emergence of what was always true about you.

The Law of Emergence states that everything is already in you—in that seed of greatness planted in the soil of your soul—and when the conditions match that seed, the seed's inherent potential naturally emerges. This is how all of nature grows, and it's how you were designed to grow too. When you use tools like visualization to manipulate the process, you're relying largely on your human imagination, which is made up of your current self-concepts, lifelong conditioning, societal beliefs, parental fantasies, and peer pressure—and this blocks the natural emergence. Imagination is certainly better than the status quo, but who you are, what you're capable of, and the vision of wealth and abundance you were born to express is beyond your imagination—you literally can't imagine it because it's outside of your known paradigm.

We don't want to limit our future by grasping too tightly to our limited ideas of what it should be. We can start with our imagination and use our highest ideas to activate the visionary vibration—and even take action in the direction of our vision—but then we must let the natural energy within our inner being (our soul) emerge, activating and radiating to shape and guide our path.

So let's begin with visualization to tap into that feeling tone of the vision:

- Find a comfortable place to sit upright (with your back straight but not stiff), close your eyes, take a few deep relaxing breaths, and begin to allow your vision to unfold in your mind's eye. If you're good at visualizing, allow yourself to fill out the picture with as much sensory input as possible (sight, sound, color, smell, touch)—really be there. If you struggle with visualizing, that's okay—just do your best to see it. And if you can't, just think about the images and activities.

    Most important, allow yourself to *feel* what it feels like to live this ideal life. How do you feel in your heart, in your body? Give yourself permission to really drop into the feeling experience. Notice the expansiveness of the energy; see if you can articulate its qualities. Is it a feeling of peace, love, joy, power, excitement, inspiration? This is the *feeling quality* you need to activate. A feeling quality is static, like love, peace, joy, power, and so on.
- Next, notice who you are *being*. This is a more dynamic quality, like being giving, spontaneous, playful. In other words, it's something you can actively be. Take a moment to see how you're

showing up in this ideal life—your behaviors, your actions, your character. What kind of a person are you being?

- Then turn your attention to what you're *doing*—not merely the one-and-done actions you are taking but the things you are doing consistently. For example, maybe in this ideal life, you notice you are exercising regularly, writing daily, having some social interaction weekly, doing date nights weekly, making a certain number of sales calls, and so on. What you're looking for are the *habits of this successful version of yourself*. If these habits aren't clear, just give yourself permission to imagine what they might be.

- Once you're aware of the feeling and being qualities, and the habits of doing, you can open your eyes and write down a list of them. Or if it works better, you can write them down as they come, then go back into the visualization to continue the process. Don't worry about getting it all right—this is a work in progress. Feel free to do this step and the other steps in phases, and as many times as needed.

Activating the Feeling Qualities

Pick one of the feeling qualities from your list and identify the people, places, activities, and objects that you believe activate these. Then repeat the exercise for the remaining feeling qualities under each of the following activation categories. (You don't have to do all of the qualities at once; you can work with one at a time if you wish. But having the complete list will be a good document to draw from as you build your actionable plan.)

- **People:** Which people make you feel more of this quality? It can be people you used to spend time with but with whom you have lost touch and would like to reconnect. It can be people you already spend time with but want to spend more time with. It can also be a type of person you want to be with more, like those who share your values or vision.

- **Places:** What environments make you feel this quality? It can be places you've been and would like to visit more, or places you want to spend time in but have reasons (aka, excuses) why you can't. These can be places in your community, your country, or beyond; and they can also be places in your home.
- **Activities:** Reflect on your life and notice the moments when you felt this quality. What were you doing? For me, when I dance, I feel energized, alive, and free. So, because my vision includes me feeling totally unleashed, I know that I need to integrate more of that activity into my life—even if it's just dancing around my kitchen every day. Make a list of the activities that make you feel this quality.
- **Objects:** Everything in your environment stimulates a response in you. The color of the walls, the pictures on your mantel, the sounds, the smells, and any other objects of the senses—including the music or media you allow in. When you become intentional about what you allow into your space, you are able to create an environment that activates your higher nature automatically. What type of music or sound makes you feel this quality? What images activate it? How about smells? For me, the smell of freshly baked bread makes me feel peaceful, the smell of newly cut grass activates joy, and the smell of certain types of incense invoke a feeling of devotion.

Activating the Being Qualities

To work with the being qualities of your big goal, take the quality you would express more of if you were living your realized vision, and ask, *What would it look like for me to be more [fill in the blank with the quality]?* For example, if you are more playful in your ideal vision, you would ask what it would look like to be more playful. You can also phrase it as, *If I was being more playful, what would that look like?* You can ask this in a general sense, or you can direct it to a specific area you're working on, such as *What would it look like for me to be more playful at work / home / in my relationship?*

As you sit with that question, meditating on it, you will start to see, feel, or sense some guidance about how you could bring more of that quality of play to that area. If you don't get anything at first, that's okay. Continue to ask, journal about it, and experiment with it. Have fun with this process—be bold, be creative, and take a leap!

The Daily GIVE: Picking the Gifts You Are Going to Give

As part of this Abundance Boot Camp, you're going to fast from "getting" and focus on "giving." That doesn't mean you can't ask for what you need; it just means that you're going to become very conscious about all the people, places, and things you externalize as your Source, and you're going to proactively reverse that flow of energy. Wherever you're trying to get something from someone or waiting for someone to give you something, you will instead work with the Seven Gifts to become the divine power plant of your own life.

Remember: The quality and quantity of your energy is the key to creation. The more of it you have—or more specifically, the more you generate—the more you can manifest the life you want. In the simplest terms, the reason the great masters like Jesus, Buddha, Lao Tzu, and others were able to perform what are considered miracles is because they were activating, integrating, and radiating higher quality energy.

If you want to create a life of more abundance—in health, wealth, love, joy, creativity, or opportunity—you need to generate a higher quality and quantity of energy.

As you understand this, you realize it's not so woo-woo to expect that when you do the inner work and activate more energy, something or someone changes across the street, across the ocean, or in some other area of our life. Through the Law of Circulation and the principles of Awakened Abundance, you become a bigger, more active power plant, generating a flood of energy through all the channels of your life—without conditions, delay, or denial. And now that you have a solid foundation of how these principles work, it's about practicing them so you can more fully GIVE (Generate Invisible Vital Energy). This process includes your use of the Seven Gifts that Give You Everything (page 81), combined with the LIFT practice (page 225).

Are you ready to begin? If so, look over the Seven Gifts listed below, and identify one to three gifts that really speak to you—either because they seem lacking or because you feel a strong charge around them. (Feel free to also go back to chapter 3 to refresh your memory of what each gift means.)

1. Giving Out
2. Giving Away
3. Giving Up
4. Giving In
5. Giving Thanks
6. Giving to Yourself
7. Forgiving

Maybe the gift of giving away all the stuff you don't use or need freaks you out. You have a closet, garage, attic, or office full of stuff that you know is weighing you down and cluttering your life, but the idea of actually letting it go brings up a primal fear or an anxiety that you don't understand or want to deal with.

Maybe you're a people pleaser or do-gooder, always giving to and taking care of others, but not meeting your needs in the process; and it feels almost blasphemous to activate the gift of giving to yourself, and selfish to fill yourself up first.

Perhaps you want to give of your time, talent, and treasure in some way—the gift of giving out—but you have a story of why you can't right now. You're waiting to have more money before you become charitable; you're waiting to have more time before you engage in service; you're waiting for some permission or opportunity before you express your talents. If so, that would be a great gift to work on.

From the Emergence paradigm, whatever you're waiting for, you're *waiting with* and *weighing down*. If you want to be a singer, don't wait for some external validation to start giving that gift; do a daily performance for your plants or a concert for your cat. If you want to be a writer, don't wait for a writing assignment; start your own free blog and begin sharing your ideas. The key is to get this energy circulating. Many of the answers and emotions you're waiting to have before you embark won't come until you start moving.

When I wanted to be a speaker, I would walk around my house in my underwear, giving talks to an invisible audience; then one day, someone gave me an audience to speak to. When I wanted to start writing books, I sat my butt down in a chair and stared at a blank screen every day, writing whatever came up. It wasn't good at first, but it got me going.

Don't get it right; just get it written.

Don't wait for magic; just start moving.

Once you have chosen the gifts you're going to work on, figure out which regular actions you're going to take for the next forty days to practice giving in these areas. If it's service, pick someone or some organization that you will commit to giving your time to on a regular basis. If you're working on giving your talents, decide what you're going to do consistently in that area (for example, writing a blog post three times a week). If it's the gift of giving to yourself, which I recommend for almost everyone, identify the area where you've been trying to get something from someone or waiting for someone to change, and start giving whatever's missing to yourself as a daily practice. If you feel like your partner isn't respecting or valuing you enough, ask yourself, *What would it look like to value and respect myself in this relationship or in general?* Meditate and journal on this until you come up with some behaviors or actions that represent you valuing and respecting yourself. Ideally, after you've done this process, you'll have a list of specific actions you can take to practice the gifts you're working on.

Step 4: Develop Your 40-Day Actionable Plan

This is where you unpack the specific actions you'll take to move toward your big goals. And it isn't about practical, reasonable actions—there are plenty of books that talk about that. This is about stretching and *leaning into* your big vision.

When I wanted to buy my dream house but couldn't afford it, I started researching possible homes, going to open houses, and talking to realtors. Family and friends who were in the same situation thought this was silly and pointless—after all, I couldn't afford it! But as I took actions *as if* my dream was real, I began to activate all kinds of new insights and possibilities; and within less than a few months, I was moving into my dream home.

I knew of a guy who used to take his son to the Ferrari dealership on a regular basis to learn about the cars and test drive them. His friend thought it was crazy and even irresponsible—that he was teaching his kid to be unrealistic. A couple years later, that guy was not only driving his own Ferrari, he had created a lifestyle that matched it.

This isn't about material gain; it's about moving toward your big goals from an abundance mind-set—from the perspective that anything you deeply desire is already real in potential; it just needs you to step into it. That said, there's no guarantee you'll get everything you go for in exactly the way you thought; but as you move from this Awakened Abundance attitude, you will transform your character and your life, and open up new doors of possibilities. So take some time to make a list of all the possible things you could do to move toward this big goal.

The 25 Ways to Manifest More

It's beyond the scope of this book to give you an entire goal-achievement workshop, but there's one practice I find helpful in exercising your ability to think creatively, innovatively, and outside the box. I call it the "25 Ways to Manifest More." It's deceptively simple, but it can be very powerful if you practice it consistently.

The basic process is to take the goal you're trying to achieve—let's say, a certain amount of money—and start listing twenty-five (or more) ways you can make it happen. Normally, we don't give ourselves permission to do this—we live within a very narrow field of possibilities. If we need more money, we think there are only a couple ways to get it (by working more hours, winning the lottery, selling a kidney!). But the universe has infinite organizing power, which means it doesn't have just one or two or a hundred ways to fulfill itself; it has an unlimited variety of ways to accomplish things.

To develop this capacity, you need to practice thinking fluently and flexibly, without any limits or conditions, and without worrying about how or the consequences. Though you may not do everything on your list, being this open to the flow of possibilities will stretch your imagination to whole new levels; and a mind stretched beyond its previous shape never goes back to the same form. In other words, you will permanently increase your ability to come up with solutions.

Your Abundance Accelerator Plan

A vision without a plan is a fantasy. So if you want to make this vision a reality, you need to turn it into an actionable plan. I call this an "Abundance Accelerator Plan," because it combines the outer actions with your inner practice to create real congruency. When your inner life and your outer life are working as one, you can truly become a force of nature.

Before we dive into this plan, I would like to talk briefly about why we tend to avoid this level of practical, numbers- and strategy-based planning. It has to do primarily with our emotions. Remember how I said everything is energy? That stack of magazines you don't want to get rid of isn't just a pile of paper; it's coagulated energy. But it's also something else—a story. A story of how you didn't follow through, wasted money, or made some kind of mistake; and it activates a pocket of emotion that you don't want to face and feel. That's the real reason you avoid taking these bold and important actions in your life.

For example, people struggling financially often don't look at the numbers because it brings them face-to-face with their core wealth and abundance wounds. People with creative blocks rarely look at their limiting habits because it forces them to confront their feelings of inadequacy and their fear of failure. People in intimate relationships often prefer to blame their partner or just withdraw rather than looking at what they want and taking total responsibility for creating it, because they fear rejection or abandonment.

By processing these goals consciously, you not only become adept at dealing with the facts and figures of your everyday life, but you become liberated and empowered at a level that would otherwise have been unavailable to you. This particular combination of the practical and transformational has proven to be a core reason the Awakened Abundance process creates real results. Ultimately, it's all about consciousness—your consciousness. If you're harboring unconscious fears, doubts, worries, or limited beliefs around having an abundance of time, wealth, love, health, creativity, or success, it's important to excavate those so you can heal, release, transmute, or integrate this energy.

So let's start building this Abundance Accelerator Plan.

As part of your plan, you will be developing a 40-day program, including daily and weekly practices that align your inner and outer activities—the specific things you're going to do as a daily routine, as well as the bigger tasks you'll do weekly to achieve your big vision. This will be made up of the various activities you have decided on from the previous exercises—but a word of caution: *Don't try to do everything at once.* If you do, you'll get overwhelmed, burned out, and give up before you create a real habit. For your inner activities, start with one feeling quality, one being quality, and one of the Seven Gifts you want to develop. To make big leaps, you just need to take small steps, consistently.

Here's an example of my daily and weekly practice (excluding my regular business activities):

- **Morning:** Meditation or prayer to make my connection with Source and set the intention for the day. Jog while visualizing my ideal life and doing affirmations (this is when I'm consciously activating the core *feelings* of my ideal vision). Drink a healthy shake and review my daily plan.
- **Afternoon:** Healthy lunch and writing practice. Another form of meditation or prayer (sometimes a moving meditation). Listen to music, dance, or work out at the gym while listening to inspiring

or educational audio books or podcasts (This is when I am doing things that allow me to step more into *being* playful and spontaneous, which are key qualities of my vision.)

- **Evening:** Another creative activity. Social time with family or friends (when I consciously practice whatever quality of being I am leaning into). Ideally, some kind of review and wrap-up of the day, and some relaxing or fun time, like watching TV. (I used to do Night Pages every night for years; now, it's more of an internal process.)

- **Weekly:** Some bigger social event or family outing, an artist date (taking myself to a movie or some other activity that inspires and feeds me), longer meditation or study time (catching up on reading, shadow work, and so on), church, some outdoor activity. (This is also where I schedule certain actions that have me moving in the direction of my emerging vision. For example, at the time of this writing, I have a vision of a beautiful property where I can do retreats, so I have been going to open houses to activate this energy.)

I don't always achieve all this or do it perfectly, but this is the basic foundation of my current practice. I try to tap back into my vision, gratitude, and prayer many times throughout the day as well—it's become a welcome habit. Your daily and weekly practice may look very different, however. You might have more outdoor activities, social interactions, or creative time; but again, don't overdo it. I didn't build this all at once but layer by layer, over time.

It's important to understand that, while you can have dramatic breakthroughs and results in forty days, this is more about building *the habits of abundance* that will allow you to achieve much more over time. It's also about creating real structure around your goals and practices, and actually putting them on your calendar. It makes them more real and more likely to happen. If you have to start small and slow, and don't get all the results you want, that's perfectly okay. What you're looking for is progress: As you go through this, do you find that you're growing in some area—that certain ways of feeling or being that were hard or nonexistent before are now becoming easier and more regular? Even a tiny movement, lived into over time, can take you in a brand-new direction. You can always do the 40-day process again, allowing it to deepen with each engagement.

Remember, being an abundance warrior is *a way of life*—a way of living that allows for a never-ending, ever-expanding upward spiral of growth and possibility.

Your Outer Action Plan

Be specific, intentional, and clear about the actions you'll schedule into your next forty days in order to move toward your big goal—actions you'll be initiating, versus reacting to outside conditions or stimuli coming to you. If you already have a full schedule, with a regular job or family obligations, take the material you excavated above and schedule it around those existing events. Many of these actions can be logical, strategic steps that are in alignment with where you currently are. But some of them can be actions you're taking to lean into the bigger vision, like my examples of shopping for dream homes or researching a European tour even before I had the means to make these a reality.

In my current business life, I have certain revenue goals, and I schedule a certain number of actions to take each week to generate that revenue: emails, calls, ads, networking with colleagues. When I want to create a new program, product, or book, I break it down and schedule creative time to focus on that. I'm also taking specific actions that stretch me beyond my current capacities, acting *as if* I'm already living my larger vision.

This section can be where you decide on the different things you're going to do to practice one or more of the Seven Gifts you're working on. If you're focusing on giving more service, for example, find a place to serve and add that to the plan. If you're working on expressing your talents more, block out some time to practice or put on a performance for friends or family. If you're developing the gift of giving to yourself and part of that would include having some conversations with a loved one, *schedule that meeting*. Don't leave it to chance. Don't wait and wish and hope things will happen. Take 100 percent responsibility for the results you want.

Setting and Tracking Qualitative Goals

When it comes to planning, scheduling, and tracking the accomplishment of concrete goals (like writing a book or building a business), it's pretty straightforward. There are clear signposts, milestones, and metrics you can follow. If you're trying to grow a particular inner quality, however, it's a bit trickier to know if you're making progress. For instance, if your goal is a greater abundance of love, for at least a week, keep track of all the areas in which you feel a lack of love and connection, or a desire for more. This includes the moments when you wish you were receiving more love and the opportunities where you could be giving more love.

As you get an overall sense of the level of love (or whatever quality you're working on) currently in your life, give it a numerical value between 0 and 100, where 0 is completely devoid of the quality and 100 is the highest possible level of expression. Maybe you feel like you're meeting your basic love needs some of the time, which feels like a 20 on the scale. And if you were meeting all your basic emotional needs in this area it might feel like Love 40. Now that's still not the ultimate level of love you want in your life (just like meeting your basic financial needs every month isn't all you aspire to), but it's the first level—the foundation.

You can do this for any area in which you want to increase your level of abundance. It's not always easy and it's rarely sexy; but if you want to make a real change, you need to become conscious about this. There's something powerful that happens just by the mere act of tracking: what you pay attention to tends to grow. So don't get too technical about this; just give it a try, and track your 40-day action plan. It can serve as a powerful barometer of your progress, giving you a clearer sense of where you've been, where you currently are, and where an adjustment might need to be made.

Step 5: Commit to Your Goal with Consistency and Congruency

Just as a vision without a plan is a fantasy, a plan that isn't on your calendar is wishful thinking. If it's not scheduled, it most likely won't get done. There are often too many competing demands, issues, and distractions that will fill your time or waste your time if you don't have clear priorities scheduled. Seriously, *don't look at this as optional.* If you really want to change your life and achieve your breakthrough abundance goal, *you must schedule everything for a while.*

As this new way of being becomes a habit—literally becomes your character—you may be able to be looser with your schedule. For example, even if exercise or meditation isn't on my calendar, I will do it every day. It's become a part of my nature, my way of life—like brushing my teeth or breathing. But until that happens, you need to remain vigilant and schedule it.

I want to stress two essential elements to achieving abundance: *commitment and consistency.* Understand that your old patterns will keep reasserting themselves, and with an almost relentless force. There are many reasons for this—it's not just psychological. It's also neurological: you have habitual, well-worn neuropathways conditioned to fire off in specific ways. So unless you're putting forth an equal measure of action on a consistent basis, those old paths will pull you back to your old ways.

Understand and accept that you won't always feel like doing what you know you should—in fact, you may have many moments and days when everything in you is rebelling. But it may also be subtle, covert. The ego is tricky—it knows how to make you think you're making rational choices when they're really emotional reactions. It sounds like, "I just don't feel like it," which we've been conditioned to believe is a good reason not to follow through. It's not. It's a cognitive disorder called "emotional reasoning."

Moving forward, once you have your plan and schedule, don't look to your emotions to determine what you will or won't do. If you've committed to exercising but you find yourself thinking, *I've had a hard day; I'm tired; I deserve to rest*, that's the ego talking. Thank it for sharing, remind it that you have a commitment, and go exercise anyway! If you act like a physically active person, you'll activate physical energy. The same with creative endeavors: Don't wait for inspiration. Act like an inspired professional, and you will activate inspiration. Even if you don't get inspired, do the work anyway. That's what a person of high character does, that's what your future self would do, and that's how a professional acts. An amateur makes excuses for why they can't; a pro gets the job done. Can you imagine a plumber telling you he can't come fix your toilet as planned because he's just "not feeling it"? You'd be looking for a new plumber pretty fast!

Create a real plan. Put it on your calendar. Commit to it consistently, no matter what, and you will look back in forty days and be amazed at the progress you've made.

CONCLUSION

UNCONDITIONAL LIVING

Life isn't about finding yourself. Life is about creating yourself.
—GEORGE BERNARD SHAW

As we near the end of this book, we're really just at the beginning of this journey. If you've been doing the work as you go, no doubt you've experienced some shifts—some aha moments—and planted new seeds of growth in you. But lasting change doesn't happen just because we read a book; it happens when we change our life. If you study any individual who has made real sustainable progress, whether it's the great leaders and innovators throughout history or your neighbor down the street, you'll discover that it didn't happen by just doing a few things here and there, or "kinda sorta" being interested in something; it happened because *they created a new way of life* that supported their emerging vision.

When Pele, the great soccer player, was asked how often he practiced to be able to do the amazing things he did on the field, he responded, "Everything is practice." In other words, he didn't become one of the greatest athletes in history by showing up a couple times a week for practice; he became great because being great was a way of life for him. Einstein didn't make some of the greatest discoveries in science by dabbling in physics or reading a few books here and there; he lived and breathed science—he prioritized his life around his studies and experiments.

The same is true of Steve Jobs, Edison, Buddha, Jesus, Shakespeare, and Mother Teresa. Regardless of what you think of these people, their ability to create a life of real abundance, success, innovation, and fulfill-ment was directly connected to the way they lived. That doesn't mean they were without flaws (some of them had major flaws) or that they didn't have real challenges (the greatest among us often have the biggest challenges), but what they all had in common was a way of life that was increasingly congruent with their vision.

Awakened Abundance is not just a system for generating wealth, becoming a highly productive and creative person, having an abun-dance of relationships and opportunities, or manifesting more in any area; it's a way of life based on the universal principles of abundance that have always existed and always will. Like learning the basic skills for riding a bike, once you master these principles, you won't have to worry as much (or at all) about having enough anymore. But to create sustainable abundance and success, you need to be committed to your vision and then build the habits that are consistent with it. If you do, you'll learn more than how to ride the bike; you'll end up with a vehi-cle that can take you where you really want to go in a more relaxed, enjoyable, (maybe even) hands-free way!

Unconditional Giving

The very nature of life is giving. That's all that life can do—give of itself—because life is already whole, complete, and infinite. It doesn't give to get anything in return, as it already has everything. As it says in Matthew 5:45, "He causes his sun to rise on the evil and the good, and sends rain on the righteous and the unrighteous." This isn't a religious statement; it's a description of principle. This is the nature of God, of the universe, of life itself. And ultimately, this is our true nature and deepest purpose—to become like life, giving of ourselves unconditionally.

This really broke through for me over the last year and a half, as I was personally going through one of the most difficult periods of my life. I think it's fair to say it was a "dark night of the soul"—every structure of my life was up for re-evaluation and change, and nothing was solid or guaranteed. It was like being a caterpillar in the chrysalis, when the caterpillar body liquefies and essentially dies to its old nature. This period of my life caused me to dig more deeply than I ever had before, praying, meditating, journaling, and contemplating the universal truth principles—seeking to pierce the veil of worldly appearances and mental and emotional patterns to find my anchor in a greater reality.

Much of my efforts seemed fruitless, like planting the Chinese bamboo seed and watering, weeding, and feeding it *for years, without results*. The fact is that the bamboo tree is making tremendous progress; it's just all happening below the surface, where a powerful root system is being built to support what will eventually emerge.

Just as the bamboo tree eventually breaks through the surface, my efforts began to bring some results. But they weren't the results I had expected. Instead of my outer world changing, it was my inner world that opened up. I still had some very challenging relationship issues, but instead of anger and fear, my response to them was a whole new level of love, compassion, and forgiveness. I also had new financial challenges because of several big shifts in my personal and professional life. And instead of seeing them turn around immediately, what opened up in me was a level of generosity I had never experienced before.

I remember walking one day across the parking lot of a store when I suddenly felt this energy of giving well up in me so strongly that I couldn't help but imagine all the ways I could give away everything I had—and it felt *so good*. I even asked some family members to keep an eye on me to make sure I didn't literally give everything away!

I didn't understand what was happening until it happened again. The second time, it was clear that it wasn't me personally generating this feeling; it wasn't coming from the personality construct called "Derek Rydall." *Life itself* was pouring through and as me. You can call it God, the universe, love—the name doesn't matter. What does matter is that I was having a direct experience of *how Source felt all the time*. This energy of giving—this boundless, inexhaustible, unconditional givingness—was the very nature of life and the true nature of everyone. I saw it and felt it and knew it clearly.

And although I was already someone committed to giving, loving, and serving, I realized even more deeply that I had to align my whole life with this truth; I had to become a place of unconditional giving, in the same way all of nature shares itself. This became my prayer—to be a place where the life, love, truth, and abundance of God could pour forth unconditionally and all-conditionally, no matter what. The result of this has been tremendous moments of inspiration and spontaneous outbreaks of gratitude so intense that they bring me to tears, and a rising level of abundance that has begun to flood my life.

To be clear, I'm not suggesting you start giving away everything you have. I'm also not saying that unconditional giving excludes the need for agreements and the honoring of those agreements. For example, if you sell products or services, I'm not encouraging you to give them away for free or without any contracts. If someone doesn't fulfill the obligations of their agreements, it's right and just to hold them accountable. Not because they're your Source, but because respecting agreements is an expression of wholeness, power, self-love, and character. Honoring agreements not only serves you but them, even if they don't humanly like it.

But within all of this human business, we must maintain the larger context of *who and what we really are*; where our good really comes from; and our greatest purpose to love, serve, and circulate our inner splendor here on Earth. It's a tricky balance to be in the world but not *of* it—to stay grounded in our daily affairs while letting our consciousness take flight. This is one of the things meant by Jesus's statement when he was asked what to do about Caesar and the issue of money. In Mark 12:17, he said, "Give back to Caesar what is Caesar's, to God what is God's."

You don't have to figure out *how* you're going to live a life of unconditional giving; you just need to set the intention and be willing to grow, expand, and serve a greater purpose—the real purpose for which you were born. You will never have less when you live this way; the universe abhors a vacuum and will fill it up as you empty yourself out. And you can't out-give God or Source, because Its capacity for giving is infinite. The more you're willing to align yourself with this, the larger your capacity will become. It'll look like you're receiving more, but what's really happening is that you're being given more so you have more to give!

It's not always easy, though. You'll be required to look at the scared and resistant places within you that are needy, greedy, stingy, and selfish. Sometimes, that'll require a level of shadow work to embrace these parts. Other times, it will require you to surrender to the impulse of generosity (with your time, talent, or treasure), even when it's uncomfortable, and looks and feels unsafe. But in all cases, if you are willing, do the work, and stay the course, you'll continue on a never-ending, ever-expanding upward spiral of progress and success—and become a shining example of what's possible for everyone.

I'd say that's a worthy goal.

As we close out this leg of the journey, I want to personally thank you for taking this trip with me. It's such an honor and a pleasure to be connected to people who are hungry to live their purpose—to make a bigger impact and realize their full potential. As you do this work on yourself, you aren't just changing your life; you're changing the collective consciousness of humanity. Every prayer, every practice, every new insight—all are making a difference for the world. For that, I'm deeply and eternally grateful to you.

Keep up the good work. Keep me posted on your progress. Stop by my website, and download more tools and trainings to support you. Leave a comment on my social media sites, check out my *Emergence* podcast on iTunes, and share what you're learning—so that I can help you take things to the next level.

Keep going, stay engaged, and stay inspired.

And until next time, remember to live authentically, love unconditionally, and follow your destiny!

ACKNOWLEDGMENTS

I want to honor and give thanks to my mom for always believing in me and supporting my dreams; to my dad for instilling in me many of the practical habits that helped me build a successful business; and to my spiritual teachers, who awakened in me a vision of what's truly possible—especially my personal mentors, Nirvana Reginald Gayle and Michael Beckwith.

This book would not have been possible without the support of my publisher, Beyond Words / Atria / Simon & Schuster; the tireless efforts of my agent, Stephany Evans at FinePrint; and the amazing work of the editors who believed in me and my work: Anna Noak, Nevin Mays, and Emily Han.

Of course, there are so many others that make my life work and make it all worthwhile, from my incredible team at Emerging Edge Media to my friends, extended family, and children. I love and appreciate you all!

NOTES

Note: Bible verses are from *The New International Version*, © 2011 by Biblica.

1. Bruce Grierson, "What If Age Is Nothing but a Mind-Set?" *The New York Times Magazine*, October 22, 2014, https://www.nytimes.com/2014/10/26/magazine/what -if-age-is-nothing-but-a-mind-set.html?_r=1.

2. Robert Rosenthal and Lenore Jacobson, "Pygmalion in the Classroom," *The Urban Review*, September 1968: 16–20, https://www.uni-muenster.de/imperia/md/content /psyifp/aeechterhoff/sommersemester2012/schluesselstudiendersozialpsychologiea /rosenthal_jacobson_pygmalionclassroom_urbrev1968.pdf.

3. Debbie Ford, AZQuotes.com, accessed March 30, 2017, http://www.azquotes.com /quote/628809.

4. Ralph Waldo Emerson, *Wikiquote*, "Ralph Waldo Emerson sourced quotes," last modified June 10, 2009, https://simple.wikiquote.org/wiki/Ralph_Waldo_Emerson.

5. Apostle Thomas, quoted in Elaine H. Pagels, "The Gospel of Thomas," From Jesus to Christ, *FRONTLINE*, PBS website, April 1998, http://www.pbs.org/wgbh/pages /frontline/shows/religion/story/thomas.html.

6. Peter Thiel, quoted in Benjamin P. Hardy, "How to Radically Change Your Goals and Success," *Inc.*, April 28, 2016, http://www.inc.com/benjamin-p-hardy/how-to-10x -your-goals-and-success-.html.

INDEX

"MANIFEST ABUNDANCE NOW!" PRACTICES

ADDITIONAL RESOURCES

To support you in getting the most out of this book—and getting real, sustainable results—I have created several free tools. To start, you can visit TheAbundanceProjectBook.com and the resource section of my website at DerekRydall.com/Resources.

For a free mini eCourse / audio course on the Law of Emergence, you can visit LawOfEmergence.com.

To download a guided Shadow Process, go to DerekRydall.com /ShadowProcess.

To get a copy of my bestselling book, *Emergence,* along with $1,791 in powerful bonuses, check out MyEmergenceBook.com.

And to register for my popular *Emergence* podcast on iTunes, go to https://itunes.apple.com/us/podcast/emergence -revolutionary-path/id878870353?mt=2.